∞

My Daily Visit with the Saints

My Daily Visit
with the
Saints

∞

Compiled by Charles Kenny

SOPHIA INSTITUTE PRESS
Manchester, New Hampshire

My Daily Visit with the Saints is an abridgment of *Half-Hours with the Saints and Servants of God* (London: Burns and Oates, 1882). The 1882 edition from which this abridgment is derived contained a number of anomalies and not a few errors of detail about the sources of the readings contained in it. In this 2017 edition we have sought, where possible, to remedy those deficiencies. We apologize for any new problems our efforts may have introduced into this superb work of spiritual readings.

Printed in the United States of America. All rights reserved.

Cover design by LUCAS Art & Design, Jenison, MI.

Biblical references in this book are taken from the Douay-Rheims edition of the Old and New Testaments. Where applicable, quotations have been cross-referenced with the differing names and enumeration in the Revised Standard Version.

Sophia Institute Press
Box 5284, Manchester, NH 03108
1-800-888-9344

www.SophiaInstitute.com

Sophia Institute Press® is a registered trademark of Sophia Institute.

Library of Congress Cataloging-in-Publication Data
To come

First printing

∞

Contents

Part 2: God the Son and God the Holy Spirit

Part 3: The Blessed Virgin Mary and Our Lady's Feasts

Part 4: Sermons on Diverse Subjects

Part 5: The World and Sin

Part 6: Vices We Should Flee From

Part 7: Virtues We Should Practice

Part 8: The Four Last Things

Part 1

∞

God's Attributes, Gifts, and Graces

∞

The Love of God

This only take care of with all diligence,
that you love the Lord your God.

— Joshua 23:11

Love is strong as death (Song of Sol. 8:6); since both equally separate the soul from the body and all terrestrial things, the only difference is that the separation is real and effectual when caused by death, whereas that occasioned by love is usually confined to the heart.

I say "usually," because divine love is sometimes so violent that it actually separates the soul from the body, and, by causing the death of those who love, it renders them infinitely happier than if it bestowed on them a thousand lives.

As the lot of the reprobate is to die in sin, that of the elect is to expire in the love and grace of God, which is effected in several ways.

Many of the saints died not only in the state of charity but in the actual exercise of divine love. St. Augustine expired in making an act of contrition, which cannot exist without love; St. Jerome, in exhorting his disciples to charity and the practice of all virtues; St. Ambrose, in conversing sweetly with his Savior, whom he had received in the Holy Eucharist. St. Anthony of Padua also expired in the act of discoursing with our Divine Lord, after having recited a hymn in honor of the ever-glorious Virgin; St. Thomas Aquinas, with his hands clasped, his eyes raised to heaven, and pronouncing these words of the Canticles, which were the last he had expounded: "Come, my beloved, let us go forth into the field" (Song of Sol. 7:11).

All the Apostles, and the greater number of the martyrs, died in prayer. Venerable Bede, having learned the hour of his death by revelation, went to the choir at the usual hour to sing the evening office, it being the feast of the Ascension. And at the very moment he had finished singing vespers, he expired, following his Guide and Master into heaven, to celebrate His praises in that abode of rest and happiness, around which the shades of night can never gather, because it is illumined by the brightness of the eternal day, which neither dawns nor ends.

John Gerson, chancellor of the University of Paris, remarkable for his learning and virtue — of whom Sixtus of Siena said that "it is difficult to decide whether the vein of piety which runs through his works surpasses his science, or whether his learning exceeds his piety" — after having explained the fifty properties of divine love mentioned in the Canticles, expired at the close of three days, smiling, and pronouncing these words of the same sacred text: "Thy love, O God, is strong as death" (Song of Sol. 8:6).

The fervor and ardor of St. Martin at the hour of his death are remarkable. St. Louis, who has proved himself as great a monarch among the saints as an eminent saint among kings, being attacked by the plague, ceased not to pray, and after receiving the viaticum, he extended his arms in the form of a cross, fixed his eyes on heaven, and, animated with love and confidence, expired in saying with the psalmist: "I will come into Thy house, O Lord; I will worship towards Thy holy temple, in Thy fear" (Ps. 5:8 [RSV = Ps. 5:7]).

St. Peter Celestine, after having endured the most cruel and incredible afflictions, seeing the end of his days approach, began to sing like the swan and terminated his song with his life, by these words of the last psalm: "Let every spirit praise the Lord" (Ps. 150:5 [RSV = 150:6]).

St. Eusebia, surnamed the Stranger, died kneeling in fervent prayer. St. Peter the Martyr yielded his last sigh in writing (with his finger, which he had dipped in his blood) the articles of the faith for which he sacrificed his life, and in saying: "Into Thy hands, O Lord, I commend my spirit" (Ps. 30:6 [RSV = Ps. 31:5]).

The great apostle of the Indies and Japan, St. Francis Xavier, expired holding a crucifix, which he tenderly embraced, and incessantly repeated in transports of love: "O Jesus, the God of my heart!"

—St. Francis De Sales (1567–1622), *Treatise on the Love of God*

∞

The saintly Father Segneri tells us that the sure way of gaining heaven, without much cost, is by making frequent acts of the love of God, and by accustoming ourselves to do everything with the intention of pleasing Him:

We shall no longer be tempted to complain that we cannot undertake such great things as we so much admire in others.

God is content if we do all we can to love Him in our sphere of life, and He asks for nothing more. You sometimes regret that you cannot practice great austerities, which no doubt are due to Him for our past sins.

Supply for these in another way. Replace those fastings and watchings by fervent acts of love; He requires nothing more.

You are engaged here below in temporal affairs; domestic cares, perchance, occupy your time. Well, do all these with the intention of pleasing Him, and God will be as content as if you had undertaken the worthy functions of an apostolate.

By what way, do you think, did the saints attain to the perfection of holiness? It was less by their heroic actions than by the great love they showed in performing their lesser duties. Our Savior praises Mary Magdalen not for having done much but for having loved much. Magdalen had not then practiced austerities, but the love of Jesus had filled her heart with torrents of tears.

—Fr. Paul Segneri, S.J. (1624–1694), *Meditations*

❧

The Holy Fear of God

With him that feareth the Lord, it shall go well in the lat-
ter end, and in the day of his death he shall be blessed.

—Sirach 1:13

The fear of the terrible judgment of God is necessary to lead a sinner back to repentance, but love must be added to fear to make this repentance perfect.

It seems to me that there is implanted in the heart of man two natures; both combined will contribute to his conversion and make it perfect and secure. There is in the heart an inferior nature, which is more worldly and which can be moved only by sensible things. Fear is for this portion of the heart, for it is contemplation of hell and the fearful consequences of vice that seizes the heart of man and turns it away from sin. But there is in this same heart a superior celestial nature, which is only susceptible of the dawn of grace. This is love; this is that divine charity that moves that portion of the heart and makes it seek God for God's sake alone.

The conversion of the heart begins with fear and finishes with love.

To return to God simply through fear is, so to say, only half the battle. In order that we may be all for God, we must combine love with fear.

Is not the love of God sufficient, says the great St. Augustine, to make us avoid sin? Was it needful to employ fear and terrible threats?

The Holy Fear of God

At least—if fear did what love should do, we should have less to complain of—what is so shocking is that nowadays we have reached that pitch of indifference that is moved neither by fear nor by love, and that the most frightful things do not make any impression on our hearts.

—Fr. Étienne de Bretteville (1630–1688), *Essays*

∞

The loss of holy fear is the mischief of all mischiefs. For this fear is a special gift of the Holy Spirit, to be sought for by prayer and penance, by tears and cries, by patience and impatience, and by the very yearnings of an earnest and familiar love. It has always seemed to me very and unexpectedly beautiful when in the special office of St. Philip Neri, knowing what manner of man he was, and what peculiar spirit he was of, it says in the antiphon of the Magnificat, "Come, my children, and I will teach you the fear of the Lord," for how else shall the saint teach us divinest love?

Let us pass in review before ourselves the ancient patriarchs and their deep awe of God; how they trembled with holy fear when God was nigh and looked upon all things over which He had so much as cast His shadow as unspeakably hallowed.

Jacob, who was so familiar with Him that he wrestled with Him, and would not let Him go until He had blessed him, stands eminent among the saints of God for the gift and grace of fear. The very ritual of the old synagogue was steeped in fear and reverence. David, the man after God's own heart, was ever praying for an increase of holy fear. Our Blessed Lord Himself, says the Apostle, in the days of His flesh was heard because He feared (Heb. 5:7). Mary and the Apostles were filled, as none others ever were, with the beauty, the tenderness, and the excess of this heavenly fear.

Hundreds of dying saints, around whose flesh and souls still clung the fair white robe of their unforfeited baptismal whiteness, trembled in every limb as they pondered the possible judgments of Infinite Purity, beneath whose judicial eye they were about to stand.

If they needed this degree of fear, what degree do we need?

Why do frustrated vocations so abound? Whence comes the multitude of unfinished saints, who lie all around us like the broken models of a sculptor's studio?

Whence so little perseverance in the devout life, and such wearying and untying even of the vows and promises whereby men have bound themselves to God?

Whence but from the lack of fear!

— Fr. Frederick William Faber (1814–1863),
The Blessed Sacrament

∞

There is nothing so bold, nothing more secure, than the fear of God.

He who fears God fears naught else; and he who has a dread of displeasing Him, or a fear of forfeiting His love, does not shrink from suffering; he cares not if he should lose all, provided he be in a state of grace.

It is said that love banishes fear (1 John 4:18), but it is the baneful fear of man, or that servile and imperfect fear that dreads the shame of sin more than the sin that brings the shame.

I say more than this. There are times when it is necessary to fortify the fear of sin by the fear of hell, in order to strengthen in us the love of God, as when we are assailed by some violent temptation, which is not so easy to overcome if we are not well grounded in the fear of God.

Let us, then, henceforth combine fear with love. These are the two supports of the soul that attach us to God, like unto His mercy and justice, which go hand in hand. Do not let us sever the one from the other, if we wish to walk on the road to heaven without swerving from the paths of perfection.

Let us often say with humility that prayer of the Church: "Make us, O Lord, keep always before our eyes the love and fear of Your holy Name."

— Fr. Nouet, S.J. (1605–1680), *Meditations*, vol. 7

∞

If a depraved mind be not shaken and humbled by the fear of God, it will never amend its habitual sins.

—St. Gregory (ca. 540–604), Homily 4 on the Gospels

∞

The Holy Will of God

Thy will be done on earth as it is in heaven.

—Matthew 6:10

Why not complain of these evils when looked at in themselves? But wherefore murmur when we look upon them as the will of God? God wills it!

Ah, that has a great weight with a man who has faith, who knows and loves God. Would a good Christian dare to say, "God wills it, but I wish it not"?

Our perfection consists in doing the will of God, and it is for us to submit. The will of God is infinitely holy. If this be the rule of all sanctity, we are then holy in proportion to our conformity to His will.

Jesus Christ is our model, and we are saintly when we are like unto Him; and we are so much the more like Him in proportion to our conformity to the will of God. Thus does He not say that He is come not to do His will, but that of His Father (see John 6:38)?

In fine, our perfection and holiness consists in charity. Charity is the fulfillment of the law, says St. Paul. Perfect charity consists in doing the will of God in the highest sense it can be placed. "He who keeps my commandments and does my will," says Jesus Christ himself, "is he who loves me" (John 14:21).

You are sometimes in anxiety; if you love God, that is a just subject of uneasiness. If you are always ready to do His will and to submit to it, then be sure that you love Him. Conformity to the will of God also makes a man happy as God, who is happiness itself.

What is it that makes God infinitely happy? It is that He does all that He wills; it is that He wills all that is good; it is that He finds in Himself all the good that He wills.

Thus a man perfectly conformed to the will of God possesses all these blessings.

He does what he wills because he wishes only for what God wills; because it fulfills also, in whatever manner it may be, His fulfillment also.

He also wishes only for that which is good, for he wills only what God wills.

In conclusion, he finds all things good in themselves; for his conformity to the will of God, united as it is to God, makes him possess God. And what benefit can fail to occur to him who possesses God?

—Fr. F. Nepveu, S.J. (1639–1708), *Réflexions Chrétiennes*

∞

Joseph, raised to the highest dignity in the court of Egypt, by his elevation came to be the terror and protector of his brothers. These of whom he had so much reason to complain—did he not consider them as only executors of the will of God, notwithstanding the outrages they inflicted on him? Did he not consider that the treason and cruelty that they employed against him proved, by the decrees of Divine Providence, to be more beneficial than their jealousy could have imagined?

It is true that they had sold him into Egypt, but it was not on account of their perfidy; rather it was by the will of God that he should be sent to this foreign land. Such were the feelings of so many saints and martyrs with regard to those by whom they had been persecuted.

They reverenced even the scourges that God had sent to chasten them. The early Christians blessed the hands that struck them.

—Fr. Jean Baptiste Massillon (1663–1742)

∞

Give us, O Lord, the will to do what Thou commandest, and to do what Thou willest.

—St. Augustine (354–430), *Confessions*

∞

The Word of God

The seed is the word of God.

—Luke 8:11

According to St. Augustine, the Divine Word falls on a weak and sensitive element, and it becomes a sacrament. This word also falls on impure hearts, and it makes them chaste; on the wicked, and makes them saints. It finds them in sin, and it converts them to God.

As in the most wonderful of our sacraments, those words "This is my Body" are transubstantiations of bread into the Body and of wine into the Blood of the Son of God, because they are not the words of the priest, but the words of Jesus Christ, offered up nevertheless by the priest; so in like manner preachers make use of moral but wondrous transubstantiations and change old sinners into new servants of God.

What miraculous wonders has not this Word produced! It falls on the heart of an adulterous David, and it makes him a royal penitent. It falls on the heart of a Magdalen; it finds her a worshipper of sin, and it makes her a model of penance. It falls on Matthew, and from a public usurer, it makes him an evangelist. You see a soul enter the Church—a soul enamored of the world and full of vanity. It enters into the Church and pays but little attention to the Word of God, and immediately a penetrating light pierces the heart, which shows the bad state in which it is. From this knowledge it sees its shame, its baseness; this shame produces the grief for having offended God, and this sorrow brings forth the resolution of a change of life.

What is the reason of this wonder, if it be not the Word of God?

The force and energy of the Word of God is such that one could say that it was all powerful. It is found in the nothingness of the ears who have listened to its voice. "It calls those which are not, as well as those which are."

It has subdued the world, overturned idolatry, converted whole nations. It has brought kings, wise men, ministers of state, under the subjection of the Gospel. It has done more than this: throughout the universe the most barbarous and savage of people have been civilized. In short, we owe to this Divine Word the conversion of the whole world and the extirpation of idolatry.

—Fr. Antoine de la Porte

∾

However enlightened and clever we may be, we must not, on account of that, neglect the assistance of holy instructions. However bright may be our intellect, we can easily go astray. However learned and scientific, we can always learn something from hearing the Word of God. If your understanding learns of nothing new, your heart will, at least, feel that you know nothing, if you do not know Jesus and Him crucified. If you are sinners, what is more capable of bringing you to a sense of your own unworthiness than listening to the voice of the missionary sent by God? If you are good, what sweeter consolation than hearing truths explained, truths that you love and practice and that become more beneficial the oftener you hear them?

Our Lord has given to the preacher of His Word a help that is not to be found elsewhere. The commonest truths in the mouth of the preacher have a strength and unction that can alone move and convert the most hardened heart.

In what disposition do you come to hear the Word of God?

Many attend to decide upon the merit or incapacity of him who announces it; many, to make unjust comparisons between this and that preacher. Some glory in being very difficult to please, in order to appear of excellent taste; they, inattentively, listen to simple explanations that are necessary to be touched upon, and all the fruit that they gather from a Christian discourse consists of disparaging remarks and pointing out the defects of the preacher. They come with an intention of finding fault and ever find something to censure and criticize.

—Fr. Jean Baptiste Massillon (1663–1742), Lenten sermon

∞

Listen with devotion to the Word of God, whether you hear it in familiar conversation with your spiritual friends or at a sermon.

Make all the profit of it you possibly can, and suffer it not to fall to the ground, but receive it into your heart as a precious balm, imitating the most holy Virgin, who preserved carefully in her heart all the words that were spoken in praise of her Son.

Remember that our Lord gathers up the words we speak to Him in our prayers, according as we gather up those He speaks to us by preaching.

Have always at hand some approved book of devotion, such as the spiritual works of St. Bonaventure, of Gerson, or of Thomas à Kempis, and read a little in them every day with as much devotion as if you were reading a letter from those saints.

—St. Francis de Sales (1567–1622), *Introduction to the Devout Life*

∞

Manna suited everybody's taste. In like manner the Word of God, which is preached to all throughout the world, supplies the wants of all kinds of persons, and according as it is listened to by those of ordinary intelligence, it will be found—as did manna of old—to be suitable to everybody's taste.

—St. Cyprian (ca. 200–258), *On the Lord's Prayer*

∞

The Law of God

Do not think that I am come to destroy the law or
the prophets. I am not come to destroy, but to fulfill.

—Matthew 5:17

The difference between the two Testaments may be explained in two words—*love* and *fear*. The one appertains to the old man, the other to the new. This is the principal difference. For the new law is that which God promises to impress upon the mind, to engrave on the heart, and is that which is written on in giving us the Holy Spirit, who diffuses the requisite charity to make us love truth and justice.

So this new law induces us to love all that it commands, while the laws engraved on a stone show only the obligations of creatures and threats in default of obedience. It is this difference that the Apostle wished to point out in his epistle to the Romans, where he says, "We have not received the spirit of bondage again in fear, but we have received the spirit of adoption of sons of God" (Rom. 8:15). The spirit of bondage is that which creates fear; the spirit of adoption is that of love. Fear makes us slaves, love makes us as children.

The new law, imprinted on the heart by the Holy Spirit, regulates the interior feelings while the laws engraved on stone can regulate only exterior actions.

Fear is not capable of changing the interior feeling; it can only act outwardly and thus force the will to do what it would not do, or even

16

what it might do. So that while exteriorly it submits to force, interiorly it resists. Although deeds and words conform to the law, the heart is opposed to it. Although the mouth and hands obey, the will is disobedient.

This is the reproach that God makes to the Jews when He says through His prophet, "This people honor me with their lips, but their hearts are far from me" (see Matt. 15:8).

The two usual methods adopted to govern mankind are fear and hope. This is why the old law does not make use solely of threats to ensure obedience, but it adds to them promises. But these promises were for temporal welfare, for sensual and gross men who sought for fleeting prosperity.

Thus we read in the twenty-third chapter of Exodus that Moses, in order to induce them to observe the law he was about to promulgate, promised them every kind of prosperity — health, long life, a numerous progeny, abundance of everything necessary, and protection from enemies, so that they might enjoy in peace and quiet all these blessings.

Now, on the contrary, the Son of God begins by preaching penance and speaks only of the kingdom of heaven. And to make us understand that His wish is that Christians should despise earthly prosperity, not expecting a reward in this life, He begins His beautiful Sermon on the Mount by saying, "Blessed are the poor in spirit," "Blessed are the meek," "Blessed are they that mourn" (Matt. 5:3–5); and "Woe to you that are rich! Woe to you that now laugh!" and to all who seek the esteem and approbation of men (Luke 6:24–25)! In this life, He leads us to expect sufferings, crosses, and persecution, and He wills that we should love what is unseen and supernatural.

— St. Augustine (354–430), *Against Adimantus*

∞

The Apostles announced to mankind a doctrine raised above human intellect. They spoke not of earthly things, but of heaven. They preached a kingdom and state that had never been understood. They discovered other riches, another poverty, another liberty, another bondage, another life and death—in fact, a change and renewal of everything.

Their teachings are far beyond that of a Plato who had traced out an idea of an absurd republic, or that of a Zenon, or those of other philosophers who had formed projects of governments and republics, and those who wished to be lawgivers.

One need but read their books to see that the devil urged them on and diffused a profound darkness in their mind, upsetting by that means the order of things and destroying the most inviolate laws of nature. And notwithstanding that these philosophers were at perfect liberty to publish their strange maxims, fearless of danger or persecution, they deemed it necessary to call to their aid the most elegant of phrases, the most pleasing eloquence, in order to impress their own ideas firmly in their minds.

The gospel that, on the contrary, preached for the poor and for all those persecuted sinners throughout the world who had been treated as slaves, and who were exposed to all kinds of danger—this gospel, I say, has all at once been received with every mark of respect by the learned as well as by the ignorant, by warriors and princes, —in a word, by Greeks and Romans, and by every savage nation.

—St. John Chrysostom (c. 349–407), *Sermon on St. Matthew*

∞

St. Jerome, in writing to the mother of Paula, says:

Begin with the Psalter, and teach your daughter how to chant the Psalms. You can read with her the Proverbs, by which she will know the moral precepts.

This can be followed by Sirach, a book so capable of inspiring her with a contempt of this world.

You can then proceed to the Gospels—these, your daughter ought ever to have in hand.

She can then read the Acts and Epistles of the Apostles. These finished, she will gladly learn by heart the Prophets and Historical books.

Lastly, she can read the Song of Songs, for she will have been prepared to understand this in a spiritual sense.

—St. Jerome (ca. 347–420)

∞

The evangelical precepts are no other than divine lessons; they are the foundation of hope, the strengthening of faith, the food of charity; the gospel is a rudder to steer our way through life and helps us to reach the harbor of salvation.

The law commands but few things, but those few should be willingly and lovingly performed.

—St. Cyprian (ca. 200–258), *On the Lord's Prayer*

∞

The Presence of God

The sinner hath provoked the Lord—
God is not before his eyes.

—Psalm 10:4–5

When one speaks of the presence of God, there are two ways of looking upon it. The first is that God is present to us, that is to say, that we think of Him, and that, in the eyes of faith, we look upon His Divine Being as intimately present in the place in which we are. The second is that we are present to God, that is to say, that He sees us and is always looking upon us, so that nothing escapes His observation—words, deeds, thoughts, desires, and intentions—and that wherever we may be, we may always have Him for a spectator, witness, and judge of all that we do. That should we act well or ill, such actions are always in His presence and before His eyes.

- *God sees me.* Ah, what a phrase is this for him who understands it well! How capable it is to control our passions, to moderate our desires, to prevent us from sinning, to sustain our courage, to animate our fervor, to regulate our conduct!
- *God sees me.* He is ever present, always mindful of me, thinks ever of me; whereas I heed Him not, I am not attentive to Him, I never think of Him. O! shame, shame!
- *God sees me.* With what respect and modesty ought I not to behave in His presence! The seraphim hide their faces with their wings, and I, a mere worm of the earth, do not tremble.

- *God sees me.* Shall I dare, in the presence of Thy glance so infinitely pure, commit deeds that I dare not even show to man? Shall I dare to sin in Thy presence, knowing that sin and the sinner is hated by Thee, and to condemn the sinner Thou hast no wish?
- *God sees me.* He penetrates into the innermost recesses of my heart; He sees therein every desire and discerns every intention. With what purity of intention, then, ought I not to perform every action!

God is present not only by the immensity of His being, but in a more efficacious manner. He is with me to help me, to support me, to act with me, to work with me. I can do nothing without Him, but I can do everything with Him. I cannot make the least movement, conceive the least desire, do the smallest action, unless He lends me His help and assistance, even when I would wish to offend Him. What condescension! Why ought I to abuse it? But He always accommodates Himself to my inclinations. He subjects Himself to my will. Is it not reasonable that I should subject my will to His? He concurs always with me. Is it not right and just that I should act in concert with Him?

Not only does God act within me, but He also acts with every creature for me. It is for me that He gives light and warmth to the sun, that He refreshes me with the breeze, that He cheers me with the fire. Should I not be unjust if I did not make use of these creations for His glory alone? Should I not be ungrateful if I basely converted such blessings into opportunities of sinning against Him who created them for me?

—Fr. F. Nepvue, S.J. (1654–1708), *Réflexions Chrétiennes*

We do our works in the presence of God when we practice the presence of God while we do them. There are six ways of practicing the presence of God, and souls should select those that are most suited to them but not try to practice more than one:

- to try to realize God as He is in heaven
- to regard ourselves in Him as in His immensity

- to look at each creature as if it were a sacrament having God hidden under it
- to think of Him and see Him by pure faith
- to look at Him as in ourselves rather than outside of us, though He is both
- to gravitate toward Him by a habitual loving mindfulness of heart, a kind of instinct that is no uncommon growth of prayer and comes sooner than would be expected when men strive to serve God out of the single motive of holy love

For the perfection of our ordinary actions, we should do these in the sight of Jesus, that is, to use the words of the missal, by Christ, with Christ, and in Christ. To do our actions by Christ is to do them in dependence upon Him, as He did everything in dependence on His Father, and by the movement of His Spirit. To do our actions with Christ is to practice the same virtues as our Lord, to clothe ourselves with the same dispositions, and to act from the same intentions, all according to the measure of the lowliness of our possibilities. To do our actions in Christ is to unite ours with His, and to offer them to God along with His, so that for the sake of His, they may be accepted on high.

—Fr. Frederick William Faber (1814–1863), *Growth in Holiness*

∞

The Providence of God

For all Thy ways are prepared, and in Thy
providence Thou hast placed Thy judgments.

—Judith 9:5

Let us place our trust in the providence of God. Let us cut off all those anxieties that serve only to torture our minds uselessly, since, whether we make ourselves uneasy or not, it is God alone who sends us all these things and who may increase them until He sees they disturb us less.

Of what use would all our cares, anxieties, and troubles be to us if they only served to torment us and made us suffer the pain of having had them?

Our cares are only the cares of an individual; those of God include the whole world. The more we trouble ourselves with our own interests, the less will God interfere.

He who is invited to a splendid banquet does not trouble himself about what he shall eat, and he who goes to a limpid spring does not make himself uneasy, for he knows he will be able to appease his thirst.

Since, then, we have the providence of God, which is richer than the most magnificent feast and more inexhaustible than the purest spring, do not be uneasy—do not cherish any misgivings.

—St. John Chrysostom (ca. 349–407), *Homilies on St. Matthew*

∞

Why fear? says St. Augustine; you have a God for a protector and His providence for a guide.

What! says the holy doctor. You fear to perish under the guidance of God, and under the protection of His providence? Is it that you know not that not a single hair can fall out without His approval (see Matt. 10:30)? Ah, if He takes so much care of things that are of little or no consequence, how safe ought we not to feel when we know with what care He watches a soul that is so precious to Him?

I am under the protection of the Lord, says the prophet; there is nothing He will not fail to supply me with. It is true that I am poor and am destitute of everything, but the Lord takes care of me, and He has undertaken to provide for my wants; nothing can happen to me — sin excepted — without His concurrence. What have I to fear?

What a host of consoling reflections we can find in the Divine Providence over His creatures! How sweet to think with what wisdom our Lord disposes of everything for His glory and our salvation! The cunning and malice of an enemy, the ill will of an envious man, a hundred accidents of this life — all end advantageously to those who love their God.

It is true that we are but exiles and travelers in this fleeting world, that we therein journey through difficult and dangerous paths, but what does God not do — yes, and daily, too — to prevent His servants from straying or from perishing? He not only is their guide and protector, but He showers down His graces and even makes use of His angels to help them. He warns them, by secret inspirations, what they should do and what they should not do, so that one would say that God is solely occupied in caring for His creatures.

The world ignores all these loving contrivances of Divine Providence. The worldlings judge of the different accidents that occur to well-to-do people in the same way they passed their judgment on the adversities of Joseph, but they did not see the resources of Divine Providence that made everything turn to the advantage of His elect — according to the words of the Apostle: "to them that love God, all things work together unto good" (Rom. 8:28).

Let all the world rise up in arms against the servants of God. What have they to fear when under the protection of their Divine Master? The malice of men cannot hurt them.

Let them employ all possible cunning to disquiet them, let them use every kind of cruel torture to destroy their bodies, even let all hell be unloosed against them. What have they to dread, if God is for them?

—Fr. Croiset, S.J. (b. ca. 1650), *Exercises of Piety*

∞

He who has given us life will give us wherewith to sustain it. He who feeds the thief, will He not feed the innocent? And if He takes care of His enemies, what will He not do for His friends? You cannot place yourself into better hands than those of Him who made you what you are. He who has been so good to you before you were what you are. Can He leave you uncared for, now that you are what He would wish you to be?

—St. Augustine (354–430), *On Psalms 6 and 38*

∞

The Service of God

My yoke is sweet, and my burden light.

—Matthew 11:30

What an honor, and how glorious it is to be in the service of so great, so good a Master.

The condition of the least of His servants is incomparably greater than that of the kings of the earth; for their greatness and prosperity finish with their lives, but the servants of God finish with their lives the pains and trials they have had to suffer in His service, and after that they find an eternal happiness and immortal crowns awaiting them.

It is then reasonable what the royal prophet assures us: that one day spent in His house and in His service is better than a thousand days spent elsewhere (see Ps. 83:11 [RSV = Ps. 84:10]).

It is true that all men esteem and love to be great, but they do not think wherein true greatness is. They deem it to be a great honor to be in the service of royalty; they pay heavy sums to be deemed the head of a firm; but they take but little pains to be a servant of God, and, what is more grievous, they often blush at the idea of fulfilling the duties of His service.

The great Apostle was elated at a time when the Christians were looked upon as scavengers of the world. And we often are confused when called upon to practice the duties of His service, and this, too, at the time when the Christian religion is dominant, and when many powerful monarchs have willingly professed it.

The Service of God

Happy are the Christians who feel the honor and acknowledge the grace that God has bestowed upon them when He has received them as His servants! O! what a good Master we have! How magnificent are His promises! How faithful He is to carry them out! How liberal are His rewards!

How happy is he who serves Him! And thrice happy is the choice he has made! O! if all men knew what it was to be a servant of God, they would have no more ardent wish or aspire to a higher honor than to be reckoned among the number of His faithful servants.

O my Lord and my God, my heart is filled with bitter grief when I call to mind the years of my past life. Alas! far from having employed them in Thy service, I am one of those unfaithful servants who have had my own self-interest in view.

However, as You are my Lord and King, I this day take an oath of allegiance, and from henceforth, swear that my wish is to live and die in Thy service.

—Henri-Marie Boudon (1624–1702), *Le Chrétien Inconnu*

∞

The service of God is not only our most important, but our sole work. This is so obvious that it requires only to be stated. Time and words would alike be wasted in the attempt to prove it. Yet, alas! even spiritual persons need to be reminded of this elementary truth. Let us subject ourselves to a brief examination of it. Are we thoroughly convinced it is true? Has our past life shown proof of it? Is our present life modeled on it? Are we taking pains that our future life shall be so?

What is the result when we compare our worldly promptitude and industry with our preference of the service of God over all other things? Are we in any way on the lookout for His greater glory, or our own greater union with Him? Is it plain at first sight that we have no object or pursuit so engrossing and so decidedly paramount as the service of God?

The spirit in which we serve Him should be entirely without reserve. Need I prove this? What is to be reserved? Can there be reserves with

God? Can His sovereignty be limited, or our love of Him ever reach the measure of enough? Is there really no corner of our heart over which He is not absolute Lord? Does He ask of us freely what He wills, and do we do our best to give Him all He asks? Have we no implicit condition with Him that He is only so far with us and no further? Is our outward life utterly and unconditionally dependent on Him? And if it is, is the kingdom of our inward intentions reposing peaceably beneath His un-questioned scepter?

It is of importance not to allow ourselves to rest in any pursuit except the service of God. By resting I mean feeling at home, reposing on what we do, forgetting that it is a mere means even when we do not err so far as to mistake it for an end, being contented with what we are, not pushing on, nor being conscious that we are fighting a battle and climbing a hill. Nothing can excuse the neglect of the duties of the position in life that God has conferred upon us. All is delusive where these are not attended to and made much of. They are as it were private sacraments to each one of us. They are our chief, often our sole, way of becoming saints.

But while we perform them with all the peaceful diligence that the presence of God inspires, we must jealously realize that they are means, not ends, subordinate and subservient to the great work of our souls. No amount of external work, not the unsleeping universal heroism of a St. Vincent de Paul, can make up for the want of attention to our own souls, such as resting in our external work would imply.

Hence we should be jealous of any great pleasure in our pursuits, even when they are works of Christian mercy and love. It is always a pleasure to do good, yet it must be watched, moderated, and kept in check, or it will do us a mischief before we are aware. The thought of eternity is a good help to this. It brings down the pride of external work, and takes the brightness and color out of our successes; and this is well, for such brightness and color are nothing more than the reflection of ourselves and our own activity.

—Fr. Frederick William Faber (1814–1863), *Growth in Holiness*

The Want of Fervor in God's Service

Because thou art lukewarm, and neither cold nor hot,
I will begin to vomit thee out of my mouth.

—Rev. 3:16

We begin at once to go back in the spiritual life when we become luke-warm or lax in the service of God. It is the first step that leads to sin and death. To languish, says St. Bernard—not the languor of love like that of the Spouse of the Canticle, not that languor of dryness that David felt when God withdrew His consolations and seemed to leave him to himself, but that lukewarmness that is culpable and voluntary, that languor that is our own doing and, through cowardice, makes us throw off the yoke of Christian regularity—induces us to neglect the ordinary exercises of piety and prayer, causes us to feel a distaste for penance, so much so that we withdraw from the sacraments and cease from performing good works. In short, it makes us feel that religion is so wearisome that we can no longer serve the Lord our God in spirit and truth.

This is what St. Bernard means when he depicts spiritual tepidity; and God wills that we should reflect on our past tepidity and attend to what His saints teach us.

The state of lukewarmness is hurtful to everyone, inasmuch as it is one of those maladies of the soul to cure which the strongest remedies are often found to be ineffectual. Such a state is also in direct opposi-tion to the grace of penance, because, in lieu of that holy fear that it ought to excite within us, it substitutes fruitless fears that result in nothing.

We must try to check the growth of tepidity by thinking of the holiest Christian duties and fortify our will by prayer and watchfulness.

In lesser attacks of lukewarmness that are not actually culpable, far from lessening our devotions, we should, on the contrary, try to be more fervent, more regular in our exercises of piety. To succeed in this, it is preferable to practice solid devotion, to encourage the most generous piety, because it often happens that he who serves God with less sensible devotion serves Him with more merit and perfection.

This lukewarmness does not come upon us suddenly. Like unto the foolish virgins mentioned in the Gospel (Matt. 25:3), it changes from a drowsiness to a deep slumber.

An indifference about our salvation, a contempt for little duties, a falling off from all that is good and hopeful, a complacency in all that is bad—all these stupefy the soul and reduce it to that state of Jonah, who slept soundly during the violent storm, when all those who were in the ship were sore afraid, and yet he remained, as it were, in a lethargic sleep.

It is in vain for a confessor to advise, vain for the preacher to exhort. If lukewarmness is accompanied by culpable negligence, the sinner will rarely, if ever, be awakened to a sense of his danger.

This is a true picture of very many who add to their indifference the torpidity of an obstinate negligence; those who do not wish to fall into open sin but take no trouble to advance in virtue; who, although absolved from past sins, still remain in a guilty negligence of their everyday duties; who do not deny the truths of our holy Faith but, in listening to exhortations, pay no attention or heed them not; who, under the pretense that they are not as bad as many others, never wish or try to imitate those who are fervent.

In conclusion, it is to such as these that the Holy Spirit alludes when He pronounces the curse on those who do the work of the Lord negligently.

—Fr. Louis Bourdaloue (1632–1704), *Passion*

The Want of Fervor in God's Service

∞

The earnestness, the zeal, the love of Mary Magdalen compelled our Savior to console her. She knew Him by His voice. O my God, what were at that moment the transports of love, the tender gratitude of that holy soul!

Those who are lukewarm in the service of God cannot realize this, because they love so little and consequently cannot know how much she loved Him. Such as these would wish to be all for Jesus, but they wish it if God will be satisfied with a divided love—if God would accept a service of their own, and not the one He desires.

They would like to be perfect, but only in their own imperfect way. They wish to rely on human prudence and, if anything, overtax their strength. They lose courage and are frightened at the least difficulty.

Vain are the desires, frivolous are the pretexts, of a heart steeped in tepidity.

—Fr. Croiset, S.J. (b. ca. 1650)

∞

Howsoever long you may have lived, howsoever persevering you have been in doing well, do not say, "It is enough; I am all right now"; for this would be as much as to say, "It is sufficient, I will now begin to slacken and fall off."

—St. Augustine (354–430), *On Psalm 69*

31

∞

God's Mercy

How great is the mercy of the Lord, and
His forgiveness to them that turn to Him.

—Sirach 17:28 (RSV = Sirach 17:29)

Mercy is the tranquility of God's omnipotence and the sweetness of His omnipresence, the fruit of His eternity and the companion of His immensity, the chief satisfaction of His justice, the triumph of His wisdom, and the patient perseverance of His love.

Wherever we go there is mercy, the peaceful, active, endless mercy of our Heavenly Father. If we work by day, we work in mercy's light; and we sleep at night in the lap of our Father's mercy. The courts of heaven gleam with its outpoured prolific beauty. Earth is covered with it, as the waters cover the bed of the stormy sea. Purgatory is, as it were, its own separate creation and is lighted by its gentle moonlight, gleaming there soft and silvery, through night and day. His mercy is simply infinite, for mercy is one of His perfections, while His love is the harmony of all.

Mercy does not tire of us, does not despair of us, does not give over its pursuit of us, takes no offense, repays evil with good, and is the ubiquitous minister of the Precious Blood of Jesus. But love seems more than this. Love fixes upon each of us, individualizes us, is something personal; but mercy is something by itself.

Love is the perfection of the uncreated in Himself. Mercy is the character of the Creator.

God's Mercy

Mercy pities, spares, makes allowances, condescends; and yet if mercy is not the reason of God's love, where else shall we find it in His infinity?

—Fr. Frederick William Faber (1814–1863), *Creator and Creature*

∞

God so pardons our sins that He blots out even the remembrance of the greatest outrage. God does not act as men do. He does not grant half a pardon.

When anyone has betrayed our trust, or has mortally offended us— howsoever we may wish to become reconciled to the offender, or may cherish an earnest desire to forgive, and strive in our heart to do so—nevertheless we find it difficult to place the same confidence in him, or to treat him with the same affection as before. There remains in the corner of our heart a tinge of bitterness from time to time, or when we call to mind what he has done to us.

Our merciful Lord is not subject to this weakness.

O! would that all sinners who sincerely repent of their past offenses could see in His heart the feelings He has for them—no resentment, no bitterness there! And how thoroughly He forgives them!

God does not stop there. Not content with forgetting our trespasses, He gives us back the merit of those good deeds that we had lost by losing His grace. He restores to us those merits and that grace with interest, and He places us in a position more advantageous than that in which we were when we fell away from Him.

I am not at all astonished that St. Mary Magdalen had not, even after thirty years had elapsed, ceased to weep for her sins, although she could not doubt but they had been remitted. I am not surprised that St. Peter should have been inconsolable even unto death for having failed in his fidelity to so good a Master, notwithstanding the certainty he had of being forgiven.

Can one be mindful that so good a Master has been offended without having one's heart torn with grief and without feeling a hatred of one's self? Can we, who have so coolly insulted Him without any reason, having, on the contrary, a thousand reasons to love Him, we, who have for so long a time abused His love, His patience, His blessings, His mercy — can we, I say, recollect this without dying of regret and repentance?

It is that thought that redoubles my grief, at having so cruelly sinned against a God who has so readily forgiven me, who has returned good for evil, and all kinds of blessings in return for every kind of evil.

Can it be that I shall ever forget the ingratitude that He has so soon forgotten? Can it be that I should forgive my infidelities, which He not only has pardoned but has urged me to accept His forgiveness many a time? In fine, can it be that I should remain satisfied after having insulted His divine goodness so often and for so long a time, a God who does not love me less today, and who loves me even more now than before I had offended Him?

—St. Claude de la Colombière (1641–1682), *Reflections*

◌∞◌

God's Mercy in Our Illnesses

My son, in thy sickness forget not thyself,
but pray to the Lord, and He shall heal thee.

—Sirach 38:9

How sweet to suffer for Jesus Christ! I cannot find words energetic enough to tell you what I feel, more especially since I have been confined in prison, where we are forced to observe a continual fast. The strength of my body has left me, but the joy of my heart increases in proportion to the prospect of a speedy death. What a happiness it will be if I am permitted to sing next Easter Sunday the *Haec Dies* in heaven!

Had you tasted the sweet delight that God has poured into our souls, you would indeed despise the good things this world affords. Since I have been in prison for His sake, I feel that I am a disciple of Jesus. I now find myself fully compensated for the pangs of hunger, by the consoling sweetness that filled my soul; and were I to be immured in prison for years, the time would appear to me to be short, so much do I desire to suffer for Him who rewards me so liberally for my pains.

Among other illnesses, I have had a fever raging within me which lasted a hundred days, without the possibility of being relieved. During all this time my joy has been so great that I find it useless to describe it in words.

—Blessed Charles Spinola (1564–1622)

My Daily Visit with the Saints

∞

When we are in good health there are two things that usually go far to stifle every sense of the fear of God, and these are the hope of a long life and the forgetfulness of eternity.

So long as the sinner is strong and well, the thought of death never enters into his mind; or, if it should, it makes but little impression upon him, because he looks upon it as an event very far off.

Then comes the judgment (which awaits until that fearful moment), and even the thought of this does not affect him, for he lives as if he never had to give an account of his misdeeds. But when he finds himself stretched on a bed of sickness, weak, languid, exhausted with pain and overcome with grief, it is then that he recollects that he is mortal; and, seeing himself so near that fearful passage that he had not before thought of, he cannot but be much alarmed at finding that he is compelled to ponder on the danger he is in, and the necessity of preparing for the salvation of his soul.

This, then, is the short road by which the Divine Mercy leads worldlings and draws them back to His service.

That libertine would have gone on carelessly for ten years more had not God in His mercy sent him a malignant fever, which has frightened him and made him return to his duty.

Doctors are accustomed to wound one part of the body in order to cure another part; they open a vein in a sound arm to relieve a feverish brain; they make use of the cupping-glass to remove inflammation; they keep a wound open in order to be able to close another; and, as St. Jerome says, the secret of their science consists in restoring health through pain.

The Son of God, who is the Physician of souls, follows the same method to cure sinners. He smites the flesh to cure the mind, and from illnesses, which are the forerunners of the death of the body, He frames a good provision for the life of the soul.

All the holy Fathers teach us that illness is the school of Christian wisdom, the dawning of virtue whereby the mind is invigorated, and the grand means of grace, which redoubles its strength through the weakness of the body. When I am weak, says St. Paul, it is then that I am strong (see 2 Cor. 12:10). I am never more vigorous in mind than when my body is exhausted with illness and wearied with weakness. More than this, illness may be said to be victorious over vice, through the triumph of grace over the passions of the soul, and a triumph of the soul over the appetites of the flesh.

It is then that the sensualist thinks more of his health than of his pleasures. It is then that the miser dreams not of his riches, but sighs for the treasure of health. It is then that the ambitious man throws aside his vanity and builds no more castles in the air. The gormandizer sobers down at the sight of death, the envious and vindictive proclaim a truce; for the pains of the body soften the bitterness of the mind.

Is it not, then, a wonderful blessing that Almighty God should allow the infirmities of the body to arrest the impetuosity of our passions?

—Fr. Nouet, S.J. (1605–1680), *Méditations*

∞

That illness has been your salvation. You have suffered, but your life has not been in danger. This is what the Lord has said, "I will strike him, and I will cure him" (Deut. 32:29).

He has struck you, your illness has awakened your faith, and that has been your cure.

—St. Ambrose (340–397), *Epistles*

∞

God's Mercy in Our Afflictions

Tribulation worketh patience;
and patience trial, and trial hope.

—Romans 5:3–4

Jesus Christ has forewarned us that we would be persecuted in this world. St. Paul, in like manner, says that all they who wish to dwell in Christ will suffer great afflictions, not only through the agency of man, but through the instrumentality of the devil and his angels.

Job emphatically says that the whole of our life here below, is one chain of temptations. Why then should we be so sensitive of tribulations, if such be the period fixed for all kinds of afflictions?

You would indeed have just cause to groan if you had passed through a life of pleasure and sensual delight—a time that our Savior had allotted for troubles, vexations, and mortifications.

If you are inactive, or apt to pine, buckle on your armor and fight courageously, If you walk on the broad path when the narrow way is recommended, what will your lot be? What fearful thoughts will be in store for you!

Cite, I entreat you, a single instance of a person who, after leading a cowardly indifferent life has participated in the reward God has promised to His elect. We must always keep in mind that our Savior warns us that the gate of heaven is small, that the road that leads to it is narrow, and that few can find it.

It is evident, therefore, that no one need go astray if he but follow the right path.

—St. John Chrysostom (ca. 349–407)

∽

To cure the blindness that almost always accompanies prosperity, the surest remedy is to be found as in the case of Tobias's gall of the fish — that is to say, in afflictions and chastisements.

When a violent fever will, as it were, liquefy your bones; when you lie on your bed prostrate and full of grievous pain, you will then see that the body for which you have so often risked your soul, that you have clothed with so much luxury, that you have pampered with so many delicacies is but a fragile vessel that the slightest accident might shatter and that, of itself, may be broken.

When a preconcerted calumny or any underhand conspiracy causes you to fall from a position to which you ambitiously aspired and may have kept up by intrigue, you will at last be convinced of the nothingness and instability of human greatness.

When age or some unforeseen calamity effaces that beauty that attracted many admirers, and that in your heart you wished to preserve, you will be forced to confess that all is vanity and vexation of spirit.

When sent adrift by a capricious master, or betrayed by a cowardly false friend, you will naturally feel contempt for those from whom you expected protection and assistance, and you will then know that one must not trust to human support; but if you wish never to be deceived, you must place all your confidence in God alone.

Losses and disgrace may be (and often are, thanks be to God) the means and cause of our conversion. They excite us to do penance, and make us feel how just is God, and that afflictions are the best victims we can offer to appease Him. They try us when we feel a natural repugnance to them. They sanctify us if we accept with humble submission both evils and remedies together. We suffer troubles, and acquire merit by our patience; occasions of conflict and victory—suffering and longanimity—knowledge and practice, go hand in hand. They are the merciful means of softening our stony hearts, and whoever resists or is insensible to the chastisements that God sends for his instruction and conversion, his mind and will, will be enveloped in impenetrable darkness. I tremble, if I dare to say so, for his salvation.

—Bishop Esprit Fléchier (1632–1710)

∞

Actual Grace

We do exhort you, that you receive not the grace of God in vain.

—2 Corinthians 6:1

St. Aelred describes the state of his soul before he resolved to leave the world, its pomps and vanities. In the life of the saint by Godescard, the saint says:

Those who looked only at the external grandeur that surrounded me — those who judged of my position in the world — knew not what was passing within me, and yet they cried out, "Oh, how enviable is the lot of that man! How happy he must be!"

But they did not see my dejection of mind; they did not know of the insupportable anguish of a heart weighed down by sin.

It was then, O my God, that I knew of the unutterable joy I felt when I found myself supported by Thy grace, and that I tasted of that peace that is now my inseparable companion.

—St. Aelred (1110–1167)

∞

The operations of grace in the conversion of a sinner are not always the same. At one time it is a sharp and piercing ray that, darting from the bosom of the Eternal Father, enlightens, strikes, humbles, and overcomes those upon whom it descends. At another time, it is a more subdued brightness that has its progression and succession, that seems to battle for victory over the dark clouds that it wishes to disperse, and after a thousand attacks, succeeded by as many repulses, it remains for some time doubtful as to which shall carry off the palm.

Now, it is a powerful God who overthrows the cedars of Lebanon; then it is the God most patient who wrestles with His servant Jacob and holds him fast in order to make him enter the right path wherein He invites him.

It is thus, O my God, that You act as the instructor, the Master of all hearts.

First proof of grace: to conquer a guilty and rebellious soul, which alone would prevent its conversion, God even makes use of its guilty passion. He seeks to excite in it those very places in which the sinner sought for pleasure and amusement. Saul in his fury runs to Damascus in order to persecute the Church, and on his road he is struck to the ground and becomes an apostle. The centurion rides up to Mount Calvary to complete the barbarous outrages of the executioners of Jesus Christ, and a ray of light descends upon him, and he confesses that He was truly the Son of God.

A soul experiences trouble and remorse in the very places wherein it vainly sought for pleasure and satisfaction.

Grace awaits, so to speak, at the gates of sin and crime; and disgust, perfidy, bitterness of soul, disgrace, and other frightful consequences are the punishments of the mercy of God, and the sinner often finds treasures of justice in the very place where he sought for his eternal loss.

Grace triumphs, when it wishes, over the greatest obstacles, because that heavenly unction changes at will our troubles into consolations, so that by means of this grace, that which was our delight, and which was to us a deadly poison, becomes a hidden manna, which feeds and strengthens us.

The Holy Spirit of God can, if He will, change the weakest of men into one so strong and powerful that nought can make him swerve from his fidelity, no danger can shake his firmness, no seductive pleasure can corrupt him. In one word, it is this, that grace, far stronger than nature, surmounts every obstacle and attracts gently and sweetly all hearts that He wishes to convert.

—Fr. Jean Baptiste Massillon (1663–1742)

∞

Grace is, par excellence, the gift of God. It is this that infinitely surpasses every gift of nature; it is the only source of our happiness, without which we can do nothing and with which, we can do everything. It is this gift that comes from on high and flows direct from the Father of Light, that converts us and makes us new men. It is that gift by which we are as we are, if, however, we are something before God, as the Apostle says, "By the grace of God I am what I am" (1 Cor. 15:10).

Yet, nevertheless (so strange it is), it is this same gift that, through our stubborn ignorance, we know not of and, through our unbearable ingratitude, we receive every day in vain. Alas! of what use is it to acknowledge its greatness and merit if we abuse it nearly every moment of our life?

It is for that, that our Savior, speaking to the Samaritan woman, chided her ignorance by saying, "Ah! woman, if you had known the nature and excellence of the gift of God" (John 4:10).

Grace triumphant must, so to speak, be subject to us. Be not shocked at this term, for it derogates nothing from the dignity of grace. It must be so subject to us as to well-nigh weary the patience of God, who waits for us for years without interfering with our free will. It selects the place and time; it seizes the most favorable opportunity to win us; it is the first to warn us, and, far from taking something away from us by force or violence, it entreats us with prayers and mild remonstrances, it accommodates itself to our weaknesses, adjusts itself to our humor, and if at last it makes us realize the blessings of heaven and the contempt for earthly joys, it is only after having convinced us by innumerable trials of the solidity of the one and the frailty of the other.

—Fr. Louis Bourdaloue (1632–1704), *On the Samaritan Woman*

∞

Sanctifying Grace

Where sin abounded, grace did more abound. That as sin hath reigned
to death, so also grace might reign by justice unto life everlasting.

—Romans 5:20–21

God, when He created man, gave him a free will, and this in so perfect a way that, without constraint, without impairing his liberty, He rules him by His power, frightens him by His threats, and wins him by His blessings.

He has an earnest wish for the salvation of all, but He waits for their consent, for their cooperation. It is to gain them that He warns them, that He encourages them, that He leads them in so wonderful a manner, so as to bring them, with His assistance, to that happiness that is their destiny.

These are the inventions of His wisdom, which the prophet Isaiah says that he will announce to the people (Isa.12).

For those who are reprobates, at one time He warns them with mildness, at another time He encourages them with kindness, and at another He corrects them with a paternal love, according to the disposition in which they are, and according to their necessities.

This loving conduct is a visible excess of the charity of our Lord, not only toward the good, but even toward the wicked, in order that they may be converted and become good.

All that contributes to our justification is an effect of His divine grace. It is that which accompanies this great work, which teaches us by exhortation, which encourages us by example, which terrifies us by chas-tisement, which moves us by miracles, which enlightens our mind, which induces us to follow wise counsels, which improves our understanding, and which inspires us with feelings conformable to the Faith that we profess.

Thus our will is subservient to grace and acts only conjointly with it; so that all these helps that God gives us require our cooperation, in order that we may begin to carry out the good resolutions that we have received from His divine inspirations. So, if we should fall into some sinful habit, we can impute our fall only to our own pusillanimity; and if we advance in virtue, we can attribute our advancement only to grace.

The help of grace is given to all in a thousand ways, be they secret or manifest. If many reject it, it is always their own fault; if some profit by it, it is the united effect of divine grace and the human will.

—St. Robert Bellarmine (1542–1621), *Opuscules*

∞

Some holy Fathers, in speaking of that passage, "And God created man according to His own image and likeness" (Gen. 1:27), say that man has two kinds of resemblance to God—the first, signified by the name of image, consists in that man by nature is endowed with an understanding and a will like unto God, capable of knowing Him and of loving Him; the second, expressed by the name of likeness, consists in that man was created in the grace of God, and this gives him a perfect resemblance to His Creator, which he had not in his natural being.

From thence it follows, that since God is the essential and unbegotten beauty, sanctifying grace is the most perfect, the noblest participator of that beauty; the soul that is endowed and adorned with it is infinitely pleasing in the eyes of God. So much so that a great saint, to whom was revealed the wondrous beauty of a soul in a state of grace, used to say that she no longer was astonished that God had willed to shed the last drop of His Precious Blood in order to cleanse it and, by His redemption, renew every trace of beauty that sin had entirely effaced.

But if God, who cannot deceive, is charmed with the beauty of a soul in a state of grace, how is it that we are so careless in enriching our souls by the practice of every virtue? Is it not lamentable that we should prefer to please a wretched being—uncomely though we be—rather than try to please the Divine Majesty by that true beauty that He is ever willing to give to those who seek Him?

We daily witness the pains that worldly-minded people take in dressing and decking out their bodies, merely for the sake of pleasing others; and often do we witness that exterior ornaments are sought after and used to hide their natural defects.

We are careful to adorn our bodies, which soon will be food for worms, and we neglect that most beautiful ornament of the soul, which is the grace of God.

—Fr. François Duneau (b. 1752), Sermon in Advent

∞

Acknowledge, O Christian, thy dignity, and after having been made participator of the divine nature, do not return to thy first state by leading a life that would tarnish thy nobility.

Is it not a gift, exceeding all other gifts, that God should call man His child, and that man should call God his Father?

—St. Leo (d. 461), *On the Nativity*

∞

Confidence in God

This is the confidence which we have towards God: that what-
soever we shall ask according to His will, He heareth us.

—1 John 5:14

Full confidence in the goodness of Almighty God is one of the sure marks of predestination.

The most criminal, corrupt, or wicked man who sincerely wishes to do penance for his past sins will find that confidence in God is an efficacious and sovereign remedy for all his miseries.

Let him be penitent, let him persevere in hope; he eventually will be saved. God has said it, God has promised it; is there any reason to doubt the word and promise of Him who is truth itself?

It is for this reason that hope has been compared to the anchor of a ship, and this comparison is consecrated by the Apostle St. Paul in his epistles. If a vessel should lose all its rigging in a tempest, if there still remain an anchor, there is hope that the crew may yet be saved.

The same thing might be said of confidence in God; and it was for want of having recourse to this that Cain and Judas perished in their sins. The first had angered God by jealousy and a cruel fratricide, but what put the climax to the curse was Cain saying in despair, "My crime is too great for any hope of pardon." The second repents of the shameful treachery he had committed against the Son of God, but, says St. Chrysostom, had he confided in the goodness of his Divine Master, had he returned to implore His mercy, our dear Redeemer, who pardoned St. Peter and who prayed for His executioners, would no doubt have led this traitor back to penance.

This confidence in God has also another advantage: it is a mighty help against temptations. "In hope you will find your strength" (see Isa. 30:15). In fine, what is more powerful than having confidence in God?

To confide in God is to lean upon Him. It is to call for His assistance, His goodness, His truth, His power.

With such arms, what can anyone fear; for what can prevail against God? It is in this confidence that one finds such fervent charity. This is easy to see by the difference there is between a presuming or a timid love and that which Holy Scripture says will banish fear.

From this proceeds the saying of the wise man: "He who is animated by charity is like unto an eagle who flies with rapidity, and who cleaves the air without hindrance."

In conclusion, did not the Apostle say to the early Christians, "Serve God with love, because to reach perfection joy and hope are the most efficacious means?"

—Fr. Vincent Houdry, S.J. (1630–1729)

∞

I feel so persuaded, O my God, that You graciously watch over those who hope in Thee, and that no one need require anything so long as they look up to Thee in all things, that I am determined for the future to lay at Your feet all my anxieties and troubles. "In peace, in the selfsame I will sleep and rest. For thou, O Lord, singularly hast settled me in hope" (Ps. 4:9–10 [RSV = Ps. 4:8]).

Men may deprive me of property and honor. Sickness may take away my strength and other means of serving You. I may even lose Your grace by sin. But never, never will I lose my hope in Thee. I will cherish it unto that dreadful moment when all hell will be unchained to snatch my soul away. "No one hath hoped in the Lord and hath been confounded" (Sir. 2:11 [RSV = Sir. 2:10]).

I know, alas! I know too well that I am weak, headstrong, and change-able. I know what temptations can do against the firmest resolution. I have seen some stars from heaven fall. But all these shall not frighten me so long as I hope in Thee.

I hold myself in readiness to meet bravely all misfortunes, because my hope is not shaken. I hope, too, that You will help me to overcome every spiritual enemy, that You will defend me against every assault, and You will make me triumph over my fiercest passions.

—St. Claude de la Colombière (1641–1682)

∞

Zeal for God

I bear them witness, that they have a zeal for
God, but not according to knowledge.

—Romans 10:2

We read in the annals of ecclesiastical history that the prefect Modestus was
sent to St. Basil, who was at that time bishop of Caesarea, with a message
from the emperor threatening him with his vengeance if he continued to exercise
his zeal for the conversion of his subjects. The prefect made specious proposals
and told the saint that much might be expected from his master's generosity if
he would but moderate his zeal. Promises succeeded menaces, for such as these
are all that man can do. St. Basil replied that where God was concerned there
is nothing more important for His servants to do than to be firm in the exercise
of their ministry. The following portion of his reply is taken from the twentieth
oration of St. Gregory Nazianzen:

"When there is a question of our essential duties, we will be as obliging
and as humble as our rules prescribe. We should be sorry to show any
arrogance, not only to emperors or kings, but even to the lowest of men.
But when the interests of God are concerned, we should recognize no human consideration, as we look to God alone. The most frightful torture,
far from alarming me, would give me joy.

"Threaten as you will, put all kinds of outrages into execution, do
your worst, go tell your master, for you will gain nothing. Were you to

reach the height of your cruel threats, you will never be able to force us to subscribe to your impious doctrines."

The prefect, astonished at the saint's firmness, told him that no one had ever spoken to him in that bold way.

"Perhaps," replied the saint, "you have never spoken to a bishop before."

—Fr. Lambert (d. 1836), adapted from *Discours Ecclésiastiques*

∞

It is an error to suppose that priests and missionaries ought alone to be zealous. There is not one who has not a mission to fulfill, without going out of his state in life; not a single person who ought not to connect his own salvation with that of his brethren. Your own sanctification is, of course, your first and greatest business. Everyone should look to this; but everyone is bound to edify his neighbor, by giving a good example. This zeal is common to all and to all conditions of life.

Are you in office? Have you inferiors? Have you the cares of a family and servants? Few professed missionaries have so much to answer for and have to give an account of their salvation as you have.

Take especial care not to neglect this duty. Do not leave it to others. Watch continually over the conduct of those whom God has confided to your care. Children, servants, inferiors are all, so to speak, so many trusts of which you are liable to render an account to your Sovereign Master. Besides the efficacy of a good example, you are called upon to give them education, instruction, and good advice.

Watch over the manners of your children and servants; with regard to morals and religion, pass over nothing; do not suffer anyone to give them bad example; check, warn, and correct with zeal and mildness.

In whatever condition of life you may be, remember that you have to fulfill the duties of an apostle. Christian charity obliges you to take to heart the salvation of your brethren, and do not forget to do all you can to obtain this desirable object.

It is not solely by preaching that the conversion of many are brought about; there are other ways much more efficacious. A kind word in season, a warning, a charitable advice, a good example, an alms—all these may be used with a zeal truly apostolic.

There is no father or mother who can fail to do an immensity of good in the home and with the servants.

What good cannot a superior in a community do, if he is animated with a pure and ardent zeal and an exemplary piety! What an immense benefit could princes do at the court and in their estates if they had at heart the truths of our holy religion! Would not honor, honesty, and justice then reign throughout their lands?

—Fr. Croiset, S.J. (b. ca. 1650), *Année Chrétienne*

∞

The will of my Father, says His Divine Son, and the reason He sent me, is to save souls and not to lose one He entrusted to me. In fact, as God has nothing more dear to Him than the salvation of men, so nothing is more pleasing to Him than to see them withdrawn from the abyss and led into the right path.

It is the favorite theme of Holy Writ, the omega of all the mysteries, the center of His love, the end of all His designs and of His labors; for which, as says St. Augustine, He created the heavens, extended the seas, and formed the foundations of the earth. And what is of greater value? For this He sent His only Son.

This is the reason that St. Gregory the Great gives when he tells us that we cannot offer to the Almighty a more pleasing service than a zeal for souls. And St. Chrysostom assures us that we can do nothing more agreeable to God than to sacrifice our life to the common benefit of all men.

Meditate awhile on this, you who have so many persons under your charge and direction; and at least, if you cannot place them in heaven, try not to lose one whom God has given to you to direct and govern, to whose hands He has confided under your care, so that you may be able to say with our Savior, "Of them whom thou hast given me, I have not lost any one" (John 18:9).

—Fr. Nouet, S.J. (1605–1680), *Méditations*

Part 2

∞

God the Son and God the Holy Spirit

∞

The Incarnation

Behold a virgin shall conceive and bear a son,
and his name shall be called Emmanuel.

—Isaiah 7:14

I have often thought of, and meditated on, the holy eagerness of the patriarchs who so sighed for the coming of the Messiah; and I felt confused and was, moreover, so penetrated with grief that I could scarcely refrain from weeping, so much was I ashamed to see the tepidity and indifference of these unhappy days.

For who among us is filled with as much joy in the fulfillment of this mystery as were the saints of the Old Testament at the promises that so called forth their longing desires?

Many, it is true, may rejoice at the celebration of this feast, but I am much afraid that it is less on account of the feast than through vanity.

—St. Bernard (1091–1153), *Sermon on the Song of Songs*

∞

The Son of God has taken upon Himself our poverty and miseries in order that we may participate in His riches. His sufferings will one day render us impassible, and His death will make us immortal.

We should find our joy in His tears, our resurrection in His tomb, our sanctification in His baptism, in accordance with what He says in the Gospel: "I sanctify myself in order that they also may be sanctified in truth" (see John 17:19).

There is not a phase in the life of our Savior that does not refer to Calvary. The Good Master was born in the stable only to die on the Cross. His life, which I should study continually, would show me all the riches of His love. I should see therein all the profound mysteries of His Incarnation and redemption. I should discover what I have cost. I should appreciate the beauty and goodness of Jesus, and I shall then cry out, "O happy fault which has procured us such a Redeemer!"[1]

—St. Athanasius (ca. 296–373)

∞

In order that nothing should be wanting to heighten the glory of this great mystery, before Jesus was born, or rather from the beginning of the world and from all ages, He had been promised to the patriarchs, He had been announced by the prophets, foretold by the sybils, represented throughout by ancient ceremonies, sacrifices, and every sacrament of the old law.

And when He deigned to descend from heaven to earth, by what circumstances, what prodigies, has not His coming been accompanied, which were but reasonable for so supreme a Majesty.

An angel sent by God has brought the glad tidings, He has been conceived of the Holy Spirit, He had chosen the purest and holiest of virgins to become incarnate in her womb, and the body He has taken has been united to the Divinity from His conception.

Pagans imagined that it was unworthy of the majesty of God to clothe Himself with a substance so degrading as our flesh. But it is easy to show

[1] "O Felix Culpa," sung within the Exultet during the Easter Vigil.

them how this humanity has been glorified, what riches it has possessed, and, far from having been a thing below the dignity of God, it has, on the contrary, considerably added to His glory, by uniting these two natures into one person.

It is in such marvels as these that the wisdom of God appears more apparent. It shows also that He alone is capable of elevating lowliness, of aggrandizing that which is nothing, of filling with honor and dignity that which was contemptible. For if, by an effect of His goodness, He had wished to humiliate Himself by becoming man, nevertheless having taken the nature of man, instead of receiving ignominy therefrom, He has, on the contrary, received an infinity of glory, since it was in His power to do what He would have wished, without making use of anything but His will alone.

But what words can describe the immensity of the various gifts with which the Holy Spirit has endowed this sacred humanity, the first and foremost being His unspeakable union with the Divine Word, which is the greatest of all the wonders that the power of God could make?

Through that, this sacred humanity has been raised above all that God has created, and beyond anything that His infinite power is capable of creating; and in order that this supreme dignity may correspond with His grandeur and magnificence, it has been made the fountain of every grace. The grace of being the universal Head of all mankind has been given to Him, in order that, through it all the treasures of heaven should be communicated to the children of Adam.

— Venerable Louis de Granada (1505–1588),
Meditations on the Love of God

∽

Here is a wonder that in itself is out of the ordinary course of nature, of which experience has not taught us, a marvel that reason ignores, of which the human intellect cannot conceive, that astonishes heaven and earth, that creates admiration even among the celestial choir. And this mystery is that Gabriel the archangel announces to Mary, "The Lord is with thee," and the accomplishment thereof is the work of the Holy Spirit.

—St. Jerome (ca. 347–420), *Sermon on the Assumption*

The Divinity of Jesus Christ

I adjure thee by the living God, that thou tell us if thou be the
Christ, the Son of God. Jesus saith to him: Thou hast said it.

—Matthew 26:63–64

Having meditated on our Lord and Savior in His eternal generation, should we not then take into consideration His temporal generation? They are both ineffable. "Who shall declare His generation?" (Isa. 53:8).

Jesus is equally great in His humiliations, because He is always God. Admiration is almost our sole portion. In fact, how wonderful it is that Jesus should have united the privileges of His divinity to the meanness and misery of our human nature, and that, without ceasing to be a God infinite, eternal, immense, immortal, and independent, He should have become a God-Man enclosed within the narrow confines of a body, of a stable, and of the swaddling clothes that enveloped Him in His infancy! That Jesus should have personally united our meanness with His grandeur, our mortality with His immortality, His divine nature with our human nature, becoming Son of Man and Son of the Virgin Mary for all eternity, as from all eternity He is Son of God and only Son of the Eternal Father! We must adore Jesus in this new condition and in this profound mystery, in the unity of His divine person and in the diversity of their natures — the one divine and eternal, the other human and temporal.

It is with this view that, raising our hearts to You, O Jesus, to pay You our homage, we adore You as receiving Your everlasting essence from the Eternal Father, and as giving Your essence and substance to human nature; that You have united to Yourself forever a union so intimate, so mighty, so glorious, and so divine.

O adorable state! O ineffable mystery! O happy moment of the Incarnation, which makes man God and God man, which gives to heaven a King of glory, to earth a Sovereign, to the angels a Redeemer, and to men a Savior!

O God, who has willed that Your only-begotten Son, who, being God from all eternity in You, should have been made man in time and eternity for us, grant us the grace of ever honoring that wondrous life and that Divine Word, in order that we may be animated with His Spirit on earth, and that we may rejoice with Him in heaven by constantly meditating on Him who is our life and glory.

—Cardinal Pierre de Bérulle (1575–1629),
On the Grandeurs of Jesus

∞

To convince the Jews that Jesus Christ was really and truly the Messiah whom they expected—promised by the law and foretold by the prophets—miracles were necessary so as to make unbelief inexcusable, and which ought to have compelled them to say with Nicodemus, "We know that Thou art come a teacher from God, for no man can do these signs which Thou dost unless God be with Him" (John 3:2). For if the Son of God was not manifested by means of miracles, His divinity would not have been acknowledged, inasmuch as the humble life of the Savior seemed to be incompatible with the Supreme Majesty.

Jesus Christ Himself—has He not said that if He had not performed works that only a God-Man could accomplish, the Jews might have had some reasonable excuse for rejecting His testimony and would not have acknowledged Him as the Messiah? His miracles, then, had authorized

His mission and manifested His divinity—although it may be said that, in fact, there have been false miracles and wicked impostors.

The miracles of the Savior are attested by unimpeachable witnesses and by authentic testimonies. The reputation of His miracles attracted around Him crowds of people who could not all be deceived, and five thousand persons witnessed the multiplication of barley loaves, with which they were fully satiated.

I am aware that the Pharisees and scribes wished to take no heed of facts that they attributed to the illusions of the devil or to the agency of magic, but what connection can there be between light and darkness?

Have there never been professors of the black art who perform prodigies? Have not magicians professed to cure the blind and raise the dead?

Besides, a man so incontestably holy as was Jesus Christ, was it meet and proper to make use of the power and ministry of the devil? And the devil, on his part, would he have made use of a man who could have made his idols powerless, his oracles mute? How, then, could you reconcile with the magic art works that are done only in confirmation of a doctrine that abhors all diabolical operations?

More than this, have not these wondrous performances been examined by the severest censors, submitted to the most rigorous critics, and to the inquiries of judges far from being favorable to Jesus?

At the sight of these miracles, how many persons of consequence among the Jews have acknowledged Him to be a Prophet sent from God? How many others who, believing in their hearts, have not dared to make a public profession of faith for fear of being banished from the synagogue? And since that time, have not Celsus, Porphyry, Julian the Apostate, Mahomet—the greatest enemies Jesus Christ ever had in the world—have they not honestly confessed that He was a man of miracles, thereby giving testimony of His doctrine, His merit, and consequently of His divinity?

∞

The angels have honored the Word Incarnate on His entry into the world, and have acknowledged how much is the Son of God above His

servants: "Being made so much better than the angels, as He hath inherited a more excellent name than they" (Heb. 1:4). They have served
Him during His mortal and suffering life, as also in the sacred position
of His immortality. This is what the following words intend to convey:
"Amen I say to you, you shall see the heaven opened, and the angels
of God ascending and descending upon the Son of Man" (John 1:51).
They have ministered to Him, I say, during the whole course of His life,
and you know the service they gave Him in the desert after the devil
had tempted Him. They consoled Him in His agony, they wept for His
death in a manner that angels only can shed tears: "The angels of peace
shall weep bitterly" (Isa. 33:7). They joyfully announced His resurrection
to His disciples. They accompanied Him everywhere while He dwelt
visibly on earth. They formed the procession and joined in the triumph
on His entry into heaven. They will be His escort on the day of the last
judgment. They will gather around Him in heaven for ever and ever.
The noblest, the highest in the choir will esteem themselves happy to be
beneath His feet, and, angels as they are, they will gladly acknowledge
a man as their King on the throne of God itself.

—Fr. Dozennes, *The Divinity of Jesus Christ*

Belief in Christ Our Lord

*Go and teach ye all nations, baptizing them in the name of
the Father, and of the Son, and of the Holy Spirit.*

—Matthew 28:19

Incredulous mortals are still to be met with, who, after the accomplishment
of all that has been foretold—after having seen the consummation of the
mysteries of Jesus Christ, the excellence of His Gospels, the manifestation
of His miracles, the wisdom of His precepts, the vanity of the pomp of ages,
the destruction of idols, the utter confusion of the Caesars, the plots of
the whole world against Him—there are, I say, still to be found men who
doubt of the truths of His holy religion. They ask for fresh miracles and
encourage those who try to confute or to ridicule what the labors of the
Apostles have effected, what the prudence of so many missionaries has
established, what innumerable miracles have confirmed, what the purity of
so many virgins has honored, what the austerity of hermits has sealed, what
the sacrifice and detachment of so many servants of God have authorized,
and what the example of so many grand saints has inspired.

It is that a religion of seventeen centuries, ever the same, ever consistent and universally accepted by the world, seems to have maintained
its authority.

For in the midst of the triumphs of Christianity there have continually risen rebellious children against it, children whom the Almighty
has given over to the pride of their self-conceit, to the misguidance of

their reason, to the corruptions of their mind, who blaspheme what they ignore, who deny what they do not understand; wicked men who pervert the grace of God and convert light to darkness; disobedient men who despise every rule, who reject all authority not their own, who defile all their ways like unto animals without reason, and who are waiting to be summoned to suffer the punishment for their blasphemy at the judgment seat of God.

The Church of Jesus Christ has found the whole universe to be docile and submissive to its precepts; the Caesars, to whom she forbade luxury; nations, on whom she enforced obedience, to whom she preached suffering; the rich, to whom she recommended poverty; the poor, to whom she enjoined resignation; all, to whom she preached mortification, penance, and self-denial. This Faith, however, and this religion, preached by twelve poor sinners without science, without talent, without support, without favor, has overcome the world and has made it acknowledge the truths of its inscrutable mysteries. And the folly of the Cross has proved to be wiser than all the wisdom of ages.

What more! My brother, all turn against the Church, yet that only serves to increase her power. To be loyal and to be a martyr was the same thing, and the more violent were the persecutions, the more it acquired strength, and the blood of the martyrs became a fruitful seed of Christianity.

—Fr. Jean Baptiste Massillon (1663–1742)

∞

It was not the eloquence of the Apostles that confirmed the Faith; their language was simple and plain. It was not the easy belief of their doctrine; it was a God crucified they preached. It was not the indulgence of their morals; for they spoke, as their Master did, of the cross, poverty, and patience. And how is it that the whole universe has surrendered to a preaching so novel and so strange? How could so many clever men have been able to submit their understanding to truths so startling? How could so many who, immersed in sensuality, so resolutely embrace a life of mortifications, if the Apostles, the messengers of God, had not been the instruments of His power, and if those divine clouds had not astonished the earth by their brightness before watering it with their rains?

Do you not wonder at the boldness that twelve poor sinners displayed when they parceled out the world among them? It is said that the successors of Alexander divided it, but it was already a world conquered; instead of this, the Apostles dispersed to conquer. One had the task of subduing Asia, another Egypt, another Judea and those countries that the conquest of nations had not reached.

What is more surprising, they all succeeded, and by what means? And this is more wondrous still: by a doctrine contrary to sense and reason (at least in appearance), by preaching a God crucified.

—Bishop Jean Louis de Fromentière (1652–1684)

∞

The Master of that religion has been crucified. His servants have been chained down like criminals, and yet for all that, His religion grows and flourishes every day.

—St. Jerome (ca. 347–420), Epistle 50

∞

The Love of Jesus for Souls

As the Father hath loved me, I also
have loved you. Abide in my love.

—John:15:9

Can we have any conception of a greater love for men than that of our Savior, since, however wicked or ungrateful we may have been, He does not cease to love us? He forgives us our trespasses so readily that one would say that He was under an obligation to us. He rewards us for our good works liberally, never revealing how much He has contributed toward their performance. He, as it were, magnifies the little services we pay Him, without letting us know the immense assistance He has given us.

Although, in fact, we have done next to nothing for Him, He does not cease to be grateful, and He showers down graces with profusion, just as if we had rendered Him some important service.

Ah! Heart of Jesus — Heart truly liberal and full of love of men — who gives us everything, and to whom we owe all, and who by His own gifts, makes Himself our debtor! After that, who could fail to love Him with all their heart, with all their mind and all their strength, and offer up repeated acts of thanksgiving for goodnesses so bountiful, love so generous?

If we ought to love our Savior for the many blessings He has bestowed upon us, we ought no less to love Him for the many misfortunes from which He has delivered us, and from which only He could have freed us.

It is He who has had compassion on us, and who, being our only resource, has taken upon Himself to pay all our debts and to expiate, by a cruel and bloody death, all our sins. It is He, then, who alone has redeemed the human race from misfortune in which He was so willingly engaged; it is He who has drawn us from hell, who, having broken our chains, has made us free. Alas! without Thee, where would we be now? We would have been cast into the darkness of the abyss. It is He who from darkness has revealed to us the light of day, who from this dark abyss has shown us the way to heaven, to which we are entitled to aspire. What would we be without Him but a mass of dust and corruption? It is He who has so cleansed us that we are like unto the angels; in one word, it is He who, making us sharers in His glory, has delivered us from every kind of misery, who has replenished us with blessings without number.

And after all this, can we possibly be ungrateful? Can we have but little love for Him? We ought indeed to look upon Him as our greatest benefactor.

If the meanest of men had rescued us from perilous danger, although without much exertion, would we not take a liking to him? What feelings of gratitude ought we not therefore to cherish for One who has rescued us from dangers without number—a Savior who, to show His love, has so generously shed every drop of His Precious Blood?

O my Savior and my God, how can we sufficiently repay You for Your infinite goodness—You who have delivered us from the tyranny of the evil one, from the bondage of sin?

For let us try to realize, if we can, what is the extent of the misery from which the Savior has delivered us. Meditate seriously for a while, and you will not be surprised. We shall wonder at His boundless love and offer up repeated acts of thanksgiving for so many blessings.

A man who walks in his sleep and, without knowing where he goes, misses stepping over the edge of a precipice, is seized with a shuddering wonder when he awakens and sees the danger he has escaped. Let us awaken and, with the light of faith, look down the precipice from which the Savior has withdrawn us—look down again, and its depth will astonish us.

Many there are who tremble with fear when they cast their glances from the extreme point of a very lofty mountainous rock. How ought we not to tremble at the sight of that abyss into which Adam had thrown us and from which our Savior has withdrawn us?

Nevertheless, the distance from heaven to hell is not so far removed as was the state of sin in which we were to the state of grace in which we are, through the merits of Jesus Christ.

—Fr. Jean Eusèbe de Nieremberg, S.J. (1590–1658), *Jesus Amabilis*

∽

The Nativity of Our Lord

And she brought forth her firstborn Son, and wrapped Him in swaddling clothes, and laid Him in a manger.

—Luke 2:7

My brethren, let us gaze upon the Son of God in the poverty of His birth. What does He not say to us there? Let us enter in spirit into the stable; we shall hear a voice issuing therefrom, saying:

Blush at having beautiful houses like unto palaces, such grand furniture, so much useless apparel, while I have only a crib instead of a bed and vile animals for company. Blush in those magnificent rooms wherein you try to be sheltered from the least inconveniences of the season, while a half-exposed stable leaves me a prey to all the hardships of a cold season.

Blush at the aversion you have for every kind of humiliation, at the precautions you take to continue in a condition that flatters your vanity, at the artifices you employ to conceal a poverty you ought to be proud of, at the contempt you display to all, who are not within the pale of your society.

Blush to bear perchance the insignia of the poverty and humiliations of Jesus Christ in your state of life and yet try to aspire to the pomp and luxury of the world shining around.

Let us contemplate this scene as faith points out. Let us enter this manger in spirit. Let us see this hidden Deity who, in the darkness of night, when all creatures are silent, in want of every necessity, is made poor to enrich us.

This Child is born in an empty stable, deserted by everyone. He is the God who created them and whom they obey. He is the everlasting Wisdom that assists at all the councils of God and which He has possessed from the beginning of time.

This divine wisdom, hidden in the limbs of an infant, was begotten in the brightness of the saints.

Ungrateful, deluded man, you who have not wished to know this divine Wisdom in the richness of His beauty, see Him now in the poverty of a stable! Laden as you have been with so many benefits and blessings, you have not recognized the hand that has spread them over you with such profusion; you have closed your ears to that striking voice that appeals to you with as many mouths as there are creatures. O man, adore thy God! His ingenious love has suggested another voice to persuade you: He teaches you through the poverty of the crib: "Now therefore, my children, hear me" (Prov. 8:32).

Ah, my brethren what does not this divine Child say, that Eternal Word that is now so silent?

No occasion to seek for rules of piety to lead us on, for we learn all that we need to know and practice in this adorable book. All the prophets, all the doctors, all the Apostles speak through the mouth of Him who has opened theirs. The stable at Bethlehem is the school where all Christians ought to study the science of salvation. All the ways to heaven, every path of virtue, begin and finish through Him who is the Alpha and the Omega, and the way, the truth, and the life, He has opened the way to heaven to all.

Providence of my God, exclaims St. Bernard, how wonderful art thou! Carnal and animal creatures have no conception of the works of God. Even wisdom itself is made flesh to make it intelligible to men of flesh.

It is no longer through men, full of a holy fear, that God proclaims His oracles; mysterious messages in shrouded language, no longer issue from the mountaintop amid thunder and lightning; these are heard no more. It is from the farther end of a grotto, it is from the height of a crib, it is in the silence of night, it is the mouth of a Child wrapped in swaddling clothes that the Incarnate Wisdom exclaims, "Behold to thee, wisdom is manifested in the flesh."

Come, ye profound philosophers, ye refined politicians, ye clever men — enter into the stable. There is your lyceum, your academy, deposit your proud learning, your studied lessons, your captious rhetoric at the feet of this adorable Doctor who exposes the vanity, errors, and littleness of everything.

Let all the fire of eloquence, all the pride of wisdom, all the subtlety of philosophy, all the refinements of policy disappear at the sight of this divine Child.

Preachers of the Gospel, happy organs of that Eternal Word who sends you; you who, as well as St. John the Baptist, are only voices to proclaim the glory of God in every temple, kneel before this Child and acknowledge the Master who has loosened the tongues of the prophets and the Apostles, who has inspired the martyrs and young virgins with words that astonished tyrants and confounded pagan philosophers; and when you shall have adored Him silently and humbly, lost in wonder, speak and consecrate every ornament of eloquence to the praise and glory of Him who has endowed you with gifts.

Happy the docile listeners who, opening their hearts to that invisible Preacher who speaks to them through your mouths, can hear the voice of our Lord in those of men!

Teach us then, O Child divine! We speak in Your place simply to exhort Christians to hear You instead of hearing us.

—Fr. Laurent Juillard du Jarry (1658–1730), *On Christmastide*

∞

Would you wish to know who is He, who is born in this way? Learn, then, who He is, and how mighty He is. It is the Word of the Eternal Father, the Creator of the universe, the Peace of the world, the Savior of men, He who is the joy and hope of the just.

The glory of this Child was that a virgin should bring Him forth into the world and the glory of the Virgin Mother was that she should have for a Son a Man who was at the same time God.

—St. Augustine (354–430), Sermon 35, *De Tempore*

The Circumcision of Our Lord

*And after eight days were accomplished that the child
should be circumcised, His name was called Jesus.*

—Luke 2:21

I am not come to destroy the law or the prophets.

—Matthew 5:17

On this, the feast of the Circumcision, our Savior, the Son of God, teaches us how we should cooperate in the great work of our salvation, and He gives us a means as divine as it is indispensable and necessary, namely, that mysterious but real circumcision of the will and heart — a circumcision for which He frames a law, of which He explains the precept, and of which He facilitates the use.

He proposes the circumcision of the heart, and He makes it necessary; for although He does abolish the old circumcision, or, to speak more correctly, the ancient circumcision finishes with Him only because He established the new, and, as St. Augustine says, He makes use of the shadow and figure only because He brings forward the light and the truth. Now this light and truth is that we should all be circumcised of heart, as the Jews were according to the flesh.

Circumcision of the heart is a cutting off of useless and inordinate desires, uneasy and fantastical wishes, immoderate and ill-regulated longings, carnal and worldly desires, criminal and unlawful wishes—all of which take root in the heart and corrupt it. This is how St. Paul understood it. And because these pernicious desires are excited in us by vain objects that delight us, by false interests that blind us, by dangerous occasions that drag us onward, and pervert us, this circumcision of the heart ought to be an entire separation from such objects, a complete renunciation of those false interests, a wise and wholesome withdrawal from those occasions, for these are what was typified in the Judaic circumcision. This is how God prepared the world when He compelled Abraham and all his descendants to be circumcised.

Now our Savior proposes this spiritual circumcision as an indispensable and requisite means to procure our salvation; for what is more necessary than to tear away, stifle, mortify, and destroy all that is the beginning and cause of damnation?

This spiritual circumcision is a circumcision that is not solely exterior, but that penetrates, so to speak, into the innermost recesses of the soul; that is no longer from the hand of man but is God's work and sanctifies man in the sight of God. It is a circumcision that consists no longer in the cutting of the flesh, but in the renouncement of the vices and the concupiscence of the flesh. It is a circumcision, of which the mind and heart are the two principals as well as the two subjects—the two principals, because it is carried out through them, and the two subjects, because it is within them; that is to say, it is a circumcision of the heart that is made, not only literally, but in the fervor of the will.

These are the animated expressions of the Apostle, who defines what may be called the new circumcision. The man of the world and a religious ought both to be circumcised at heart. But to compare the wants of the one with the other, this circumcision of the heart is in one sense more indispensably necessary for the man of the world than for the religious, who, by the vows of his profession, has renounced everything. The man of the world has stronger passions to fight against than a religious does, since he has before him more opportunities of exciting them. Because the man of the world is much more exposed to be tempted than a religious, consequently he ought to watch over himself and should continually try to deny himself and endeavor to persevere.

After the first step a religious has taken — after that first sacrifice that has deprived him of everything — it would seem that there was nothing more to be done; but you in the world, what have you hitherto given to God, or what further sacrifices have you not to make and offer to God?

— Fr. Louis Bourdaloue (1632–1704), *On the Circumcision*

∞

The Child Jesus' blood shedding in the circumcision was another penance of His infancy that, for many reasons, may be regarded as a pattern for the unnecessary mortifications of the saints, if, indeed, any mortification can be strictly deemed unnecessary, even for the most innocent of the sons of men. He needed not the rite. He who was God Himself required no ceremonial covenant with God. That Flesh, which was already united to a divine Person, needed no consecration.

It was a strange, separate, unaccountable blood shedding, standing, as it seems, in a peculiar relation to the other blood sheddings; as it was not only no part of the redemption of the world, but was utterly detached from the Passion.

It did not keep the compact with the Father, which was death, and nothing short of death, so that the drops that were shed were not shed to the saving of souls.

Was it the homage of the Infancy to the Passion? Was it, like the bloody sweat upon Mount Olivet, an outburst of the Sacred Heart's impatience for the plenitude of Calvary?

To Him truly it was pain, to His Mother sorrow, to Joseph a heavenly perplexity, to the angels a wonder, and to the saints a pattern and a mystery.

— Fr. Frederick William Faber (1814–1863), *Bethlehem*

∞

Jesus Christ is circumcised as the son of Abraham. He is called Jesus, as the Son of God.

He whom no one can convict of sin, He who had no necessity to be circumcised, nevertheless makes use of the cure for sin and consents to suffer a shameful and painful remedy.

We, on the contrary, who do not blush at the hideousness of sin, are ashamed of doing penance, a sign of extreme folly. Thus we are slaves of sin, and we blush at the remedy, which is still more criminal.

—St. Bernard (1091–1153), *On the Circumcision*

The Holy Name of Jesus

You are justified in the name of our Lord Jesus Christ.

—1 Corinthians 6:11

There is no work, says St. Paul, but that we should begin by invoking this holy Name: "All whatsoever you do in word or in work, all things do ye in the name of the Lord Jesus" (Col. 3:17). Here, then, is the best method we can adopt in our work and in the whole conduct of our life. If, to make our life happy, we ought to bless Jesus, morning, noon, and night, we cannot draw down His blessing more effectually than by invoking His holy Name, which is the price of His blood and of His life.

It is true that, to do this worthily, we have need of His help; but He is too jealous of His glory to refuse even this, and we need not fear that He will fail to assist us, since it is He Himself who has inspired us.

Let us then open our hearts to Him, in order that He may engrave thereon His holy Name; and if you earnestly wish to receive His divine inspirations, make yourself worthy of His promises.

Let us be thoroughly convinced that the greatest honor we can pay to the Son of God, in His quality of Redeemer, is to embrace courageously every means that He holds out to us to save our souls. Our happiness is so mixed up with His glory that we cannot be lost without doing Him an injustice and snatching from Him that which is dearest to Him, namely, our eternal salvation.

If we have this holy Name deeply engraved on our hearts, it will not be difficult to imagine that it should be often on our lips, that is to say, that we should invoke it often and that we should do our best to impress it upon the hearts of others; for it is so sweet a perfume that it seeks only to be spread far and wide; it is a spring so limpid that nothing makes it more plentiful and clearer than when many come to slake their thirst; it is a light that ought to illuminate the universe.

O! what a joy to be able to contribute in some degree to the glory of Jesus, and to the veneration of His most holy Name! O! that I could induce all men to pay Him homage and that I could hear every tongue proclaim His praises!

Here is the best and foremost of all my desires, that at the holy Name of Jesus every knee should bow, in heaven, on earth, in hell; and that every tongue should confess that the Lord Jesus is in the glory of His Father (see Phil. 2:10–11).

A true devotion to the holy Name will help to obtain our own sanctification; for in saving our own souls, we accomplish the greatest desire of our Savior, and we contribute on our part to do that which adds an additional glory to Him, which is our own salvation.

Our salvation depends, on the one part, on Him; on the other, on ourselves. On His part He has abundantly supplied us with all that is necessary to complete the work of that grand, important, and sole hope of a happy eternity. He has cured all our infirmities. He has given us preservatives and wholesome remedies against all our vicious habits. He has delivered us from the power of the devil. He has reconciled us with His Eternal Father. He has paid all our debts. He has surmounted every obstacle to our salvation, and, through excess of love, He has shed His Blood, and after suffering excruciating pains He has expired on the Cross. But, after all, if we do not make a good use of His graces, all that He has done and suffered will be in vain, inasmuch as we deprive Him of the glory of His holy Name.

In addition to this, the most solid devotion to the holy Name of Jesus is to love and try zealously to obtain the salvation of our neighbor. Nothing is so dear to the Sacred Heart as the salvation of a soul. His life so full of hardships, His death so cruel, are evident proofs of this.

How careful should those be who have been called to the ministry of God's Word and to other functions that contribute to the salvation of souls who have been ransomed by His Precious Blood.

How glorious to be employed in His service, to have the power of dispensing the merits of His sufferings and death.

You whose vocation it is to work continually for the salvation of those souls entrusted to your care, think seriously how sad it would be if one soul should perish through your negligence. But what would it be if, instead of saving souls, your conduct through life should be a cause of scandal?

O! let us think of what we are and what we ought to be. We ought to be as so many saviors of men in our interaction with the world, edifying them by our example, instructing them, succoring them, praying always for them, and by our ardor and zeal doing our best to secure their salvation.

Listen, then, to the voice of the Blood of that Redeemer who beseeches you, by virtue of His Name and the excess of His love, to help Him to make His Name efficacious by saving souls and by making them partakers of the fruit of His Precious Blood.

—Fr. Nouet, S.J. (1605–1680), "The Man of Prayer"

The Feast of the Epiphany

All they from Saba shall come, bringing gold and
frankincense, and showing forth praises to the Lord.

—Isaiah 60:6

It will readily be admitted that the lights and graces that the Magi received were immense and extraordinary, since they were enlightened outwardly as well as inwardly. But, truly, could less have been done to convince the Gentiles or to draw them to the knowledge of a God-man whom they had not as yet seen command the waves of the sea, or raise the dead, or restore sight to the blind—a God who only visibly showed Himself as an ordinary child, silent, poor, and weak?

Nevertheless, if the Magi had had the same indifference that the majority of Christians have for heavenly things, they would have perhaps looked upon the star only as a curiosity, and they would have met perchance to seek for natural causes to account for its appearance. They would not have hastened to set out on so long a journey, and in delaying to obey the secret order that impelled them onward, they would have lost the greatest of blessings.

—St. Augustine (354–430), Sermon 35, *De Tempore*

∞

St. Chrysostom assures us that God caused the star to appear in order to convince the Jews of their infidelity and to show them that their ingratitude was inexcusable. For as Jesus Christ came upon earth to call the whole world to the knowledge of His name, and to be acknowledged and adored by all nations, He opens the gate of faith to the Gentiles, and He instructs His chosen people through the medium of foreigners.

God, seeing the indifference with which the Jews listened to all the prophecies that promised the birth of the Savior, summoned the wise men from the East to seek for the King of the Jews in the midst of the Jews. And He willed that Persia should teach the former what they did not care to learn from the oracles of their prophets, in order that, if they had among them any men of goodwill, this visit of the kings might lead them to believe, and if they wished still to be obstinate, no excuse would be of any avail. For what could they think or say when they witnessed these Magi, guided only by a star, seeking and adoring Him whom they had rejected?

—St. John Chrysostom (ca. 349–407), *On Matthew 2*

∞

No obstacle seemed to be too formidable for the Magi to overcome, no difficulty could shake their resolution; for as soon as they saw the star, they felt an inward secret inspiration and immediately they left their kingdoms and carried with them the offerings they intended to present to Him whom the Scripture calls "the King of kings and the Lord of lords" (1 Tim. 6:15; Rev. 19:16).

They generously faced danger or death by asking for the King of the Jews in the capital of Judea.

Happy Magi! exclaims one of the Fathers, who, in the presence of a cruel king, boldly proclaimed themselves to be confessors of the faith.

The same grace that our Lord has given to pagans, it may be truly said that He has given to us many and many a time. For example, the edifying examples we see, the sermons we hear, the good books we read, the holy inspirations we feel, the pious reflections we make are as so many stars that shine and guide us on our way.

He calls us, says St. Gregory, through the writings of the Fathers, through the voice of pastors, through the illnesses that He sends us, through adversities that well-nigh overwhelm us. See, continues this holy doctor, by how many stars we are invited to go to Jesus Christ!

Now, if we wish to imitate our holy kings in the fidelity that they displayed in corresponding to the grace of God, let us unhesitatingly follow the star that is meant to guide us on our way.

What is this way, if it be not the narrow path that leads to eternal life?

Let us hasten to enter thereon, and when once we are there, let nothing discourage us or tempt us to go back, but let us walk on steadily and perseveringly, until we have found our Savior Jesus Christ.

But, alas! we do the reverse of this. Far from paying attention to the workings of grace, far from having our eyes open to perceive the star, far from having the courage to follow its guidance immediately, some shut their eyes on purpose not to see the light, and others put off to another time the carrying out of the good resolutions that it suggests to them.

—Fr. Montmorel, *Homilies*

∝

Jesus' Infancy and Hidden Life

He went down with them, and came to Nazareth,
and was subject to them.

—Luke 2:51

It is surprising that the Son of God, having come on earth simply to glorify His Father by redeeming mankind, should have passed nearly all His life in obscurity. During all this time could He not have traveled through the world to teach men by His doctrine, to edify them by His example, to convince them by His miracles, and to draw them to the knowledge of the true God?

The carpenter's shop: Was it a dwelling worthy of a Savior? A hidden and unknown life: Was this to be the life of a Messiah? And so long a retreat: Was it necessary for a God made man?

It must be so, since He who is wisdom itself and does all things with consummate prudence has made the choice. Who is it who had the glory of His Father more at heart than His only-begotten Son? And who knew better than He did how to promote it? The salvation of man: Was not that the object of His Incarnation? And was He ignorant that the conversion of the universe ought to have been His work?

We must therefore come to the conclusion that a hidden life up to the age of thirty was more glorious to God than the most striking miracles and that the work of our salvation required that silence and obscurity during all that time.

What is more glorious, what more instructive, than the mystery of this hidden life? The Eternal Father wished to be glorified by the hidden life of His Son; the Savior prefers this obscurity to all the marvels of an active life.

Ah! great God, when shall we be convinced that perfection and merit does not consist in doing or in suffering great things for Your glory, but in wishing and doing all that pleases You?

The Savior glorified His Father quite as much in the poor workshop at Nazareth as He did afterward in Judea through His preachings and miracles.

O my God, how foolish are they who feel inclined to show their zeal only in performing mighty works of charity! Such as these would say that a hidden life extinguishes fervor.

The will of God is sought for by those who put their trust in Him, but how many virtues are included in this one! The Son of God was strictly obedient to Mary and Joseph; this is an abridgment of His life, from the age of twelve to thirty years. Would not one say that obedience is above every other virtue? For one cannot doubt but that during that time, Jesus Christ would have possessed every virtue.

Scripture seems to include all in saying that He was perfectly obedient! Ah! my God, how important is this lesson, but it is not relished! How consoling, my Lord, is Your example, but it is not followed! I have only to obey, and I am sure of pleasing You.

How short is the path to perfection! I have only to obey, and from that time I practice every virtue! A complete victory over the strongest temptations is attached to obedience: we are humble, we are solidly grounded in virtue, when we are obedient.

As for the other wonders that Jesus worked during that time, He has kept them so hidden that we can but have a confused knowledge of them. The finest paintings are faded when exposed to too much light and air; but a hidden life is always safe, and it is God alone who can help us to it.

To be talked of by the world, to be successful, to be praised is, for those who seek it, the reward for purely exterior good works. If we wish to possess God as a reward, let us remember that He alone must be our witness.

—Fr. Croiset, S.J. (b. ca. 1650), *Retreats*

∞

The love of solitude and the love of silence are two virtues, of which the Son of God gives us the example in His hidden life. There are two kinds of solitude. The first is that of the heart, which can be practiced, even among the talk and hum of a busy world, by a holy contemplative mind not affected by outward observances. The second is that of the body, which effectually separates us from the conversation and sight of men, but this will be of little use to us if separated from the first.

Our Savior has so practiced both the one and the other that it ought to induce us to follow His example. See Him in Nazareth, where He leads a hidden life; He is content with a village, a mean-looking house, a vile employment. What conversions could He not effect by the mere efficacy of His Word! Nevertheless, He lives silently, to teach us to love retreat; and this we should never shrink from, when the glory of God, or the salvation of our neighbor, or any pressing want, is concerned.

Try to be fond of retirement, so that you may examine your conscience effectually. You need not be afraid of losing your time or of burying your talents.

Jesus did not lose the fruit of the least of His labors when He began His public life, from having been a recluse until He was thirty years of age.

—Fr. Nouet, S.J. (1605–1680), *The Man of Prayer*

∞

The Transfiguration of Our Lord

And after six days Jesus taketh unto him Peter,
and James, and John, and bringeth them up into a high
mountain apart. And he was transfigured before them.

—Matthew 17:1–2

The primary intention of the Savior in showing Himself clothed with glory, and His face shining as the sun, was to manifest a ray of that glory that He had concealed under the veil of His human body — a happiness He had prepared in His kingdom for all those who should be faithful in His service.

He wished also to urge them to carry the cross, and to teach them that God gives to His saints, even in this world, a foretaste of the delights and joys of the next. He wished to teach them that the life of those who follow Jesus is indeed a cross, but a cross accompanied with heavenly consolations and interior joys so sweet that it corresponds with what He Himself said, that His yoke is easy and His burden light (Matt. 11:30). After that, should we hesitate to enter into the service of so liberal a Master — we who know that we shall one day partake of His glory, and that perhaps He will give us henceforth a merciful foretaste of the happiness He has prepared for us?

Let us consider for a moment how our Lord and Savior was transfigured. It was by allowing the beauty of His soul, which He had always concealed, to irradiate and spread itself over His body. No sooner had it appeared than

His face did shine as the sun, and His garments became white as snow. The evangelist would have said more brilliant than the sun, had there been anything more luminous to which he could have compared it.

But let us offer up a thousand acts of thanksgiving to that Divine Redeemer, who, for love of us, has up to now deprived Himself of that glory so justly His due on this day of His Transfiguration. He deemed it right and just to manifest His glory, although only for a short time, in order to be able to finish the work of our salvation.

Could You, my Savior, have shown me a greater love by depriving Your sacred body of a glory so just, so grand, so legitimate, with the sole view of sacrificing it for me upon the Cross?

O! why could I not give up every earthly joy for the love of You? For then I would one day be rewarded in Thy abode of glory.

∞

The holy prophets Moses and Elijah appeared on Mount Tabor clothed in glory and majesty. It may be that their luminous presence contributed to increase the glory of a Savior whom they acknowledged as their Redeemer, or it may have been to show that the saints should one day share in the happiness of their Master, inasmuch as they participated in His labors and sufferings on earth.

Who can describe the joy that filled their hearts when they saw before their eyes Him for whom they sighed for so many ages, with what humility and deference they adored Him as their God, and what thanksgivings did they not offer to Him as their Redeemer?

These holy prophets spoke, says the evangelist, of the excess that He was to accomplish in Jerusalem; that is to say, of the Passion He had to endure on Mount Calvary, the theater of His sufferings. Redeemer of mankind, what are You saying to them on this joyful occasion? What connection can there be between Your Passion and Your glory? If music in mourning is disagreeable (Sir. 22:6), are sad discourses bearable in a time of joy?

But I see now what it is. Your sweet music is in reference to Your death, because the love You feel for us impels You to find a pleasure in the greatest suffering. And by that You wish to teach us that You have never had a moment of repose without some mixture of pain and that the joys of this life that You have implanted in the hearts of Your faithful servants are intended to prepare them for many crosses. Again, as he who ardently loves willingly speaks of the object of his affection, so because You, O Lord, loved nothing so much as crosses, You experienced no greater pleasure than to converse about that Cross whereon You would soon be nailed for love of us.

The place on which our Savior was transfigured was a retired spot, suitable for prayer, to show that God does not reveal His glory in public but in a retreat, when we are the better weaned from earthly joys and are the more likely to reach perfection. Thus Moses and Elijah had the happiness of seeing God, not in a crowded city, but on the top of a deserted mountain.

How true it is that it is most important that we should try to love solitude and retirement, that we should raise our hearts and say with David, "Who will give me wings like a dove, and I will fly and be at rest?" (Ps. 54:7 [RSV = Ps. 55:6]).

—Fr. Louis du Pont, S.J. (1554–1624), *Meditations*

The Washing of the Feet

Before the festival day of the pasch, Jesus, knowing that his
hour was come, . . . riseth from supper, and, laying aside his
garments, and having taken a towel, girded himself. After that,
he putteth water into a basin, and began to wash the feet of his
disciples, and to wipe them with the towel wherewith he was girded.

—John 13:1, 4–5

Here is, my brothers, a spectacle worthy of attracting the attention of a Christian, and to which St. Gregory the Great invites heaven and earth to be a witness of the example that a Man-God gives to all. It is not a light capable of surprising us by its grandeur and magnificence. The pomp and splendor that usually excite our curiosity and attract our notice have no share here. But it is the mighty that is abased; it is the Sovereign of the universe who is willing to perform the meanest service to poor sinners—a Master who bends His knee to His disciples. In a word, it is Jesus at the feet of His Apostles, in order to wash them with those very hands that had created heaven and earth and fixed the stars in the firmament above.

This spectacle deserves our admiration because it shows us something grand, rare, and new, on which we should gaze and reverently meditate, on a ceremony that is carried out and renewed year after year on this day and in every church.

Surprising sight, which shows us the Most High Majesty of the world in the lowest of humiliations!

O wondrous charity! Since this Savior finds nothing better calculated to win their hearts than by washing their feet, knowing that He had to give them His own Body as the most precious pledge of His love; but still a sight full of mystery and instruction, as the Savior says Himself to the first of His disciples, "What I do, thou knowest not now, but thou shalt know hereafter" (John 13:7).

In fact, He gave them the knowledge by explaining what He commanded them to do hereafter. And I dare to say that it required no less than His example to lead them to the practice of Christian humility, of which they were as yet ignorant of its practice and value: "For I have given you an example, that as I have done to you, so you do also" (John 13:15).

The Son of God had already given a rule of conduct to His disciples, namely, to take the last place without disputing about precedence or rank. But in this mystery, He gives us an example of a deeper humility, for He lowers Himself so as to wash the feet of those who were not worthy to wash His. And it would seem that He took upon Himself, as a rule for His humiliations, the eminence of His dignity and rank, which He retains over all His creatures. Ah! I will not hesitate to say that after that, this last place that He takes has really come to be the place of honor, since it is that of a God made man; that a similar humiliation exalts us, since it makes us like unto a God humiliated; and that those acts of humility we practice in imitation of Him are really glorious actions, since they attract the attention of God and deserve His praise.

After that, a Christian who ought to be convinced of this truth — will he be scrupulous on a point of honor, and will he believe that it is dishonorable to practice Christian humility? Will he be able to excuse himself from performing duties so essential to Christianity on the ground or plea of his merit, his position, his character, or his reputation? Will he blush to serve the poor, or visit the sick in a hospital? Will he feel ashamed to perform similar humiliating duties to which his religion calls him, duties that the example of his God obliges him to perform, since He is the model we ought to imitate?

What a shame rather, for a Christian to be always scrupulous on a point of honor; always ready to wrangle for precedence of rank or honor, resolved to yield to no one, and to hold in contempt those who are beneath him. And thus, at last he will fear to lose his reputation, if he were to follow the example of his Savior, by practicing any act of humility. Ah! unworthy pretext of a Christian, and hurtful to Christianity, which is grounded on humility and self-abasement.

—Fr. Vincent Houdry, S.J. (1630–1729), *On Christian Morals*

∞

Moses and Elijah, that is to say, the Law and the Prophets, appeared conversing with Jesus, in order that by the presence of these persons should be accomplished what is said in Deuteronomy 19:15: "In the mouth of two or three witnesses, every word shall stand."

Peter, emboldened by the revelation of so many mysteries, full of contempt for all worldly things, raises his desires and heart to heaven, and, in a holy transport of joy, exclaims, "It is good, O Lord, to be here" (Matt. 17:4).

—St. Leo (d. 461), *On the Transfiguration*

∽

The Passion of Our Lord

He humbled himself, becoming obedient unto
death, even to the death of the cross.

—Philippians 2:8

An inward grief seized the heart of the Savior of the world. He walked in silence to the place called Gethsemani, where, finding that His mortal strength succumbed to the extreme anguish of His soul, He was perforce constrained to appeal to His Apostles, as if to ask them for some relief. "My soul is sorrowful unto death" said He, "and I feel that I must give way to the sadness coming over Me" (see Matt. 26:28). But receiving no consolation from them, He again withdrew apart, not so much to hide His trouble and His fear, as to retreat within Himself.

See Him now in a corner of this garden, how pale He is! How He staggers! How He trembles and falls upon His face! See His face quite wet with tears; His very clothes are saturated with a bloody sweat, which flows in streams upon the ground!

He lifts His hands and raises His voice to heaven. He twice goes back to His disciples to complain how little He is assisted and twice returns to His retreat; but no rest, no calm succeeds.

I know not, my brethren, what is your idea, but I confess that this mystery astonishes me and is beyond all comprehension. When I look upon a God humiliated, a God sorrowful even unto death, my mind, shallow as it is, has no difficulty in unraveling this enigma. But a God troubled in His soul, struck with fear, and sad even unto death troubles me exceedingly, and I am lost in thought.

What! this Messiah whom God sent down on earth to be our Master and example; this Savior who has come into the world to suffer; this Savior who has shown so much impatience to shed His Bood for love of us—now that His hour has come, seems to be wanting in resolution. See Him extended full length upon the earth, bathed in His Blood, suffering for three hours a cruel agony, and unceasingly repeating those words, "Let this chalice pass away."

O! my Savior and my God, the support of the weak, the strength even of the strong—mighty soul whose generous feelings are so raised above every infirmity of man—tell us, I beseech Thee, what may be the cause of so keen, so deep a grief. For I cannot really believe that fear alone of that death, which You have taught us to despise, could have caused You so great an agony.

—St. Claude de la Colombière (1641–1682)

∽

In your mind's eye draw a lively picture of the Passion of Jesus Christ. In this sketch, you can represent the lance that has pierced His heart, the thongs and cords that are so embedded in His flesh that the thorns and nails are steeped in blood.

Surely, if you think of these sad circumstances of His death, and gaze attentively, you must indeed be moved. Gratitude would compel you to be so; for, after His having endured so many tortures for your sake, the least you can do is to compassionate His sufferings. Justice requires it, for if you feel compassion for any of your brethren, what do you not owe to the Son of God, who, through excess of love, was made man and took His place as your friend and brother? Humanity alone would prompt you, for if you saw the lowest of your fellow creatures in the condition to which His love for you had reduced Him, you surely would have pitied him.

St. Gregory of Nyssa could never see the painting of the sacrifice of Isaac without shedding tears of compassion and tenderness, for he thought of that innocent victim who laid bare his neck and awaited the death blow from the hands of his own father. If this so moved his pity, is not the sight of Jesus dying on the Cross infinitely more pitiable?

Oh, what sufferings has He not endured! Who could sufficiently appreciate the excessive goodness and mercy that induced Him to bear such a heavy weight of dolors? Cast your eye on His many wounds. See the streams of blood that trickle down. Look at His face, so disfigured with spittle, mud, and blood. Taste the bitterness of the gall they gave Him to drink. Listen to the blows of the heavy hammer as it drives the nail through His tender feet. Listen to those loving complaints He sends up to heaven: "My God, my God, why hast thou forsaken me?" to teach you the excess of those interior griefs that you cannot see or understand (Matt. 27:46)!

Remember that He is innocent, that He is the Son of a God who is the God of glory. And if you can gaze on this, His bed of suffering, without weeping for your sins, you must confess that you are unfeeling and hardhearted.

However great may be our miseries, however painful may be the misfortunes we have to endure, whether deserved or not, the remedy we find in the Cross and sufferings of our Savior is infinitely greater and more powerful.

One single drop of the blood He shed for us was capable of paying all our debts, sufficient to blot out all our sins, and powerful enough to extinguish all the flames of hell. What would be the value of that deluge of blood that He has poured over us with such profusion? If each drop can save a million worlds, the whole mass of that Precious Blood: will it not be able to save a sinner?

You cannot doubt the efficacy of so potent a remedy, since it is of inestimable value, nor of the sufficiency of your ransom, since what He has given is beyond all price. Every river, when it flows into the sea, loses its name, because, when compared with the mighty ocean, it is as nothing;

and so the greatest sins vanish and disappear when they are drowned in the ocean of divine mercy. And if you doubt this still, you are ignorant of the value of the sufferings and death of the Son of God.

Do you not know that the Apostle says: His blood calls for mercy for every sinner, even to those who have been put to death, and it cries out with so loud and powerful a voice that it drowns the noise and clamor of our sins? Do you not know, in fine, that He "gave himself a redemption for all" (1 Tim. 2:6), and consequently that His blood, His sufferings, His death, and His satisfactions are all yours?

Put, then, your trust in Him without troubling yourself about your miseries. Avail yourself of His blood, more powerful than Abel's. Make good use of so powerful a voice, and do not fear that His Father will reject you, but only fear that you yourself will refuse. "See that you refuse him not that speaketh" (Heb. 12:25).

For if those who rejected Him when He spoke on earth have not been able to avoid being punished, so we who reject Him when He speaks to us of heaven will have a lesser chance of being saved.

—Fr. Nouet, S.J. (1605–1680), *Sur la Passion*

∞

Jesus Risen

*The Son of man shall be betrayed into the hands of men; and
they shall kill him, and the third day he shall rise again.*

—Matthew 17:21–22

He is risen; he is not here.

—Mark 16:6

The Resurrection of Jesus Christ fully confirms the fact of His divinity.

You will say, perhaps, that the Savior of the world, during His mortal
life, surely worked a sufficient number of miracles to prove that He was
the Son of God. Devils cast out, those born blind cured, those, after a
death of four days, raised again to life: were not these so many manifest
demonstrations, so many palpable proofs, of the divine power that dwelt
within Him? What need, then, of the more striking proof in His Resurrection to confirm this belief?

I say that the divinity of Jesus Christ was especially attached to His
Resurrection: "Who was predestinated the Son of God by his resurrection
from the dead" (Rom. 1:4). Why? Because the Resurrection of the Savior
was the proof that this God-Man had expressly given to the Jews to make
them acknowledge His divinity; because this proof was in fact the most
natural, the most convincing of His divinity; because of all the miracles of
Jesus Christ worked by virtue of His divinity, there was not one that had
been so incontestably evident as that of His Resurrection of His body; and

98

because it is that of all which has most contributed to the propagation of the Faith and to the establishment of the gospel, the substance and main point of which is to believe in Jesus Christ and to confess His divinity.

It is not, therefore, without reason that Jesus Christ especially insisted on this sign, to make it appear that He was God and the Son of God. In fact, it appertains only to a God to say, as He does, "I have power to lay down my life, and I have power to take it up again" (John 10:18). A God alone, I say, would express Himself in this way.

Before Christ came into the world, men were seen who had been raised from death to life, but these were recalled to life by other men. Elisha, by the mere breath of his mouth, reanimated the dead body of the Shunamite's son, and through the fervent prayer of Elisha, the child of the widow of Zarephath, who died of exhaustion and a decay of nature, was restored to his sorrowing mother full of vigor and health (2 Kings 4:17–37; 1 Kings 17:17–23).

But, as St. Ambrose remarks, they who were restored to life were so restored through the means of extraordinary virtues, and those who worked these miracles performed them solely by virtue of given graces.

The unheard-of miracle was that the same man should have worked a double miracle, not only of rising from the dead, but of raising Himself from the tomb; and this is what had never been seen or heard of. And this was the miracle that God reserved for His Son, in order to proclaim to the world that He was at one and the same time, both God and man; man, because He had risen from the dead, and God, inasmuch as He had raised Himself from death to life.

∞

It is true that we shall rise again from the dead, because Jesus Christ is risen again; and in order to crown our hopes, I add that we shall rise like unto Jesus and that His resurrection is the model of our own.

For, asks St. Augustine, why had God willed that the resurrection of His Son should have been so obvious, and why was the Son of God so desirous to make it known and to make it public? Ah! answers the holy doctor, it was in order to show us clearly and evidently in His own person the just extent of our pretensions. It is in order to show us what He is, what we ought to be, or what we can become. I have, then, only to represent to myself whatever is most striking, great, and admirable, in the triumph of my Savior. I have only to contemplate that glorified humanity, that body, material as it is, invested with every spiritual essence, emitting beams of living light and crowned with an everlasting splendor. Such, then, is the happy state to which I shall one day be raised, and such is the consolatory promise that faith makes me.

Now our bodies are subject to corruption and rottenness; now they are subject to suffering and grief; now they are weak and subject to death; now they are only lumps of flesh, vile and contemptible.

But then, by a quick and most marvelous change, they will have, if I may venture so to speak, the same incorruptibility as a God, the same impassibility, the same immortality, the same subtlety, the same brightness: "[He] will reform the body of our lowness, made like to the body of his glory" (Phil. 3:21).

All that, nevertheless on one condition, and that is that we should so labor in the present life to sanctify our bodies by mortification and Christian penitence. For, if we have indulged these bodies and afforded them whatever a sensual appetite demanded, and, thereby made them bodies of sin, they will rise, but how? As objects of horror, to the confusion and shame of the soul, to share in her torment, after having participated in her crimes.

—Fr. Louis Bourdaloue (1632–1704), *On the Resurrection*

∞

The Sacred Heart and Wounds

You shall draw waters with joy out of the Savior's fountains.

—Isaiah 12:3

It is in the adorable Heart of Jesus that we shall find every help for our necessities, every remedy for the cure of our ills, the most powerful assistance against the assaults of our enemies, the sweetest consolation to soothe our sufferings, the purest delight to fill our souls with joy.

Are you in sorrow? Do your enemies persecute you?

Does the recollection of your past sins disturb you? Is your heart troubled or full of fear?

Throw yourself, so to speak, in the wounds of Jesus Christ, even into His Sacred Heart. It is a sanctuary; it is the retreat for holy souls and a place of refuge wherein your soul is safe.

It is of Him and through Him that we should ask for all we require. It is through Him and in Him that we should offer to the Eternal Father all we do, because this Sacred Heart is the treasury of every supernatural gift, the source of every grace.

It is the channel through which we unite ourselves more intimately to God and through which God communicates Himself more freely.

It is, in fine, to this Sacred Heart that we should continually strive to unite ours—no longer wishing to have other desires or sentiments than those of Jesus—and then we may be sure that His will and His Sacred Heart may, so to speak, merge into our heart, and that the two will be as one. Draw waters at leisure out of the Savior's fountains: you will never exhaust them.

—St. Peter Damien (988–1073)

∞

St. Bernard calls the wounds of our Savior fountains of mercy; not only to tell us that He has received them through an extraordinary display of mercy and goodness but also to show us:

- that they are a fresh motive for His Heart to take compassion on us
- that, since He received them, He is more alive to our misfortunes, when He remembers that He died for us
- that He sees in the scars of His wounds the proof of His love and the price of our salvation.

No! He wishes to lose neither the price of His Precious Blood nor the objects of His love.

Consequently, what more powerful and efficacious motive can there be for a sinner who sincerely wishes to repent than to think of the wounds of the Savior?

The holy Fathers call these wounds our eyes and our tears—our tears, because they impart an abiding sorrow for sin; our eyes, because we see in these scars, either what our Savior has done for us or what we have done against Him.

I see a Heart wounded for us and a Heart wounded by us. I see, O God, the wounds that You have received from the hands of the executioners. But I also see the wounds I have made by my own hands, since it is certain that with every sin I commit, I reopen Your wounds, for so Your prophet makes this reproach to sinners: "They have added to the grief of my wounds" (Ps. 68:27 [RSV = Ps. 69:26]), as much as to say, "I do not complain of my nails or of my thorns; your sins have added new griefs to my first torments and have made wounds that renew and widen the first."

The Sacred Heart and Wounds

Can we, then, be astonished, if holy penitents have wept bitterly when they looked on the Sacred Wounds of the Savior? "Whither shall I go from thy Spirit? or whither shall I flee from thy face?" (Ps. 138:7 [RSV = Ps. 139:7]). This is what the penitent David said: O my God! whither shall I flee so that I may be sheltered from Thy anger and safe from the terror of my sins? If I ascend into heaven, Thou art there; if I descend into hell, Thou art there; even when I enter into Your Heart, I meet the reflection of Your justice in the alarm my conscience conjures up.

St. Jerome replies to this question and to this perplexity, that it is only in the wounds of the Savior that we can find this hope. These are the sanctuaries, where so many sinners have flown for refuge from the just anger of God, and wherein we ought to shelter ourselves, and that for two reasons: firstly, because we see in the depth of His scars a loving readiness to forgive us, and give us comfort; secondly, because we find in these sacred sources all-powerful testimonies of His mercy and goodness for men, in which we may easily participate, if only we diligently try to make ourselves worthy of His promises.

—Fr. Jacques Biroat (d. 1666), Panegyric on St. Thomas

The Sacred Heart of Jesus has been wounded in order that by means of the visible wound we may see the invisible wound of His divine love. Who would not love this Heart so wounded for the love of us? Who would not return love for love, to a Savior who has done so much for us?

Thy side, O Lord, has been pierced, in order that we should find an entry into Thy Sacred Heart. O! how sweet and good it is to seek repose in that Heart divine!

From my Savior's sacred wounds, I find out His Heart's secret: I now can fathom the depths of God's goodness, for the bowels of mercy that caused Him to come down from heaven to dwell with us are open to me.

—St. Bernard (1091–1153), On the Passion

The Mystery of the Cross

And bearing his own cross, he went forth to
that place which is called Calvary.

—John 19:17

Let no one, my brethren, blush at those sacred and adorable marks of our redemption. The Cross of Jesus Christ is the source of every blessing; through that, we live; through that, we are what we are. Let us carry the Cross of Jesus and adorn ourselves with so glorious a crown. It is the seal and fulfillment of everything that appertains to our salvation.

If we are regenerated in the waters of baptism, the Cross is there present. If we approach the table of the Lord to receive His holy Body, it there appears. If we receive the imposition of hands to consecrate us as ministers of God, it is still there. In fact, we see in everything that adorable sign that is, at once, the cause and emblem of our victory.

We have it in our houses, we hang it and paint it on our walls, we engrave it on our doors, and we should ever carry it in our hearts, for the Cross is a sacred monument that recalls to memory the work of our salvation, the regaining of our ancient freedom, and the infinite mercy of Jesus Christ.

When, then, you make the Sign of the Cross on your forehead, arm yourself with a saintly boldness, and reinstall your soul in its old liberty, for you are not ignorant that the Cross is a prize beyond all price. Consider the price given for your ransom, and you will never more be slave to any man on earth. This reward and ransom is the Cross. You should not, then, carelessly make the sign on your forehead, but you should impress it on your heart with the love of a fervent faith. Nothing impure will dare to molest you on seeing the weapon that overcomes all things.

Be not, then, ashamed of the Cross, in order that Jesus Christ be not ashamed of you when He will come, clothed in the Majesty of His glory, accompanied by this sign of our redemption, which will then shine more brilliant than the sun. Engrave it in your heart; lovingly embrace that which procured the salvation of our souls; for it is the Cross that has saved and converted all the world. It is that which has banished heresy and unbelief, has reestablished truth, has made a heaven on earth, and has transformed men into angels. It is by means of the Cross that the devils have ceased to appear formidable and are now only to be despised; it is through the Cross that death is now no longer death, but only a long sleep. In fine, it is through the Cross that all our enemies have been conquered.

If you find, then, anyone who says, "What! You worship the Cross?" answer him with a tone of voice that betokens firmness: "Yes, I do worship it and shall never cease to do so." If he laughs at you, pity him, and shed tears for his blindness; and say boldly, "We protest before heaven and earth that our glory is in the Cross, that it is the source of all our blessings, our every hope, and that it is that which has crowned every saint.

—St. John Chrysostom (ca. 349–407), *On Matthew 16*

∞

All those who belong to Jesus Christ are fastened with Him to the Cross. A Christian during the whole course of his life should, like unto Jesus, be on the Cross. It would be an act of rashness to descend therefrom, since Jesus Christ did not descend, even when the Jews offered to believe in Him. The time for driving out the nails of His Cross was only after death. There is, then, no time to extract the nails while we live; we must wait until our sacrifice is consummated.

This Cross to which the servant of God is attached is His glory, as the Apostle said, "But God forbid that I should glory, save in the cross of our Lord Jesus Christ" (Gal. 6:14).

This Cross, I say, to which the servant of God should be fastened, is not for forty days but for life; therefore, he who looks piously upon it should consider it as a treasure, because it teaches him Christ crucified, and he will despise everything to acquire a knowledge that is to be learned only in the school of the Cross.

Formerly, it was looked upon as an object of horror, but Jesus Christ has made it so worthy of respect and veneration that kings and princes have forbidden the punishment of crucifixion to be continued, in order to do honor to those faithful servants who gloried in a punishment that our Lord and Savior has so ennobled. And this wood to which the Jews had nailed our Lord, accompanied as it was by so many outrages and insults, has become so worthy of honor that kings have imprinted it on their foreheads, and in union with the lowest of their subjects they look upon the Cross of Jesus Christ as the ship that will guide and carry them safely into harbor.

So strong sometimes are the storms of life that strength of arm is of no avail, and there is no other means to save us from shipwreck than trusting in the Cross of Jesus Christ, by which we are consecrated.

—St. Augustine (354–430), Sermons 75 and 88

∞

The Ascension

*And the Lord Jesus, after he had spoken to them, was taken
up into heaven, and sitteth on the right hand of God.*

—Mark 16:19

Instead of saying what was uppermost in my mind, why cannot I repeat the discourse that Jesus Christ made to His disciples before His Ascension? It would give you more pleasure and would doubtless be useful for you to hear:

> Although I leave you, my dear disciples, to go to my Father, it is nevertheless not without pain that I leave you. Whatever glory may await me in heaven, if your interests were not allied to mine, I could not so readily resolve to separate myself from you. I came down upon earth when I thought that my presence was necessary. If I ascend to heaven, it is because I know that henceforth I shall be more useful to you when away; independently of this, the Holy Spirit will soon descend and take my place, and you will not long remain unconsoled.
>
> Go, my Apostles, go and teach all nations the truths I have taught you. Go and undeceive so many poor unfortunates who are steeped in vice and ignorance. Do this so effectually that of all the souls I have redeemed there shall not be found one lost one. Fear neither the boasted knowledge of doctors and philosophers, nor

the power of the great ones of the world. I will give you wherewith to confound the pride of both one and the other. It is true that you will have to suffer much, but the helps you will receive from me will soften and sweeten every pain. Go, then, and merit the rich crowns I am going to prepare for you.

The Apostles and disciples did not long enjoy the pleasure of hearing Him; for the Savior having raised His hand to give them His final blessing, He began to rise, and soon was lost among the clouds.

If the father of the prodigal son testified so much joy, and made so grand a feast for a son who had not only dishonored him but had been the disgrace of all his kindred, by having squandered his property in shameful debaucheries, what must have been the welcome that the Eternal Father gave His only Son, who, to please Him, was worn out with the fatigues of a poor and suffering life; a Son who, to increase the glory of His Father, zealously bore the cruelest torments; an innocent Son who has saved so many sinners and who, by His death, has opened the way to heaven to all mankind?

It was then that this God of majesty acknowledged Him for His Son, that He announced to all the celestial choir that He was their King, that all should bend to His authority and be submissive to His power, that He should be the Master of the heaven He had opened, of the hell that He had overcome, and of the earth that He had sanctified.

We can easily believe that all the happy spirits cried out, "The Lamb that was slain is worthy to receive power, and divinity, and wisdom, and strength, and honor, and glory, and benediction" (Rev. 5:12). The Lamb who has suffered death is worthy to receive divine honors, to rule with strength, with wisdom, with absolute authority; it is right that we should treat Him with homage and respect, that He should be raised to the highest pinnacle of glory, and that all heaven should ring and re-echo His praises forever and forever.

It was at the sound of this welcome that the Son of Man was introduced into heaven, where no man had before been seen and where that numerous band of saints He had delivered from limbo followed Him, and were received with all the honors that were due to the merits of their Redeemer and to their own merits too.

—St. Claude de la Colombière (1641–1682),
Sermon on the Ascension

∞

It is not solely for Yourself, Lord, that You reenter into Your kingdom; it is for us You ascend, as our Chief, and You go, according to the promise You have made, to prepare for Your elect the mansions that are destined for them. You ascend as our Mediator, and for us You present to Your Father the fruits of that superabundant redemption that has reconciled heaven and earth. You ascend as our Guide, and in showing us the boundary to which we ought to reach, You trace the road on which we ought to walk.

Adorable Master of that Militant Church You have established on earth, by the labors of Your mortal life, give us a share in the glory of that Church Triumphant that You begin to collect in heaven, and of which You will be the everlasting happiness. We are Your members, and wheresoever the general is to be found, there also should be his soldiers.

Without You, without the hope and happiness of possessing and seeing You, what peace could we enjoy in this valley of tears wherein we dwell? And what can the world offer in comparison with that heavenly beatitude that reigns in You and with You?

Ah! dear Lord, when will the day come when I shall bid farewell to this place of banishment? When will You appear to me in all Your glory?

I languish in expectation; the world to me is now as nothing, and my heart is already with You in heaven.

—Fr. Louis le Valois (1639–1700), *Entretien sur l'Ascension*

∞

The Ascension is the glorious terminus of the voyage of the Son of God.

My brethren, let us follow the Lamb wheresoever He goes; let us follow Him suffering with patience; let us follow Him rising; let us follow Him still more eagerly when He ascends to heaven. And let us raise our hearts to God the Father, in whom His glory reigns.

—St. Bernard (1091–1153), *On the Assumption*

The Descent of the Holy Spirit

But the Paraclete, the Holy Spirit, whom the Father will
send in my name, he will teach you all things.

—John 14:26

The Apostles left the supper room in Jerusalem filled with the Holy Spirit. They had within them a treasury of knowledge — stores of graces and spiritual gifts that they could distribute throughout the land. And they went to preach to all nations, having become a living faith and like so many books, animated by the grace of the Holy Spirit.

This is why they announce, with such a marvelous certainty, mysteries of which the old philosophers had no conception, and they publish them not to fifteen or twenty persons, but to cities and to the entire populace, to Greeks, to barbarians, in inhabited towns and in the middle of the deserts.

But more than this, they announce and preach to men a doctrine far above human intelligence. They speak of nothing terrestrial, but only of the things of heaven. They preach a state and kingdom of which they never heard before. They disclose other riches and another poverty, another liberty and another slavery, another life and another death, a new world and quite a new mode of life — in fact, a complete change and renewal of everything.

—St. John Chrysostom (ca. 349–407), *On St. Matthew's Gospel*

My Daily Visit with the Saints

∞

Scarcely had the Savior opened heaven to take His place at the right hand of His Father than He reopens it, to give to His disciples a share — if not of His majesty and glory, at least of the abundance of His graces.

Being unable to descend to them, and unwilling that they should ascend to Him, He sends them another Self to console and instruct them, to protect and sanctify them.

Thus the Church finds herself happily situated between Jesus Christ and the Holy Spirit, drawn by the one, conducted by the other. They divide between them, says St. Bernard, the office and employment of their love for our salvation. Jesus dwells in the abode of His glory and acts as our Intercessor and everlasting Mediator near His Father. The Holy Spirit dwells in our midst, to be our Consoler and Ruler. One prepares in heaven the crowns He has destined for the elect; the Other encourages them and gives them strength to fight bravely.

The One has entered into the depth of the sanctuary to consummate the functions of His priesthood; the Other fashions here below spiritual and holy victims. The One, high in heaven, carries man to the bosom of God, to give him a certain pledge of his glory and of his blessed immortality; the Other, sent from heaven, brings God down to the bosom of man, in order to cleanse him and fill him with light and grace: this is the mystery the Church celebrates on this, our Whitsuntide.

The Holy Spirit is sent to bear testimony to the person, divinity, and doctrine of Jesus Christ. He bears testimony of His birth, for by virtue of His power He formed His adorable body in the womb of a Virgin.

He bears testimony of His death by manifesting its efficacy; of His glory, He is the pledge; of His charity, He is the dispenser; of His truth, He is the witness par excellence. "It is the Spirit," says St. John, "which testifieth that Christ is the truth" and that everything, excepting Jesus, is falsehood (1 John 5:6).

What is this world that the Gospels so often condemn, but a union of vanity and falsehood? Its pleasures are illusions, its promises are trifling amusements; its caresses, treasons; its joys, mere follies; its sadness, despair; its maxims, nought but errors; its laws, unruly; its good works, hypocrisy.

Such is the spirit of the world, but the Spirit of Jesus Christ is truth itself. Its promises are faithful, its hopes are certain, its laws are just, its works are holy, its joys are solid; and all that He is, all that He says, all that He does, all that He ordains, forms a body immutable, holy, and everlastingly true, and of this the Holy Spirit testifies as well as that of His doctrine.

—Bishop Esprit Fléchier (1632–1710),
Sermon on the feast of Pentecost

∞

The Most Holy Trinity

And there are three who give testimony in heaven:
the Father, the Word, and the Holy Spirit.
And these three are one.

—1 John 5:7

All the passages in the Old Testament in which the divinity of the Son of God and of the Holy Spirit is established equally, teach the truth of the mystery of the most Holy Trinity.

In Isaiah, does not the Son of God bear, even after His Incarnation, the name of God strong and powerful, the Father of eternity? In the Psalms the Lord has said, "This day have I begotten thee" (Ps. 2:7). "The Lord said to my Lord, Sit thou at my right hand" (Ps. 109:1 [RSV = Ps. 110:1]) are words of which the Savior himself made use, in order to confound the Jews, and from which He has extracted a proof of His divinity.

With regard to the Holy Spirit, is not His divinity also declared in several passages of the Old Testament, where He is called the Spirit of the Lord, the Spirit of God, and which make Him appear at one time as the Author of the fertility of all nature: "And the Spirit of God moved over the waters" (Gen. 1:2); at another time as the Author of all the grandeurs and beauty that is seen in the heavens?

God, says the holy man Job, has ornamented the heavens by His Spirit (Job 26:13) and at another time is the Author of the sanctification of men, and the source of grace, and their salvation.

But with all that, it must be confessed that the revelation made of the mystery of the Holy Trinity in the Old Testament is obscure in comparison with what has been revealed to us in the New, where the Three Divine Persons have been so distinctly traced out, and so clearly proposed to our faith, as being not only the chief end, but the principal object of our adoration.

First of all, what is clearer than the manifestation that was made at the baptism of the Savior, where the heavens open to make us notice and distinguish at the same time these Three Divine Persons: the Father in this voice: "This is my beloved Son, in whom I am well pleased" (Matt. 17:5); the Son in that Man-God marked and pointed out in that voice; the Holy Spirit under the form of a dove visibly descending on the Savior?

Secondly, are not the heavens opened for us in giving testimonies, and to make us acknowledge, with St. John, that there are Three who give testimony in heaven: the Father, the Son, and the Holy Spirit, and that these Three are One (1 John 5:7)? Has not the Father opened the heavens, and has He not made His voice heard both on Mount Tabor and on the River Jordan (Matt. 3:17; 17:5)? Has the Son not opened the heavens, to show Himself at the stoning of St. Stephen? And has not this proto-martyr had the joy and happiness of seeing Him sitting on the right hand of His Father, and this, too, when he was in bodily suffering (Acts 7:55)? Has the Holy Spirit not also opened the heavens to manifest Himself to men, when He descended brilliantly and visibly in the form of parted tongues as it were of fire, and sat upon every one of the Apostles; and then to the Gentiles even, and that for several times, and "the apostles began to speak with diverse tongues" (Acts 2:4) and accompanying this with the gift of working many miracles?

Besides these, to be convinced that these witnesses from heaven are only One, we need only read in the New Testament the striking proofs of the divinity of the Son and the Holy Spirit, so often, so clearly expounded. In addition to this, those words of Jesus in the Gospel include the whole of this doctrine: "I and the Father are one" (John 10:30).

—Fr. Vincent Houdry, S.J. (1630–1729)

∞

Does the darkness of this mystery weaken our faith? Can we question or doubt of what God teaches us, because we cannot understand it? This is not the opinion of the holy Fathers, nor of the Doctors, who maintain that there can be no faith without obscurity.

What would be the merit and virtue of faith, says St. Leo, if it consisted merely of believing self-evident truths? Would it be making a great sacrifice to God if, by following His judgment, it would agree with our own; or if we recognized truths that it would be folly to deny? Would it not be treating our Lord in the most insolent and unworthy manner, even in a worldly point of view, were we to ask Him for a reason for all He said, and rather than wishing to believe His Word, we would defy Him, or rather require Him to give palpable proofs of all that He has deigned to reveal?

What rashness and boldness, to determine to submit to the judgment of reason only, thus wishing to place that weak ray of intelligence that God has given us in opposition to that infinite abyss of splendor that enlightens everything and cannot be fathomed.

O eternal and immutable Truth, You have revealed to Your Church the adorable mystery of the Trinity and have commanded all the faithful to believe what You have revealed.

And a petty mind, whose views are so narrow and confined, ignorant of the commonest things, easily disturbed, daily deceived in the discussion of trifling affairs, ever in want of being led, redressed, and corrected daily — this poor weak mind, I say, will dare to examine the decrees of his Creator and will deliberate if he ought to add faith to his opinions, because he cannot comprehend it!

O my God! I confess that I can understand nothing of this great mystery, that it far surpasses my intelligence; but nevertheless I firmly believe all that You have said, although my senses are opposed to my belief, although my weak reason seems to fight against it, although I have no other proof than Your word.

The Most Holy Trinity

I feel so certain of the truth of this divine mystery that I do not hesitate to found on this belief every hope of my eternal happiness.

This mystery is incomprehensible and must be adored with an unreasoning belief.

—St. Claude de la Colombière (1641–1682)

Part 3

∞

The Blessed Virgin Mary
and Our Lady's Feasts

∞

Devotion to Our Blessed Lady

From henceforth all generations shall call me blessed.

—Luke 1:48

There is no nation, no state or condition, that has not called Mary "blessed." Pagans, Greeks, barbarians—the noble, the rich, and the poor—have honored her, have invoked her aid. Angels, men, heaven, and earth have striven to show her their respect and homage.

Certainly a devotion must be good when it is so universal a practice among the faithful. And if St. Augustine makes use of the uniformity and extent of the belief of all Catholic nations as a proof that they must belong to the true Church, it is also an evident proof of the solidity and holiness of devotion to our Blessed Lady to see the universal piety of the faithful.

There are millions who daily implore her motherly protection; an innumerable number of zealous voices call upon us to share in their devotion; the Holy Spirit of God, encourages men of every condition of life in every nation.

We may safely say that heaven resounds with her glory, and the universe re-echoes its praises. All nations who adore God pay honors to the wonders done to her: Europe, Asia, Africa, and America have all been struck with astonishment at the "great things that He that is mighty hath done to her" (Luke 1:49).

It must not be supposed that the devotion to the Blessed Virgin is merely a devotion practiced by simple or ignorant people. Crowned heads have considered it a great honor to be devoted to her and to acknowledge her as their Lady and their Queen.

The canticle, which says in a general way, "All generations shall call me blessed" (Luke 1:48), does not seek any blind submission to our faith. To believe it does not call for any stretch of imagination; it needs only to be seen. Even at first sight, it is apparent that what the Blessed Virgin foretold has long been accomplished. So many monuments raised to her honor, so many churches consecrated in her name, so many hands busy in writing her praises, so many preachers glad to eulogize her virtues—all these form so many authentic testimonies to the truth of her prophecy.

Here you see the happiness of the ever Blessed Virgin universally acknowledged.

O! what a consolation it is for me, when I think of the many honors you, my dearest Mother, have received in every part of the world, where the gospel has been preached or where your Son is adored! What a joy it is, when I read of the many sanctuaries that have been consecrated to your honor and glory, of the many feasts that the Church has set apart for you, of the many holy confraternities, military orders, and religious communities that honor you with an especial worship and are consecrated to your service!

Since we have spoken of monarchs who have done much to spread devotion to the Blessed Virgin, do not let us forget that glorious St. Louis the Just, who solemnly consecrated himself, his kingdom, and his subjects to this Queen of Heaven, and who, to give a striking proof of his love for her, placed his crown and scepter on the altar of Notre-Dame in Paris and left especial directions that an annual commemoration of this event should be made in all the churches of France on the feast of her glorious Assumption. His successor, Louis the Great, ratified and confirmed this by an additional decree, in which he beseeches every prelate of his kingdom to exhort his people to cherish a fervent love for, and to practice an especial devotion to, the holy Mother of God.

The whole Christian world has, throughout all ages, shown its devotion to the Blessed Virgin. And this devotion has been authorized by a great number of miracles, which are so many illustrious and striking testimonies that God permits, approves, and draws from it His own glory. Not only the holy Fathers and Doctors, but the whole Church, have exerted themselves to pay her due honor and proclaim aloud her praises, and this the Church has always done, while, on the other hand, the baneful spirit of heresy has ever tried to cloud the glory of Mary. So many grand and glorious treatises have been written on this subject that it would be difficult to enumerate the books that have been published respecting this devotion.

To those who complain of these multitudes of books, the holy Fathers, and St. Bernard in particular, reply that if all men were forced to speak or write of this devotion, they never could say enough.

From this we must come to the conclusion that devotion to the Blessed Virgin is really the devotion of the Church. And this is nevertheless certified by the particular care she takes to honor her, and by the praises she bestows upon her. In fact, the Church's attention is quite pointed in this respect: it not only does honor to her mysteries and celebrates her feasts with great solemnity, but, as if all these solemnities were not sufficient to satisfy her devotion, she sets apart one day in the week to be consecrated to her memory.

But above all, the miracles that God has worked and still works daily, in favor of this devotion, evidently prove that Mary should be honored in every age and by all the faithful, God being unable to work miracles to authorize error or impiety.

Besides, when I speak of miracles, I speak of incontestable miracles, supported by an authority that it would be rash to challenge, such as those that are approved by ecclesiastical powers after a careful and strict examination, or those that we gather from the testimony of authors celebrated for their wonderful learning and rare sanctity.

Some have been related even in councils, as in the Second Council of Nicaea. This sufficiently denotes that it is very useful to speak of them, to write about them, and to preach about them, when they are legitimately approved of. And this the Church has done in general councils.

—Fr. Henri-Marie Boudon (b. 1624),
On Devotion to the Mother of God

∞

If you follow Mary, you will not swerve from the right path. If you pray to her, you will not fall into despair. If she holds you, you will not fall. If she protects you, you need not fear. If she leads you, you will never weary. And if she befriends you, you will be safe.

—St. Bernard (1091–1153), *De Aquae Ductu*

∞

The Immaculate Conception

The Lord possessed me in the beginning of his ways,
before he made anything from the beginning.

—Prov. 8:22

In this mystery it seems to me to be fitting and proper to apply to Our Lady's Immaculate Conception those words of the prophet, "the unspotted mirror of God's majesty" (Wisd. 7:26).

These words have been applied to the Uncreated Wisdom, that is to say, to the Word Incarnate, who is the substantial image of His Father and the mirror of His divine perfections, because He is begotten in a splendor more pure and brilliant than the light. They, however, can be applied in a just proportion to the glorious Virgin, since Mary was conceived without sin, exempt from its original stain, and destined to be the Mother of a Son who is as far removed from sin as light is from darkness. Consequently, Mary can be rightly called an unspotted mirror. Her conception also corresponds with the eternal and temporal conception of that God-Man, who is to be her Son, and also represents perfectly the sanctity, purity, majesty, and the noblest attributes of God Himself.

To show that the conception of Mary is this unspotted mirror that the wise man has pictured in the eternal conception of the Divine Word, the following reasoning would suffice: God was not willing, nor would He allow, that the body of the Blessed Virgin should be purer or more exempt from every stain than her soul. Now, the purity of her body has been the most perfect that can be imagined; it equaled, nay surpassed, those of the angels, and, if we may believe some of the early Fathers, it reached even to the infinite. Then, far from having contracted the least stain of sin, she was truly an unspotted mirror.

That God should have willed that Mary's body should not be endowed with a more excellent purity than that of her soul is not what could reasonably be expected of His wisdom, since the soul is the noblest part of man.

If the body, according to the expression of the Apostle, is a beautiful vase, the soul is the most precious of liquors that ought to fill it; and consequently the virginal body of Mary, whose purity surpassed that of angels and was near unto God, as St. Bernard says, had to contain a soul still purer, inasmuch as the purity of the body, without the purity of the soul, can have no value or consideration with God.

O! great God, could it have been indeed possible that You, who had taken so many pains to endow a purity of body to her whom You had chosen to be Your Mother, and at the same time allowed her soul to be soiled with a stain as infamous as that of original sin; that the one should be purer than the light of the stars, and the other more vile than the slime of which the first man was formed; that the purity of the one should have been capable of bringing You from heaven to earth, and that the defilement of the other would have discouraged You from coming down; and, in conclusion, that the woman whom You had chosen for Your Mother should have been, even for a moment, a slave of the devil?

No, I cannot believe it. You have too great a horror of sin, even to tolerate the shadow; You love innocence and holiness too much to consent to be born of a sinner, and to give an apparent opportunity of accusing You on a subject of which You are so sensitive.

—Fr. Vincent Houdry, S.J. (1630–1729)

The Immaculate Conception

∞

There is something in Mary that moves and affects me much more than this privilege of having been exempt from original sin—something that adds additional luster to this first prerogative. Mary received this grace from the very first moment of her conception. It was a wondrous gift, but what appears to me to be still more wonderful is that she kept this grace, until the last moment of her life, as pure, as entire, as when she first received it—no sin, no imperfection, no weakness, no surprise has ever done her harm.

It is a wonder to see water springing from the bosom of the earth as clear, as fresh, as if it fell from heaven. But it is a thing unheard of, that this same water from the well, after having bedewed the fields and dirty places, should flow at last into the sea, without a taint of smell, as unpolluted, as when it issued from the spring.

This is, however, what our Blessed Lady has done. She lived in this valley of tears for more than sixty years—this, too, in the midst of the same sins and occasions of sins that corrupt daily even innocent souls—without ever losing the purity of her heart. Her humility and patience were put to proofs without a parallel, and she gained fresh luster from every trial. The Holy Spirit gave her the preference among the many virgins without losing her honor. She had her joys, but she had her dolors too, and through these, she never lost for a single moment, the peace and tranquility of her soul.

Let us contrast ourselves with this holy and immaculate Mother. She received grace with life, and, what is more glorious still, she kept it intact until she died.

And we, alas! have been conceived and brought into the world in sin; and we have received the grace of the sacrament of Baptism, which made us friends of God.

But, what is more lamentable, we lose the benefit of this grace, almost as soon as we have received it, and then pass the remainder of our days in the dread uncertainty of forgiveness. For it must be confessed, to our shame, that we for the most part remain in a state of grace only so long as we are unacquainted with sin.

—St. Claude de la Colombière (1641–1682)

∞

All men are conceived in sin, and we do not read of anyone who was sanctified in his mother's womb, excepting Jeremiah and St. John the Baptist, although there is no doubt that the Blessed Virgin, enclosed in her mother's womb, should have been purified by a much more sublime degree of sanctification, seeing that she was to be the sanctuary where God the Son was to be made flesh.

—St. Bernard (1091–1153), *On the Nativity of St. John the Baptist*

The Nativity of Mary

And there shall come forth a rod out of the root of
Jesse, and a flower shall rise up out of his root.

—Isaiah 11:1

It seems to be just and reasonable that the Church should celebrate a great feast on the Nativity of the Blessed Virgin; for one may say, with St. Augustine, that this day is the natal day of the Redemption of mankind. The Church looks upon this Virgin as the powerful and beneficial morning star, which arises for the benefit of the world—like a beautiful orb that begins to shine in the midst of the dreadful turmoil of the universe, that begins to calm the storm, dissipate the darkness, and promises to guide us safely into port.

The Church looks upon her as the blessed Aurora that is to be soon followed by the Sun of justice, to enlighten every nation by the glory of her graces.

In reality, the birth of Mary is a glorious pledge of the reconciliation of the Creator with the creature; it is a sure sign of God's mercy for us; it is assuredly a precious omen of our salvation.

The newborn Virgin is, so to speak, a mysterious rainbow formed by the clouds of nature and the light of grace that God brings forth to assure us that henceforth it is His will to change the deluge of His wrath into the gentle rain of grace and benediction.

It is, then, most proper that the Church should rejoice greatly on this her natal day, and she wishes that we should render unto Mary due honors and gratitude.

∞

It was the birth of the Holy Virgin that the Chosen People had expected for ages, that the prophets had foretold with joy, and for which the saints of the Old Testament had sighed with so much fervency.

We have almost a right to believe that the angels — in token of the joy of heaven — brought down the news to Joachim and St. Anna, since the parents of Isaac, Samson, and St. John the Baptist had received a similar favor.

It need not be doubted that the news may have been accompanied by numerous marvels throughout the land, that in a short time there would be a mighty and glorious change. What a motive for joy for the world when it sees that come forth that was to give it its Savior, Redeemer, and King! What a subject for wrath for the devils when they see that beautiful star of Jacob arise, of which one of their prophets had even threatened them. "A star shall rise out of Jacob," says Balaam (Num. 24:17). They took her for a fatal comet that foretold the ruin of their empire and the end of their tyranny.

∞

It is true that Mary is still a weak child, to whom nature has but given sobs and tears, in order to bewail the miseries of a life into which she enters, and in this respect she is inferior to the angels who enjoy eternal happiness.

But she is destined to bear Him whom the heavens and the earth cannot contain; she is chosen to give birth to that God on whom the seraphim cannot gaze without trembling. It is this that places her infinitely higher than all the choirs of angels, and it can be said of her as was said of her Son: "Being made so much better than the angels, as he hath inherited a more excellent name than they" (Heb. 1:4).

The Nativity of Mary

Yes, this sacred quality of Mother of God to which she is destined raises her above all that is glorious in the nature of all the celestial choir.

Also it is from this beauteous title of Mother of God that she derives all the advantages and inherits the grandeur of being above all other creatures, and it is with this view that God causes her to be born this day.

Of every outward blessing that the world calls fortune, the Blessed Virgin was almost entirely destitute. She was not born in a fine palace; neither was she clothed in purple; she did not make her entry into the world under a canopy; around her bed you did not see a crowd of officers and servants.

She was born lowly and obscure. She begins the lessons that her Divine Son would finish in the crib at Bethlehem. She teaches us to despise the vanities of the world, since man in his cradle is more miserable and prouder than all animals. She plainly tells us that outward pomp and fine clothing serve only to feed our pride without decreasing our misery.

O! how well does poverty sit on the Mother of that God-Man, who by His humility will overthrow the pride of the devil; who by His nakedness, weakness, and poverty will shame the vanity of the world, with its luxuries and superfluities!

The riches of our Lady are all in her soul. "All the glory of the King's daughter is within" (Ps. 44:14 [RSV = Ps. 45:13]). It is within her that God shows His generosity; it is therein He has displayed all the treasures of His grace.

—Fr. Antoine Verjus, S.J. (1652–1706), *Panégyriques*

The Holy Name of Mary

And the virgin's name was Mary.

—Luke 1:27

Who is it who, having loved and honored the holy name of Mary, has not experienced what St. Ephrem has written about it with so much fervor? That it is really the heavenly star that shines through the surrounding darkness: how often has it not made us think more of God and our duties? That it is truly the harbor of refuge, wherein those who are threatened with danger can take shelter: how often, when violently tempted by the evil one, have we not been strengthened by invoking the name of Mary; for is not Mary our Mediatrix?

Many and many a time has not Mary, through her powerful intercession, made our peace with God, whom we have so often offended by our repeated falls, that she is the help of the afflicted and the consolation of the wretched?

We could fill volumes, were we to quote instances of all those who, finding themselves well-nigh wrecked with sadness and grief, have found a safe port by invoking the name of Mary. Would you see people constantly crowding to places that are consecrated to God under this holy name if they did not find that those who invoke it are relieved from all human miseries?

And why should not this holy name be so salutary, since it is so nearly allied to the Savior? Whosoever speaks of Mary speaks of the Mother of the Redeemer, speaks of a priceless treasure that encloses within itself the infinite wealth of the Father of mercies, and the remedy for every ill.

God wishes that these graces should come through Mary, and He has made her our Mediatrix.

If, then, you wish to know what a host of graces are enclosed in the name of Mary, look what a treasure of heavenly riches God has enclosed in her chaste womb.

Who among us, if he could see the sacred persons of Jesus and His holy Mother, would not immediately throw himself at their feet, and after embracing them would not pour out his heart to them?

It is true that we can have no longer their bodily presence, now that death has deprived us of both one and the other; but have we not a consolation near at hand? Can we not, in the place of their visible presence, invoke their names, impress them on our memory, engrave them in our hearts, pronounce them often with respect and love?

Indeed, we know that the old philosophers believed that names were but the representation of things, that they recalled to mind the idea and the form, and that men had invented their use in order that we might, in a certain way, place persons before our eyes, discuss with them on matters we know or have known, notwithstanding the length of distance or the question of time. By this innocent artifice, means have been found of producing everything by means of words and phrases, in imitation of the first being, which brought forth His own image, that is to say, His Word.

We also give to things a new being; we recall persons who are near or who are far off. The tongue and speech form a picture to the ears of things that we cannot see; we draw them from the tomb; we recall them from ages long passed away; we summon them to life when we will.

In a word, by means of names, we have found out the way of immortalizing everything; we give them a species of being, over which memory or death have no empire.

Who will, then, prevent you from making use of this holy artifice with regard to two persons whose names ought to be dearer to us than anything else in this world? I mean those of Jesus and Mary.

Should we not have their blessed names ever on our lips? Such would be the case if we had them deeply engraved on our hearts.

Fill us, Holy Mary, with the love of your holy name; fill us with the fire of divine love. At the sound of your name, my conscience will awaken, my love will be set on fire.

Mary! O name so many times attacked, but always victorious, ever glorious! Mary! O name always beneficial to my soul, which tranquillizes my fears, which helps me in my trouble! Every day will I pronounce it, and to it I will add the sacred name of Jesus. The Son will remind me of the Mother, and the Mother will remind me of the Son.

Those sacred names of Jesus and Mary I will engrave upon my heart, and when I breathe my last sigh, those names will be ever on my lips and will be names of blessing and salvation.

—Fr. D'Argentan, *Grandeurs de la Vierge*

∞

The Presentation of Mary

Behold, I come to do Thy will, O God.
—Hebrews 10:9

If angels and men could have mingled all that was virtuous and holy—if they could have gathered together every grace, merit, and perfection, they could not have given to God a more acceptable offering than was made on the Presentation of the Blessed Virgin to the Temple.

Yes! it must be confessed, O Lord, that before your Divine Son had come into the world and was made a victim for our sins on the Cross, Mary alone was deemed worthy of being an acceptable sacrifice.

The blood of oxen and sheep, the pouring out of liquors, and the perfume of spices, were things too material to please You. The sacrifices of Abel, Noah, and other patriarchs; the magnificence of David, and the holy profusion of Solomon well deserved Your favorable notice, but all these, were incapable of fully satisfying You.

It is true that Abraham and Isaac gained Your affection—the one, willing to sacrifice his only son, the other submissively agreeing to be immolated for Your glory. I know that You graciously accepted the offering that Manoah made to You of Samson, and also that of Anne when she presented her little Samuel to You. But however excellent these victims may have been, they nevertheless have slight blemishes and failed in possessing that perfect purity, without which they could not be worthy of You.

There was only Mary, in whom You found no stain of sin, or, rather, there was no one but Mary, who could have been a victim, sufficiently holy and pure, to supply for the defects of others and to fill in what was wanting in them to appease You, namely, the anticipation of the glorious sacrifice of the Cross.

Receive, then, this innocent dove that is to be soon followed by the spotless Lamb. Receive the lamentations of the one, and then You will receive the blood of the other. Receive the vows of the holiest of creatures; receive the offering of a virgin who is to be the Mother of a God, and then You will receive the sacrifice of God made man.

We ought certainly to believe that Mary does not enter into the Temple by compulsion, neither should we imagine that she entered therein in obedience to the will of her parents. Charity presses her on more strongly than the obligation she was under to fulfill her vows, and had they not presented her, she would have been drawn thither solely by her immense love.

She had long sighed for this happiness, and in the transports of her fervor she said repeatedly to herself: When shall I be enclosed in that sacred Temple, where God has fixed His dwelling, and where He has fixed mine? Dear Lord, do not delay to grant me the possession of that happiness, the postponement of which causes me such painful longing. "These things I remembered and poured out my soul in me; for I shall go over to the place of the wonderful tabernacle, even to the house of God" (Ps. 41:5 [RSV = Ps. 42:4]).

At length the happy day having arrived, do not ask me if she was transported with joy. Far from waiting for the commands of her parents to prepare herself for the fulfillment of their vows, she was the first to warn them and to urge them onward.

It was wonderful, indeed, to see a child of three years endowed with so firm a resolve—to see her leave the comforts of home without a sigh; to forego the caresses of her relations; to bid adieu to her dearest companions; to tear herself away from the arms of a father who loved her more than his eyes, and of a mother for whom she had the tenderest affection. All these, she resigns with tears of joy.

The Presentation of Mary

Picture to yourself the feelings of Joachim and Anna when they approached the high priest in order to place their daughter in his arms; how their souls are troubled with a divided love—one a love divine, the other a human love. Joachim, who has for so many years been ignorant of the sweet name of father, and who now would soon be deprived of his darling pet; Anna, too, venerable in age and piety, after a barrenness of years had now become the happiest of mothers—she, too, was on the point of losing all her joy and comfort. Joachim sighed and sobbed, and Anna shed tears of grief.

But the generous Virgin is unmoved. She sees the tears her parents shed, she hears the sighs without a sign of weakness, their sobs she listens to, without shaking her courage. She knows full well that these dear ones are well-nigh heartbroken, but grace is working within her, and a love much stronger is growing now, for God calls the Blessed Virgin to His service. She thinks not of a father's tenderness; she heeds not a mother's love; she knows and looks to God alone, to whom she wishes to sacrifice herself.

—Fr. Vincent Houdry, S.J. (1630–1729), *Discourses*

∞

The Annunciation

Hail, Mary, full of grace; the Lord is with thee.
—Luke 1:28

An angel presented himself to Mary, and she was troubled. Scarcely had he begun to speak to her than fear seized her, so that she felt within her a host of perplexing thoughts: "She was troubled at his saying, and thought within herself, what manner of salutation this should be" (Luke 1:29).

If Mary had been one of those worldly persons, who are virgins only in body, but not so in spirit, this visit she received would not have surprised her much, and the praises bestowed upon her, instead of astonishing her, would have agreeably flattered her. But the profession she had made as a virgin was undertaken solely with the view of devoting herself entirely to God.

The rules that had been prescribed, which were to renounce the manners and customs of a profane age, had been strictly kept. Her exact and severe regularity, her attention never to relax in the least duty, the preservation of an irreproachable conduct that was proof against the slightest censure, the modesty and bashfulness that were with her supernatural; the opinion she had formed that praises bestowed on her sex and favorably received, that praises even tolerated and quietly listened to, were to her a secret and contagious poison—all these caused her a trouble that she was not ashamed of showing, because being troubled in that way, she manifested the true character of a virgin faithful to God.

On Mary's answer depended the accomplishment of this glorious mystery. This consent was, in the order of the eternal decrees of God, one of the conditions required for the Incarnation of the Word; and this is the essential obligation we are under to this Queen of virgins, since it is of faith that it is through her that Jesus Christ has been given to us, and it is to her we are indebted for this Divine Savior. For if the Son, even of God, descends from His glory in heaven; if He enters into the chaste tabernacle of Mary to be made flesh, it is at the moment she has said, and because she has said it, "Behold the handmaid of the Lord, be it done to me according to thy word" (Luke 1:38).

It is not in consequence of this answer and consent of Mary that the Son of God came down from heaven and became incarnate. Mary conceived the Word first through the humility of her heart, and secondly through the purity of her body.

It is humility, says St. Augustine, that on the part of man should be the first and most necessary acquirement when conferring with God. If, then, God chose Mary to be His mother, it was that she alone appeared to Him to possess that perfect humility that He required. In fact, as St. Bernard remarks, a God who was on the point of humiliating Himself even to the excess of clothing Himself with our flesh ought to have an infinite liking for humility.

But what is there so peculiar in Mary's humility?

Why, first of all, it was a humility joined to a fullness of grace; she was saluted as full of grace, and she replies that she is the handmaid of the Lord. Secondly, it was also a humility highly honorable; an angel comes to tell her that she will be Mother of God, and she gives herself the title only of handmaid of the Lord.

This is what delighted heaven; this it is that determined the Word of God to leave the bosom of His Father and enclose Himself in the womb of Mary. While she humiliates herself before God, the Son of God empties Himself in her. "Emptied himself, taking the form of a servant" (Phil. 2:7).

From all this, let us learn to be humble. A mother of God humble, a God emptied! What a lesson for us! Without humility, there is no Christianity, no religion, since without humility, we would not have had the Incarnation or a God made man.

Secondly, Mary conceived the Word through the purity of her body and through her virginity. The prophet had foretold that the Messiah should be born of a virgin. And it was, says St. Bernard, essential, that a God by making Himself man should have had a virgin for a mother, since any other conception than that would not have suited the dignity of God and would have dimmed the brightness and glory of His divinity. Also, according to the beautiful idea of St. Bernard, the whole of this mystery passes between God, an angel, and Mary, which traces out for us three characteristics of the most perfect purity.

From this, what conclusion can we come to? Why, that, God being of Himself the essence of purity, it was necessary that a union so wonderful should be in harmony, and this was accomplished when the Word was made flesh. God, in this mystery, even gives the preference to virginal purity by choosing a virgin mother and by deputing an angel to be His ambassador.

Do not be astonished, continues St. Bernard, since the purity of this Virgin was so meritorious that it raised her above the level of angels. The angels are naturally pure, by a privilege of beatitude and glory, but Mary was so by election and virtue, so much so that she was troubled at the sight of an angel; this was the effect of her watchfulness to preserve the treasure of her purity. She was also ready to renounce the dignity of divine maternity rather than cease to be a virgin, and thus it was that God felt induced to descend into her in order that the Word should be made flesh.

—Fr. Louis Bourdaloue (1632–1704),
From his two sermons on the Annunciation

The Annunciation

∞

Imagine what it is to be a Son of God, and you can have some idea what it is to be His Mother. The excellence of the one will make you understand the excellence of the other.

—St. Gregory (ca. 540–604), *On the First Book of Kings*

∞

The Visitation

*Whence is this to me, that the mother
of my Lord should come to me?*

—Luke 1:43

St. Ambrose says that in this mystery there are two visits to be thought of—that of Jesus to St. John, and that of Mary to St. Elizabeth. St. John was in need of Jesus, and Elizabeth wanted Mary.

But how could these two children meet, enclosed, as they both were, in their mothers' wombs? How could two pregnant women, separated as they were from each other by roads almost inaccessible—how could they see each other, during a season so rigorous?

You know it well, my brethren. Jesus secretly instills in the heart of Mary a wish to visit her cousin Elizabeth—the greatness of her new dignity, a long fatiguing journey delays her not—the precious burden she begins to carry relieving, as says St. Augustine, instead of hindering her. Supported by this secret movement of grace that helps her on, she surmounts every obstacle and at length arrives at the house of Zechariah.

The presence of Jesus causes John to leap for joy in his mother's womb, and Elizabeth was filled with the Holy Spirit at the sight of Mary.

Mary's joy, humility, and gratitude shone forth in a manner quite divine in that wonderful canticle she gave in answer to the blessings of Elizabeth. What mysteries, what instructions, are included in this our Gospel history!

The Visitation

St. Ambrose was in ecstasy when he meditated on this celebrated visit, signalized as it was by so many mysteries, prophecies, and wonders. This holy bishop seems to display all his charming eloquence in describing what took place at the interview of those illustrious mothers, one of which gave birth to the greatest among the children of men, and the other to a God made man for the salvation of all. Elizabeth, says this Father, is the first to hear the voice of Mary, but John, even before that, is sensible of the grace of Jesus—the one rejoices at the Blessed Virgin's visit, the other leaps for joy at the visit of his Savior.

The two mothers proclaim aloud the marvels of divine grace, and the two children feel or produce the workings of the said grace. Jesus Christ fills St. John with the grace attached to the ministry of the Precursor, and St. John anticipates its functions in a wondrous manner. Elizabeth and Mary, interiorly animated by the spirit of their children, extract from their interview a series of oracles and prophecies.

—Fr. Laurent Juillard du Jarry (1658–1730), *On the Visitation*

∽

Ponder on the words that St. Elizabeth utters, and judge from them how the Holy Spirit must have moved her. She seems, as it were, to shout with rapture (see Luke 1:43):

Whence is this to me, that the mother of my Lord should come to me? I am only the mother of the servant, and behold the mother of the Almighty Monarch comes to visit me! O charity unequaled, profound humility of the mother and her Son to visit me, their unworthy servant! O happy, happy house that is so filled with such precious favors from heaven, in which the Savior of mankind pays His first visit on earth, and through the hands of the Blessed Virgin. Whence is this to me! O adorable Providence, which has so graciously given me this happiness!

I have often remarked that one of her best precautions was to prepare for the reception of this abundance of grace by making a long retreat of five months, thus hiding herself from the turmoil of the world. The evangelist would not have mentioned this without a purpose, for we read in the first chapter of St. Luke: "And after those days Elizabeth, his wife conceived, and hid herself five months" (Luke 1:24).

If that great saint had been distracted with the cares of the world, if she had not been in her house, when the Son of God, within the pure body of His holy Mother, came to honor her with a visit, she would, perhaps, have been deprived of all His favors; but she received graces in abundance, because God found her praying in solitude.

Happy is the soul who loves to be in retreat, thus flying from the noise and bustle of the world.

It is while she is in retreat that God visits her, and that she rejoices in God: "I will allure her and will lead her into the wilderness, and I will speak to her heart" (Hos. 2:14).

—Fr. D'Argentan, Conférence

◌

The Purification

And after the days of her purification, according to the
law of Moses, were accomplished, they carried him
to Jerusalem, to present him to the Lord.

—Luke 2:22

Mary, in obedience to the Law of Moses, sacrifices even her own honor, since by the Purification, she appears in the same condition as that of other women. Thus the brightness of her virginity was obscured; of that virginity of which she was so jealous in the mystery of the Incarnation; of that virginity whose glory is to shine outwardly, and not show the least stain. She consents to risk her reputation and her name, and of all the humiliations, that one, I dare to say, was the most difficult to bear—to be pure as the sun before God, and to appear impure, before the eyes of men. Such is, nevertheless, the sacrifice this holiest of virgins makes.

Now, this law of God, my brethren, does not compel us to do anything so humiliating. It wishes that we should appear as we are; that, being essentially submissive to the supreme control of God, we should not blush at duties that His law requires and at services that we are bound to perform. Especially, being impure sinners, we should not be ashamed to perform practices of penance that are to cleanse us, to reconcile us with God, and to help us to pay off the debt of His divine justice.

But what do we do? By a strange reversing, we wish to be sinners, and yet appear to be good. Mary gives up all desire of outside show, provided she is assured that the treasure of her virginity is preserved, and we, often even in the most trifling things, are but too anxious to keep up appearances.

Consider the many virtues she practices in this mystery: she hides her glory, not wishing to appear what she is; she emblazons her humility by appearing to be what she is not.

She is Mother of God, and she appears only as the mother of a man; she comes to be purified in company with other mothers, although she is the purest of virgins. Dispensed from this humiliating law, she nevertheless carries it out to the very letter.

However dear that adorable Son may be, she offers Him up for us, even unto death, by presenting Him to the Eternal Father, as a propitiatory victim. It costs her much to hear the saddest and most heartrending prediction made on Him, and with what resignation did she not consent? O Lord, how conformed is the spirit of the Mother with the spirit of the Son, and how both are different from ours. We wish to appear what we are not; our pride cannot brook the idea of appearing as we are. Luxury, pomp, ambition, and vanity accompany us even to the foot of the altar.

We are, however, charmed with the deep humility of the Blessed Virgin. Shall we never be but cold and indifferent admirers of the sublimest virtues? Does our love of purity inspire us with a great delicacy of conscience? What do we do to acquire and cherish so necessary and delicate a virtue? Only those who are clean of heart shall see God.

—Fr. Louis Bourdaloue (1632–1704), *On the Purification*

∽

Mary had spent twelve years of her sinless life in the courts of the Temple. It was there that she had outwardly dedicated her virginity to God. It was there she meditated over the ancient Scriptures and learned the secrets of the Messiah. She was coming back to the Temple again, still virgin, yet, mystery of grace! a mother with a child. She came to be purified, she who was purer than the untrodden snow on Lebanon. She came to present her child to God, and do for the Creator what no creature but herself could do: give Him a gift fully equal to Himself.

When the second Temple was built, the ancients of the people lifted their voices and wept, because its glory was not equal to the glory of the first. But the first Temple had never seen such a day as that which was now dawning on the Temple of Herod. The glory of the Holy of Holies was but a symbol of the real glory, which Mary was now bearing thitherward in her arms. But she had two offerings with her. She bore one, and Joseph the other. She bore her child, and he, the pair of turtledoves, or two young pigeons, for her purification (Luke 2:24). Many saw them pass. But there was nothing singular in them, nothing especially attractive to the eyes of the beholders. So it always is, where God is. Now that He is visible, He is, in truth, except to faith and love, just as invisible, as He ever was.

∞

Mary made her offerings and "performed all things according to the law of the Lord" (Luke 2:39). For the Spirit of Jesus was a spirit of obedience; and although the brightness of angelic innocence was dull beside the whiteness of her purity, she obeyed the law of God in the ceremony of her purification, the more readily as it was a concealment of her graces. But she bore also in her arms her true turtledove, to do for Him likewise "according to the custom of the law" (Luke 2:27).

She placed Him in the arms of the aged priest Simeon, as she has done since in vision to so many of the saints, and the full light broke on Simeon's soul. Weak with age, he threw his arms around his God. He bore the whole weight of the Creator, and yet stood upright. The sight of that infant face was nothing less than the glory of heaven. The Holy Spirit had kept His promise. Simeon had seen, nay, was at that moment handling, "the Lord's Christ." O blessed priest! worn down with age, wearied with thy long years of waiting for the "Consolation of Israel," kept alive in days that were out of harmony with thy spirit, even as St. John the evangelist was after thee, surely He who made thee, He who is so soon to judge thee, He whom thou art folding so proudly in thine arms, must have sent the strength of His omnipotence into thy heart, else thou wouldst never have been able to stand the flood of strong gladness that at that moment broke in upon thy spirit!

—Fr. Frederick William Faber (1814–1863),
The Foot of the Cross

∞

The Seven Dolors of Mary

And thy own soul a sword shall pierce.

—Luke 2:35

If we sincerely wish to be really and truly the children of Mary, we cannot do better than try to imitate our Mother. Let us ascend to Calvary; let us constantly remain with her at the foot of the Cross; let us share with her in the sufferings of Jesus; and let us impress on our hearts the image of the Crucified One.

If St. John had not ascended Mount Calvary, the Savior would not have given Mary to us in so marked a manner. We cannot hope to be fervent children of Mary if we are not to be found with her on Mount Calvary. It is there that she has adopted us — it is there only that she will acknowledge that we are her children.

You deceived yourself, O great Apostle, when you said on Mount Tabor, that you wished to be always there: "It is good to be here" (see Luke 9:33). You did not know then that the glory of Tabor is reserved for a happy eternity and that Calvary is the sole inheritance of God's children on earth.

It is at the foot of the Cross that Mary can say, "Look and make it according to the pattern, that was shewn thee in the mount" (Exod. 25:40). If you wish to be my children, imitate the example that I give you. Be firm and constant at the foot of the Cross; and know that if you keep away or stand aloof, you can be neither a child of God nor a child of Mary.

If we simply were compelled to compassionate our dying Savior, we would find many a tenderhearted Christian who would be easily led to practices of piety. But it is not merely a question of compassion. We must not endeavor to imitate: we must be crucified with Jesus Christ. If Mary does not see within us the likeness of her dear crucified Son, she will not acknowledge us as her children: "For whom he foreknew, he also predestinated to be made conformable to the image of his Son" (Rom. 8:29).

If that be true, can we believe that we are children of Mary? Alas! very far from being on Calvary and at the foot of the Cross, we are at the feet of earthly idols to whom we offer a continual sacrifice; and, far from being an image of Jesus crucified, we are more like to the evil one.

Ah, holy Virgin! since you have suffered so much to be our Mother, obtain for us favors from your Son, so that He may make us worthy to be your children; and, after having accompanied and imitated you on Calvary, we may, through your powerful intercession, be found worthy to reign with you in heaven.

—Essais de Sermons, Lent

∞

The first thing that strikes us about our Lady's Dolors is their immensity, not in its literal meaning, but in the sense in which we commonly use with reference to created things. It is to her sorrows that the Church applies those words of Jeremiah: "O all ye that pass by the way, attend and see if there be any sorrow like to my sorrow. To what shall I compare thee, and to what shall I liken thee, O daughter of Jerusalem? To what shall I equal thee, that I may comfort thee, O virgin daughter of Sion? for great as the sea is thy broken-heartedness: who shall heal thee?" (Lam. 1:12; 2:13).

Mary's love is spoken of as that which many waters could not quench. In like manner, the saints and Doctors of the Church have spoken of the greatness of her sorrows. St. Anselm says that whatever cruelty was exercised upon the bodies of the martyrs was light, or rather it was as nothing, compared with the cruelty of Mary's passion. St. Bernardine of Siena says that so great was the dolor of the Blessed Virgin that if it was subdivided and parceled out among all creatures capable of suffering, they would perish instantly. An angel revealed to St. Bridget that if our Lord had not miraculously supported His Mother, it would not have been possible for her to live through her martyrdom.

It would be easy to multiply similar passages, both from the revelations of the saints and the writings of the Doctors of the Church.

Where is Mary to look with her soul's eye for consolation? Nay, her soul's eye must look where her body's eye is fixed already. It is bent on Jesus, and it is that very sight that is her torture. She sees His human nature, and she is the Mother, the Mother beyond all other mothers, loving as never mother loved before, as all mothers together could not love, if they might compact their myriad loves into one intense nameless act. He is her Son, and such a Son, and in so marvelous a way her Son. He is her treasure and her all. What a fund of misery—keen, quick, deadly, unequaled—was there in that sight! And yet there was far more than that. There was His divine nature.

Yes, He is God. She saw that, through the darkness of the eclipse. But then the blood, the spittings, the earth stains, the unseemly scars, the livid, many-colored bruises—what did all that mean on a Person only and eternally divine? It is vain to think of giving a name to such misery as then flooded her soul. Jesus, the joy of the martyrs, is the executioner of His Mother. Twice over, to say the least, if not a third time also, did He crucify her, once by His human nature, once by His divine, if indeed body and soul did not make two crucifixions from the human nature only. No martyrdom was ever like to this. No given number of martyrdoms approach to a comparison with it.

It is a sum of sorrow that material units, ever so many added together, ever so often multiplied, do not go to form. It is a question of kind as well as of degree. And hers was a kind of sorrow that has only certain affinities to any other kinds of sorrow and is simply without a name, except the name that the simple children of the Church call it by—the Dolors of Mary.

—Fr. Frederick William Faber (1814–1863), *The Foot of the Cross*

The Assumption

Who is she that cometh forth as the morning ris-
ing, fair as the moon, bright as the sun?

—Song of Solomon 6:9

The Holy Spirit had enkindled so ardent a flame in the heart of the Blessed Virgin that it was really a continuous miracle that she sustained so impetuous a heavenly fire without dying, and this repeatedly burst forth from her breast. For if St. Ephrem cried out in his desert cell, and placed his hands over his heart lest it should burst and split; if St. Francis of Assisi thought that he would die of joy when he heard an angel sing a strain of the celestial choir; if St. Francis Xavier, laying bare his bosom to breathe more freely, and looking up to heaven, beseeched his merciful Lord and Master to be sparing of His favors, and to remind Him that a human heart could not endure such a flood of consoling light; what must our Blessed Lady have felt, she who received more than all the saints put together? How was it that she did not expire at every moment? How was it that she was not consumed with the flames of love divine, more especially as the Son of God, who is love itself, had willed and chosen to dwell for nine long months in her virginal womb? Cannot we say, with St. Bernard, that her chaste interior was laden with love, that she had neither heart nor life, if we be allowed to say so; but that love was her heart, and to live for God and love Him too, was one and the same thing?

The life of the Seraphim consists in seeing God, in loving Him always, in enjoying an eternity of bliss; and, as St. Gregory observes, wherever they go, they never go out of God—they fly in the bosom of His immensity; they dwell in His heart; they exercise their divine functions in the sanctuary of His divinity.

This was, then, veritably the life of the Blessed Virgin. She shared the rank of the blessed in heaven, far, far above the state of mortals who lived on earth. Her heart was ever near to God, and God was always in her heart. Her sleep was one continual dream of love, and she could say with the spouse in the Canticle: "I sleep and my heart watcheth" (Song of Sol. 5:2).

Doubtless the death of Mary was a greater miracle, for to what can we attribute the cause? Who can tell the cause of so wonderful a death? Can we attribute the cause to sin? Oh no; she is innocence itself; her conception was immaculate, her birth was stainless, her life without reproach; and never having been a slave of sin, she needed not pay the debt of nature. To sickness? No; she was never ill, and her body was exempt from the gradual decay of nature. To agony? No; death would appear to be too welcome to be painful. Is it to the shafts of divine love? But love was the mainstay of her life—how could it have caused her death? To her Son's Cross? But if she was to die, why did she not die on Calvary?

It is certain that never a mother loved her son so much, because no mother had a son who was hers alone—no mother had a son so loving, so perfect; there never was a mother, who had a heart so inflamed with the fire of divine love. Many mothers have died either with grief at seeing their children die, or with fear at seeing them on the point of dying.

How was it, then, that the Blessed Virgin did not die at the death of her Son, she who loved Him so, she who saw Him suffer such a cruel death? You will tell me, with St. Bernardine, that to live without Him was a greater martyrdom than dying with Him; because in dying with Him she would have been martyred only once, but in surviving Him, every moment of her life was simply a torture.

The Assumption

What wonder, then, that her life was a species of death, and that death, thus reversing the order of nature, was a renewal of her life?

∞

It is impossible for anyone to describe the excess of glory and the sublimity of the ever Blessed Virgin's throne. We need not be astonished, as Arnold de Chartres remarks, because her glory exceeds that of all others. She has a rank of her own. Her pedestal is raised considerably higher than that of the angels. The glory she possesses is not solely a glory like that of the Word Incarnate; it is in a certain way similar.

King of glory, it is certain that magnificence and grandeur are inherent to Your holy habitation. You have given striking proofs of this, on the feast of the Assumption of Your holy Mother. You have crowned her Queen of all saints; there is no one but the King who precedes her. She is so glorious that one would say that it is the glory of God itself, or rather that God had her with His own glory. She is so great and powerful near You that she herself cannot fathom the extent of her power.

—Fr. Nouet, S.J. (1605–1680), *Vie de Jésus dans les Saints*

∞

The Holy Rosary

It is better, therefore, that two should be together than
one, for they have the advantage of their society.

—Eccles. 4:9

I cannot conceive a man being spiritual who does not habitually say the
Rosary. It may be called the queen of indulgenced devotions. First, consider its importance, as an especially Catholic devotion, as so peculiarly
giving us a Catholic turn of mind by keeping Jesus and Mary perpetually
before us, and as a singular help to final perseverance, if we continue the
recital of it, as various revelations show.

Next consider its institution by St. Dominic in 1214, by revelation,
for the purpose of combating heresy, and the success that attended it. Its
matter and form are no less striking. Its matter consists of the Pater, the
Ave, and the Gloria, whose authors are our Blessed Lord Himself, St.
Gabriel, St. Elizabeth, the Council of Ephesus, and the whole Church, led
in the West by St. Damasus. Its form is a complete abridgment of the Gospel, consisting of fifteen mysteries in decades, expressing the three great
phases of the work of redemption, joy, sorrow, and glory. Its peculiarity
is the next attractive feature about it. It unites mental with vocal prayer.
It is a devotional compendium of theology. It is an efficacious practice
of the presence of God. It is one chief channel of the conditions of the
Incarnation among the faithful. It shows the true nature of devotion to
our Blessed Lady and is a means of realizing the Communion of Saints.

Its ends are the love of Jesus, reparation to the Sacred Humanity for the outrages of heresy, and a continual affectionate thanksgiving to the most Holy Trinity, for the benefit of the Incarnation.

It is sanctioned by the Church, by miracles, by indulgences, by the conversion of sinners, and by the usage of the saints. See also how much the method of reciting it involves. We should first make a picture of the mystery and always put our Blessed Lady into the picture, for the Rosary is hers. We should couple some duty or virtue with each mystery and fix beforehand on some soul in purgatory to whom to apply the vast indulgences.

Meanwhile, we must not strain our minds, or be scrupulous, for to say the Rosary well is quite a thing that requires learning. Remember always, as the *Raccolta*[2] teaches, that the fifteenth is the coronation of Mary, and not merely the glory of the saints.

— Fr. Frederick William Faber (1814–1863), *Growth in Holiness*

∞

The first founders of the holy Rosary, filled with the grace of the Holy Spirit, and all on fire with divine love, made their appearance as new Apostles ready to sacrifice their lives and shed their blood for the love of Jesus Christ, for the honor of the Church, and for the defense of their Faith.

It is a truth that is easy of proof by a fact perhaps the most memorable that may have happened in France since God was therein known. The spirit of heresy, which is inseparable from the spirit of rebellion, had spread far and wide among the Albigenses. These heretics, not being able to defend themselves by argument or by Holy Scripture, resolved to support their errors by fire and sword. The king of Aragon, the counts of Toulouse and Armagnac, many other sovereigns and great lords increased

---

[2] The Raccolta is a book of prayers and practices to which popes have attached indulgences.

this party, and, uniting their forces, they succeeded in collecting a force of one hundred thousand men.

Terror spreads around, and the storm equally threatens religion and the state. Success must be decided, on one side or the other.

Who will dare to oppose this torrent? Who will disperse the tempest? Fear not; the God of armies, who formerly sent Simon Maccabee to pro-tect the Jews and to save the synagogue, raised up Simon de Montfort, the Maccabee of France, for the protection of the Church and the Catholics.

The ever Blessed Virgin, on the other hand, giving the Rosary to St. Dominic, repeated these consoling words: "Take this holy sword, a gift from God, wherewith thou shalt overthrow the adversaries of my people" (2 Macc. 15:16).

This promise was not fruitless; this Rosary was like Gideon's sword which, under the form of blades of barley, caused such havoc in the camp of the Madianites. In fact, it may be said that if this immense heretical army was overthrown and cut to pieces, it was owing more to the efficacy of the Rosary than to the power of the crusade. The Count de Montfort's army was strong in numbers, but the piety of his soldiers, and the help they received from above, made them as brave as lions. He did what Judas Maccabeus did: "He armed every one of them, not with defense of shield and spear, but with very good speeches and ex-hortations" (2 Macc. 15:11). He armed them with the Rosary, too, and at once gave the signal to charge. Invoking the Name of the Lord, they fearlessly attacked the enemy; with prayers on their lips, confident of victory, and sword in hand, they overthrew the enemy's squadrons one after the other, galloped over the bodies of the slain, and gained one of the most famous of victories — a victory that saved the kingdom and was the triumph of religion.

Holy Virgin, the Church is indeed in the right to sing your praises — it is to you alone that we can attribute the defeat of every heresy.

The Rosary is the most powerful, and at the same time the most efficacious, of daily devotions, since all kinds of favors are granted to those who recite it devoutly and regularly. If you wish to know what particular graces we obtain therefrom, the following are those that the Blessed Alain de la Roche learned from the Blessed Virgin herself: holiness of life, integrity of purpose, contempt of the world, and peace of Christian homes.

—Fr. Nicolas de Dijon (d. 1696), *On the Rosary*

∞

Our Lady of Mount Carmel

All her domestics are clothed with double garments.

—Proverbs 31:21

I know full well that we have within ourselves certain signs of our predestination. Nevertheless they are but conjectures that tend to strengthen our hope but do not entirely dissipate the just fears that God wills that we should have when we think of His impenetrable judgments. No one, says St. Gregory, so long as he remains on earth, can positively know what is decreed in heaven as to his predestination, or as to his eternal loss. This is the sad condition in which we live here below; we are certain of soon finishing our career in this place of exile, without really knowing if we shall ever see our own true country.

We must not lose sight of this tuition if we wish to prevent faults into which we are sure to fall, without that.

Our dear Lady of Mount Carmel has placed no limits to our hope in becoming her children. The promise she has made of protecting us is not limited by any condition. She has engaged that she will not suffer us to be unhappy for all eternity; that is to say, she gives us every hope of our salvation that we can possibly have in this life. She promises by that, that if we persevere in her service, we shall infallibly persevere in grace.

But what do you say of so magnificent a promise? Has the Blessed Virgin explained it to your satisfaction, or do you cherish some scruple? When, to calm the anxiety that the uncertainty of your salvation causes you, you would have dictated to our Blessed Lady the promises she has made, could you have chosen more formal promises?

The holy Fathers, when they have spoken in general terms of the power of the Blessed Virgin, have made use of expressions quite as strong and quite as favorable. St. Bonaventure does not give any other limit to the power of Mary than the almighty power of God. St. Antoninus assures us that God does not make a favor when He listens to her prayers, but He grants them as an indispensable duty, and that she would not know what it is to be refused. St. Anselm asserts that a true servant of Mary cannot be lost.

Here you have opinions sufficiently capable of inducing you to place entire confidence in the Mother of Mercy; but however learned and holy these men may have been who have given us these splendid testimonials, they fall short of the promises our Blessed Lady made to St. Simon Stock, and of these I am about to speak. They teach me that I have nothing to fear if the Blessed Virgin takes an interest in me, but that is not sufficient to appease my uneasiness; I wish to know if she does so really.

She gives me here manifest and visible proofs. It depends upon myself to take it in its right sense. She has attached to this scapular her protection, for she says, "He who is clothed with this habit shall not endure everlasting fire."

I am not, then, astonished that at the first report of so magnificent a promise Christians from all parts flocked to the holy community of Mount Carmel, to whom she had entrusted so precious a treasure.

Noblemen, princes, kings even, who have as much to fear for their salvation as the commonest of men, eagerly desired to participate in the privileges of these holy religious — they whose grandeurs exposed them daily to so many dangers.

—St. Claude de la Colombière (1641–1682)

∽

This scapular imposes upon all members of the Confraternity of Mount Carmel the obligation of leading a pious and truly Christian life by renouncing the maxims of the world as did the early Christians when they received the sacrament of Baptism and were clothed in a habit appropriate for the ceremony.

But many never think of this, and to this may be attributed the cause of their not fulfilling the duties of their profession. We must, from time to time, call to mind our engagements, in order to fulfill the promises we made when we received the habit.

Once upon a time, a powerful monarch, when he was urged to perform some action unworthy of his high rank, immediately displayed his regal tunic to those who had solicited him: "Should I be worthy to wear this purple robe," said he, "if I had soiled it by even a single cowardly deed? Would it not make me blush every day of my life, if I had dishonored it merely for the purpose of avoiding death? Could I ever look upon it without feeling an inward reproach, that even for one day I was unworthy to wear it?" Then rising, he wrapped his mantle around him and said that he would prefer to die gloriously rather than lower his dignity by performing an unworthy action.

This, my dear brothers, ought to be our sentiment when we wear so holy a habit; it ought to distinguish us from men of the world; it ought to put us on our guard. Does this habit reproach me? Will it not make me blush at the awful judgment seat of God? This would be our case if, after the promises we made, we should relax and fall. Let us then keep up the holiness of this habit by an exact observance of all the duties of our state of life.

—Sermons on Every Subject

Part 4

∞

Sermons on Diverse Subjects

∞

The Holy Catholic Church

Behold I am with you at all times,
even to the consummation of the world.

—Matthew 28:20

The Christians of the primitive Church enticed the pagans, not only by their generous and unconquerable patience, but also by the holiness of their lives. And the heretics, as corrupt in their manners as they were in their belief, were the cause that the name of Jesus Christ was blasphemed among the Gentiles, and that the light and brightness of the Church was blackened by an infinity of calumnies.

Read ecclesiastical history, and you will not find an age in which hell has not vomited forth some new heresy, and where the devil has not succeeded in seducing some member of the Church to arm and fight against the body. You will see that there is not a single article of the Creed that has not been assailed, not one article of faith for whose destruction the devil has not even distorted the words of Holy Scripture and the power of the Word of God.

As for myself, I confess that nothing demonstrates the goodness and miraculous protection of Almighty God as much as the preservation and augmentation of the Church in the midst of heresies.

A vast number of heresies have attacked the Church, a thousand storms have raged over her, but in the midst of tempests, this ship, although battered by many rolling billows, has not been shattered or engulfed. Truth remains, errors pass away. All these heresies, aided by the eloquence, doctrine, and subtlety of their authors, supported by the powerful influence of the great and the noble, sustained by the armies of emperors, have passed away, or are passing away. All these heresies have made much noise, and, by the impetuosity of the infected waters, have carried away all those who were not strongly bound to the Church. They have floated with the stream, as says St. Jerome.

And this is the reason: they are the muddy waters that have for their source the invention of man, and not the pure and limpid stream that comes from God, who is the Fountain and Source of all sanctity.

If the Apostles, and those apostolic men who were eminent for their sanctity, had not been the instruments of Almighty God, but in reality the authors of the Church, the Church would have failed when those apostolic men were no more.

Besides—for we need not dissemble—how many times has it not been seen that those who held the places of Apostles were not inheritors of their virtues, but, on the contrary, lived in a way totally opposed to the lives of saints? Their faults, nevertheless, have never introduced error in the doctrine of which they were the depositaries and oracles, and the corruption of their manners have never tarnished the faith that had been entrusted to them.

It is strange, but true, that in all sects the doctrine is congenial to the hearts of those who taught it. It is not thus in the Christian religion. We must, then, acknowledge that its preservation does not depend on men. But there is a secret and divine virtue that sustains it in sanctity and that causes it to last, in spite of the continual efforts of those who conspire its destruction, whether it be from within or without.

—Fr. Claude Texier, S.J. (1610–1687)

∞

What blindness! that each heretic forms his own idea of religion, according to his private judgment, by refusing to subscribe to the tenets of the Church; that each one becomes the judge and umpire of eternal truths; that from some particular tenet he frames a form of worship, and introduces ceremonies, to adore the God Almighty, or to appease His justice; that he undertakes to reform, interpret, and reverse the precepts of the law and Christian morals that God has revealed to His Church, and that the inspired writers have left us!

Heretics have understood this anomaly, for after having refused to obey the legitimate successor of St. Peter (for whom Jesus Christ has prayed that his faith might not fail [Luke 22:32]), they have been compelled to establish heads of their sects, so that they may see in their congresses and synods (which, by the by, they hold without any right, or without any old established form) the same power they cannot endure to see in the Catholic Church; and they recognize the rebels and heresiarchs as their masters and interpreters of their religions.

— Bishop Esprit Fléchier (1632–1710), *Life of Cardinal Commenden*

∞

The Treasures of the Church

A dispensation is committed to me.

—1 Corinthians 9:17

It must be now or never, that we must imitate the Apostle and accomplish by penitential works what is wanting in the Passion of our Lord and Savior.

We must implore of God the remission and indulgence of our sins, by offering satisfactions proportionate to the offense, as says St. Cyprian.

A jubilee is an indulgence made up of the Precious Blood, tears, fasts, prayers, and alms of a penitent sinner; these exhaust the vengeance of God's justice and extinguish the fire of His anger. Now, there are two ways of satisfying the justice of Almighty God — one is the ordinary way; the other is the extraordinary.

The ordinary way is the path strewn with penances, fasts, prayers, and almsdeeds; there is nothing too guilty that these will not but prove useful and serviceable. But there is an extraordinary way, a path of grace and a mixture of mercy and justice. It is extraordinary, because with little, it does much, and the justice of God is satisfied with this little.

From these I calculate that there must be a great distinction between ordinary penance and a jubilee. The first is that penance works slowly; it takes time. Today a fast, tomorrow another, as one who pays his debts by installments. Now, in the indulgences of a jubilee, we have an abridgment of God's mercy. It makes quick work of His mercies; it is a way in which what would have taken years of penance in the ordinary way we can expiate and satisfy at this acceptable time (the indulgence proclaimed) in a day.

Some Fathers of the Church, in speaking of penance, call it a shortening of eternal punishment, because what we owe to the justice of God in eternity, we expiate by means of penance in a few days. But we venture to say that an indulgence is still a further abridgment of penance, because penance costs us more than an indulgence. Another distinction is that it is difficult and harassing to expiate our sins by sharp penances, but it becomes easy of satisfaction through indulgences; one is a rigorous baptism, the other a merciful baptism.

Thus we can distinguish three kinds of baptism. The baptism by water costs nothing to the recipient, the baptism of penance costs much, and the baptism of an indulgence is between the two: we therein find a full remission of our sins, but at very little cost.

It is a mingling of the satisfactions of Jesus Christ and those of the sinner, and the little that the sinner contributes is worth very much. It is not, however, on account of our own satisfactions that jubilees have been established; it is chiefly on those of our Savior, because He has merited that indulgence for us through His Precious Blood and has left us the treasures of His own merits to defray all costs.

If you ask me why our Lord and Savior has given the power of applying the merits of His Precious Blood by indulgences and jubilees to His vicars, the sovereign pontiffs, I would answer that He wishes to save us the more easily.

It was not sufficient for Him to have extinguished the eternal flames of hell, but He wishes further that His Blood should serve to liquidate the debts of temporal punishment, which are owing to the justice of God.

In the primitive Church, when Christians were full of zeal and fervor, there was not so much occasion for jubilees for expiating their past sins; they cheerfully submitted to the strictest penances and had no other wish to satisfy divine justice than by practicing rigorous austerities. But because, in the course of time, charity grew cold, jubilees and indulgences were needed, in order that we might be able to be reconciled to God, and to satisfy fully His justice.

As the jubilee was given to Christians through an extraordinary flow of divine mercy, we must remark that, according to Holy Scripture, there is in God a mercy that, on account of its grand result, is called great: according to Thy great mercy.

Now this great mercy of our Lord and God is like one of those grand and noble rivers that seem to be ever full, but, at certain seasons of the year, the tide runs so high that the water overflows the banks and fertilizes the fields around.

Thus we may say that it is at the time of a jubilee that the Divine Mercy inundates the Christian people and overwhelms the faithful with a deluge of graces. This abundant stream of God's merciful goodness does not wash only the roots of those trees growing on its banks, as the psalmist says — that is to say, it does not communicate itself to the good and fervent alone, but it is intended for the greatest of sinners, those who are the furthest removed from Him.

—Fr. Claude Texier, S.J. (1610–1687), *Dominicale*

The Ministry of God's Church

He that heareth you, heareth me;
and he that despiseth you, despiseth me.

—Luke 10:16

Chronicles mentions that the priests and Levites were sanctified to carry the ark of the Lord, the God of Israel (1 Chron. 15:2).

If the priests of the Old Testament, who offered up the incense and the common bread were required to be holy, if they were to be sanctified to carry the ark of the Lord God of Israel, ought not the priests of the New Testament to be truly sanctified, for do they not offer up the Heavenly Bread, the Bread of Life, the only Son of God, and have they not the honor of carrying daily the Lord of the ark, even the very God of Israel? In another place it is said, "Purify yourselves, you who have charge of the vessels of the sanctuary." You do not carry solely the vessels of the Lord, my brethren; you carry the Lord Himself, you bear Him in your hands, you carry Him on your tongues, you enclose Him in your hearts. How, then, dare you carry Him with unclean hands, on indiscreet tongues, in corrupted hearts? How can you be so cruel as to carry Him with you in the world, which is His enemy, and wherein sin and abomination dwell?

The high priest said one day: As I have always lived far apart from the world, I fancied that my brethren lived as I did; but I have been surprised by persons of the first consideration who have come to find me out, and who have told me, that not only the people of Israel, but the priests and

171

Levites, have not separated themselves from the people of the lands and from their abominations. I was so deeply moved by this news, continues this holy man, that "I rent my mantle and my coat, and plucked off the hairs of my head and my beard, and I sat down mourning" (Ezra 9:1, 3).

Priests should be holy, says God, because I am holy, and being holy I wish my ministers to be holy, and I cannot endure any but holy men to approach me or my altars. Sanctity is a necessary appendage for the priest, and the want of holiness is a species of irregularity that is unbearable, and that I cannot suffer.

Let not those who have not the courage to try to become saints be rash enough to be priests of my altars: "They shall not come near to me, to do the office of priest to me; neither shall they come near to any of my holy things that are by the holy of holies" (Ezek. 44:13). This is as much as to say that priests who are not holy do an injury to God; they tarnish the glory of His name; they defile His temple, altar, and sacrifice; they scandalize His religion; they do violence to His sanctity; and they offend His Divine Majesty.

There is no condition of life more noble, more exalted, than that of being a priest of Jesus Christ. There is also no state that requires more preparation. They belong to God by a particular consecration; consequently, they ought to be more attached to Him. They are privileged to approach near to God, and they ought to be of the purest. They beseech and appease God for all the faithful, so they ought to be worthy of His propitiation for themselves.

They represent Jesus Christ; they ought to enter into His spirit. They dispense and offer up the holy mysteries; from these they ought to gather its first fruits. As they should be masters of the spiritual life, it is only right that they should fix it in their own hearts and by their actions show that they love all that is spiritual. They reprove and correct others, so their conduct should be irreproachable. They have received more graces, so they should be more grateful. Their sins attract attention, and thus they should be the more cautious. It is difficult for them to retrieve themselves if they fall, and they ought to preserve their innocence, with fear and trembling.

Reflections such as these should induce those whom God has called to this holy state to exercise the greatest care imaginable.

Idleness and disgust usually follow haste and imprudence, says St. Bernard. He who usurps the office of priesthood will be a useless possessor of such a dignity. Not having consulted God, he will not be the work of God's own hand; and having closed the entrance of grace, he will be unable to fulfill properly and faithfully those functions that the grace of God can alone enable him to accomplish.

On the other hand, a genuine vocation engenders zeal, and it is difficult for him who has devoted himself entirely to the service of God not to make it his sole business to serve and honor Him.

The priesthood of Jesus Christ is not a sinecure, but a ministry of toil and trouble, which includes a multiplicity of essential duties difficult to carry out.

"Be thou vigilant and labor in all things," says the Apostle to Timothy, exhorting him to strengthen himself in his laborious vocation, through the merits of Jesus Christ, and to "labor as a good soldier of Jesus Christ," which will enable him to resist all the powers of darkness (2 Tim. 4:5; 2:3). "Do the work of an evangelist," preaching the Word of God, after having impressed it upon his own heart, and rendered it manifest by his own deeds. "Fulfill thy ministry," not so much to keep the faith, as to preserve it pure and holy: mysteries of our Lord and Savior that must be carried out with fear, and secrets of conscience that must be religiously concealed. "Keep that which is committed to thy trust," and be prepared to carry out any amount of duty that truth, justice, and charity may impose upon you (1 Tim. 6:20).

— Bishop Esprit Fléchier (1632–1710), *Panegyrics*

∞

The clergy are called by that name, either because they are a portion of the inheritance of the Lord or because the Lord is their portion. He, therefore, who is thus of the inheritances of the Lord, or he who has God for his portion, should show himself to be worthy of possessing God, and that God should possess him.

He who engages to serve the Church as a minister of Christ knows well at first the meaning of the title, and by understanding the full significance of the name of priest, it enforces the fulfillment of every duty of his office.

—St. Jerome (ca. 347–420), *Epistle ad Nepotianum*

∞

Material Churches

How lovely are thy tabernacles, O Lord of hosts! My soul
longeth and fainteth for the courts of the Lord.

—Psalm 83:2–3

Unfortunately, there are people who go to church without humility or prudence. They assist at the grand services as if they were going to the theater. Instead of thinking of the feast, or with any idea of being attentive, they ridicule all they see. Loaded as they are with sins, they insolently stride across the threshold of those sacred gates, according to the language of the prophet; they affect a grand air, as if they were persons of distinction, and this, too, in those places where all worldly importance should cease to be.

They hurry on the crowd in order to be a near witness of the ceremonies, rather than having a wish to participate in heavenly graces. They push even to the altar rails, not through an earnest eager devotion, but through a vain curiosity. They bring in with them a worldly heart; and when even they are coldly speaking and praying to Almighty God, they are thinking more of themselves and of their vanities. In fact, they have no scruples in going in, and they drag in with them their iniquities without compunction or remorse.

What shall I say of those impieties that are committed daily in the presence of Jesus in the tabernacle, who, all invisible as He is, is no less to be adored? What shall I say of those profane remarks disturbing the holy and venerable silence of the sacred mysteries, interrupting the meditations of the faithful, reaching even to the sanctuary, and distracting the attention of the ministers who are attending on the celebrant?

What of those mincing airs and indecorous postures that so scandalize the good, that are, according to the words of Jesus Christ, the desolation of those holy places, where angels assist with fear and trembling? What shall I say of those affected ways, of seeing and wishing to be seen, that convert the house of God into a place of rendezvous for immodest glances and guilty thoughts?

With no small amount of indignation, we see some Christians (if I may dare to call them Christians), who scarcely deign to bend a knee when Jesus is exposed for the adoration of the faithful, as if to dispute the homage that is due to Him, as if it pricked their conscience and reminded them of the little feeling of religion that may be left within them.

Worldly persons, more gaily decked out than the altars even, display proudly their luxurious finery and often seem proud of their indecent attire, and this too, before the poor and humble Jesus, hidden in the Holy Sacrament of the Eucharist.

We see sinners entering heart and soul into conversations that only rekindle their bad passions, and thus commit fresh sins even in front of those tribunals of penance, wherein they should confess and weep for them.

It thus happens that the very means of our salvation become the instruments of our loss; that the church, which is the place wherein we should sanctify ourselves, becomes the theater of our delinquencies; that prayers are turned into sins; that even the sacrifice of our Lord, which is the source of all graces, becomes a subject of condemnation; and that nothing in His judgment can perhaps more add to our guilt than our having entered His temple and assisted unworthily at His mysteries.

How many there are who go to church in order to keep up a certain decorous reputation, because it is customary, because it would not do to offend the world, bad as it is — a world that piques itself on certain rules of decorum and a desire to keep up an outward show of religion!

How many there are who acknowledge and practice an exterior worship, who glorify God with their lips, whose prayers are heartless, who give up their minds to voluntary distractions, speak without thinking, pray without knowing what they are saying, and expect that God listens to them when they do not listen to themselves! This is what St. Cyprian says: How many there are who, when they make an act of devotion, fancy they do honor to the church they frequent, who are always in the most conspicuous seats, and who approach to God merely to be seen by men!

How many there are, who come to church because they are forced to come, who consider the long service of a great feast a bore, and who grumble because they are under the necessity of hearing a sermon, or of remaining until the grand High Mass is over! Is not all this an abuse of holy things?

We should enter God's temple in order to become holy. It seems to me that all therein should conduce to our sanctification. That baptismal font that reminds us of the origin of our spiritual regeneration and puts us in mind of the grace and obligations of our baptism. Those altars that teach us that we have a heart wherein Jesus wishes to dwell, and wherein we can offer as many sacrifices as we have temptations. Those confessionals: do they not invite us to sigh for our sins; do they not make us long to be bathed in the Precious Blood of Jesus? That pulpit: does it not preach to us that we should be new men, engendered by the Word of God? That divine and adorable tabernacle: does it not lovingly entreat us to kneel and pray before Him with great purity of intention and to ask for the grace to love Him more and more?

—Bishop Esprit Fléchier (1632–1710),
Dedication of St. James Major Church

∽

You have the church, which is a refuge, and, if I may dare to say so, is a heaven in miniature. You have a sacrifice offered up and consummated. You have the house wherein the Holy Spirit showers down abundant graces. You have the tombs and relics of the martyrs and saints, and many other things, which should induce you to return from a state of sin and indifference to that of grace and justice.

— St. John Chrysostom (ca. 349–407), Homily 69

∞

Sundays and Holidays

*Blessed is the man who observes the
Sabbath Day, who keeps his hands pure,
and who abstains from any kind of sin.*

—Isaiah 56:2

Sunday has succeeded to the Sabbath. It is forbidden on that holy day to do any servile work, and all are under the strict obligation of attending the Divine Office. After having spent six days in the tumult of temporal affairs, is it not just and right to devote one day for the purpose of collecting one's thoughts and of thinking of spiritual things?

You work during six days, says the Lord, and in those six days you do all that you have to do. But the seventh day is consecrated to the Lord your God.

To celebrate Sundays and holidays properly, your chief aim should be to avoid all that is evil and to do good.

It is true that there can be no time when it is permitted to do wrong and that we are always obliged to do good; still, it is also true that we have particular obligations on fixed days to avoid the one with greater care and to do the other with greater zeal.

Alas! who would credit it if one did not see it with his own eyes? Christians think that they satisfy the obligation of keeping Sunday by merely abstaining from manual labor, as though they acted solely from a wise policy or to give rest to a tired body, not from any wish of strengthening the soul, after it has been weakened by the worry and cares of business.

It is also true that many whose profession consists chiefly of head work, or those who have nought else to do but play and amuse themselves, make no difference on feast days, except hearing a Mass in a hurried way, their minds thinking of worldly things, their hearts filled with frivolities. We can even affirm that, generally speaking, more harm is done on Sundays and holy days. It is this that caused St. Chrysostom to say that the Sabbath, which had been set apart for cleansing our souls from sins committed during the week, was a day set apart for the commission of greater sins.

How do most people follow this precept? Instead of employing Sunday for the expiation of their faults, we may safely say, especially of those engaged in mercenary occupations, that it is a day for adding sin to sins. They spend the day in all kinds of sensuality and give themselves up to drunken joy.

Our Lord could now say what He said in former times to the Jews through the mouth of His prophet Isaiah: "I hate your solemnities of the first day of the month, and all your other feasts; they have become burdensome, and I am weary of enduring them" (Isa. 1:14).

Mark these words, "your solemnities," as if our Lord had said: You have made my feasts your feasts, and the days that ought to be consecrated to my glory, you devote to the satiety of your passions.

As regards manual labor, it is not bad in itself, and it is not to condemn it that God forbids it on days that are consecrated holy. It is not also that He approves of idleness, which of itself is a great evil. But it is in order that all work or employment, however good in itself, must yield for a time to one more excellent—a work for which man is created—which is to know God, to adore, honor, and love Him above all. This is the chief end of the law.

You shall work for six days in the week, and during that time you can do your work and provide for your wants. But the seventh day is the

Lord's day, and you must relinquish labor to offer Him your love, adoration, and homage.

— Fr. Montmorel, Sermon on the Sixteenth Sunday after Pentecost

∞

When God created the world, He worked for six days, after which Scripture says that He rested on the seventh. But in what consisted this rest of God? Here it is: "And God saw all the things that he had made, and they were very good" (Gen. 1:31). God took a general review of all His works and found them to be good and perfect. He found His rest in His approval. This is what we should imitate.

Leave off your servile work, and take a survey of your conduct throughout the past week. See if you can say with God that all that you have done during these six days is good. Examine if you have been faithful to God and your neighbor; if you have fulfilled the duties of your state of life; if there has been any injustice in your employment or business.

After this examination, give your approval to that which has been good, rectify that which has been faulty, and consecrate the rest of the day in renewals of love to God, so that He may be propitious to us. Do this also, in reparation for the many dissipations you have complacently indulged in.

— *Les Discours Chrétiennes*

∞

Fasting and Abstinence

Prayer with fasting is holy and pleasing to God.

—Tobit 12:8

The lesson that the Son of God teaches us in the desert shows us that the best methods of resisting temptations are by fasting and mortification of the body. Subdue the flesh, and you weaken the devil; for he can do nothing if we deprive him of his weapons.

Let it not be said that fasting and mortification are intended only for religious bodies; for since our Savior has deigned to make use of this remedy (although He had no need of it), no one of whatever rank or condition can be dispensed from this obligation. If persons of quality, or people in business, were exempt from the temptations and attacks of the evil one, it might be allowable to treat their bodies delicately; but since the enemy tempts them more than others, they require ever to be on the defensive, and consequently fasting is to them the more necessary.

The chief objects of fasting are to mortify the body, to deaden the passions, and to keep the soul in a state of grace. To live, then, in pleasures and gaiety during the holy season of Lent, and to continue in sin, is contrary to the spirit of fasting and to the intentions of our holy mother the Church.

How miserable are they who poison so efficacious a remedy, and who deliberately refuse to make use of a cure that the Church gives them for the purpose of overcoming the world, the flesh, and the devil!

Fasting and Abstinence

As the first man was condemned for not having abstained from eating, notwithstanding the express command of God, so the Creator has fixed on fasting as a reparation for this first sin. It is the best means of avoiding the consequences of original sin, the best remedy to restore peace of mind, to control the passions, and to bring our flesh under subjection.

Overeating and overdrinking have made the devil victorious throughout the world, but fasting drives him away; for does not St. Matthew say in his Gospel that "this kind is not cast out, but by prayer and fasting" (Matt. 17:20)?

We read in the annals of ecclesiastical history of an edifying circumstance that occurred in Constantinople under the reign of the emperor Justinian. It is therein related that this city was visited by a terrible famine and that, the season of Lent having come round, before God had withdrawn the frightful scourge, the emperor caused all the meat markets to be thrown open, and he issued an edict to the effect that he granted leave from abstinence during Lent for that year only.

But how do you think so humane and considerate an order was received by the people? O! happy age! O my God, is there a spark now left of this ancient fervor? Would you believe it, ye Christians of our century, that in this vast city, weakened as it had been by so dire a calamity, there was not to be found a single Christian, I say not one, who wished to take advantage of the favor granted? And yet this was not all; for no sooner was the dispensation published than the whole body of Christians besieged the palace and implored the emperor to revoke the edict and restore the old laws, since they were ready to die rather than break them.

Not to speak of those who absolutely refuse to obey the precepts of the Church, there are many, alas! who seek for dispensation from abstinence and other penances without any reasonable excuse. And it is my firm belief that of those who ask for leave without necessity, there would not be found one single person who properly fulfilled the Easter obligation.

What! ye pleasure seekers, during the forty days you have continued in the same sins, nay added sin to sin, deliberately and with all the coolness that acts of so long a duration cannot fail to have. And yet you wish me to believe that all of a sudden, perhaps in a single night, your heart is so changed that it detests the past frightful dissipations and that the horror of the excess equals the pleasure you had in committing sin.

If you were on your deathbed, I would question the sincerity of your contrition, after committing sins so recently, so openly, and after showing such a manifest contempt for the precepts of the Church.

And now that you are in good health, you would wish to persuade me that you are willing to begin afresh, if the fast recommenced, and you wish to persuade me to believe that your repentance is sincere.

As for myself, I believe it to be false, and I should hesitate to pronounce the absolution, for fear of profaning the Precious Blood of our Lord, unless indeed I saw that you were ready to fast for forty days after the feast, as a proof of your repentance.

—St. Claude de la Colombière (1641–1682)

∞

Baptism

*Going therefore, teach ye all nations, baptizing them in the
name of the Father, and of the Son, and of the Holy Spirit.*

—Matthew 28:19

Let us try to preserve the noble birth we have inherited from our baptism.

If an earthly potentate had found you poor and begging, and had suddenly adopted you as his son, you would soon forget your past misery; you would no longer think of your lowly hut, however great may have been the difference between these things.

Think, then, no more of your first state, since the one to which you have been called is comparatively more illustrious than regal dignity. For he who has summoned you is the King of angels, and the property He has reserved for you is not only far beyond our comprehension, but even beyond all that words can express. He does not help you to pass from one station of life to one higher, as this potentate could have done; but He raises you from earth to heaven, from a mortal life to an immortal life, a life so glorious and inexpressible that it will not be known, until we gain possession of it.

How then, being partakers of these grand blessings, can we presume to think of the riches of this world, and how can we trifle away our time in frivolous and vain amusements? What excuses will remain, or rather, what punishments ought we not to suffer, if, after having received so wondrous a grace, we should return to that first condition from which we have been so fortunately — so mercifully — withdrawn? You will not be punished simply as a sinful man, but as a rebellious child of God; and the lofty eminence of the dignity to which you were raised will serve only to increase your punishment.

— St. John Chrysostom (ca. 349–407), *Sermon 12 on St. Matthew*

∞

What is it to be a Christian?

It is a man who has a close affinity with God and through baptism becomes His Son. What more exalted, what more grand! What Jesus Christ is by nature, the Christian is by adoption. He receives, through spiritual regeneration, the likeness of that which the Word receives through eternal generation. We have received, says St. Paul, the spirit of adoption of sons, whereby we dare to call God our Father, and, if sons, heirs also (Rom. 8:15, 17).

The birth of Jesus Christ in Mary, says St. Augustine, is the model of our second birth, which is made through baptism. They proceed from the same source, which is the Holy Spirit: one was made in the bosom of Mary, who is virgin and mother, and the other is made in the bosom of the Church, which is pure and fruitful. The end of the first is Christ, that is to say, a Man-God; the end of the second is a Christian, that is to say, a man divine. Could God, asks St. John, have carried His love and our happiness further than by making us really and truly children of God? Could we push our ingratitude and unworthiness further than by disgracing that glorious title by a behavior, as criminal as it would be shameful?

A Christian is one who has a close affinity to Jesus Christ, of whom he is, through baptism, made a member.

What more glorious? All Christians, says St. Paul, are but one body, of which Jesus is the Head. They become members by this sacrament that unites them to Him, by a genuine union, since it forms an article of faith; by a very real union, since the Holy Spirit is its source; by an intimate union, since through it we are animated by the Spirit of Jesus Christ and dwell within Him—a union, in short, sublime, since the Redeemer compares it to the union that He Himself has with His Father. So that, as says St. Peter, we by that become partakers of the divine nature (2 Pet. 1:4).

If Jesus Christ, who obtains for us all these advantages, had not Himself secured them for us, could we have believed in them? But if we do believe them, should we not have a more exalted idea of them, and ought not our conduct to be conformable to our belief?

Through baptism, a Christian becomes a temple of the Holy Spirit. Do you not know, says the Apostle, that your bodies are temples of the Holy Spirit, who dwells within you (1 Cor. 6:19)? Thus it is that the same ceremonies are made use of in baptism as in the consecration of churches. Through exorcism, the devil is expelled from the soul of him who is made a Christian. It is consecrated by the holy chrism, a figure of the anointing of grace by which the Holy Spirit spreads around the heart. It takes possession of it by that mysterious breathing of the priest who baptizes. It then becomes the source and object of the worship that the faithful pay Him in that temple, through acts of faith, hope, and charity. It is that Holy Spirit who prays in him, by moanings so efficacious; and on account of that they are so very meritorious that they are able to impart an undoubted right to the possession of God. Could God honor man more than by making him a child of God, brother of a Man-God, and temple of the Holy Spirit? Also, St. John tells us that through baptism we enter into fellowship with the Father, and the Son, and consequently with the Holy Spirit.

What glorious fellowship! What exultation! What happiness!

—Fr. F. Nepvue, S.J. (1654–1708), *Réflexions Chrétiennes*

∞

Through the Sacrament of Baptism you become the temple of the Holy Spirit. Take care not to drive such a guest away by your sins and thus become a slave of the devil, because the price of your redemption is the Precious Blood of Jesus.

Acknowledge your dignity, O Christian, and, having been clothed with a nature quite divine, do not return, I entreat you, to your old vileness, by leading a life that would lower the rank to which you have been raised.

Remember whose chief and body you are the member of. Remember that, having been withdrawn from the power of darkness, you have been transferred to the light of the kingdom of God.

—St. Leo (d. 461), *On the Nativity*

꘎

The Sacrament of Penance

He that hideth his sins shall not prosper; but he that shall
confess and forsake them, shall obtain mercy.

—Proverbs 28:13

St. Chrysostom, in his fifth homily on the epistle to the Corinthians, asks, Whence comes it that we confess our secret sins, and that on this depends our judgment? The judges of the land do not act thus, for they never pass sentence or deliver their judgment until there is a verdict.

But, says the saintly doctor, we have rules that earthly judges have not; for we do not profess to punish as they do, but are content to submit to the Church, which imposes a penance for crimes.

The royal prophet, wishing to avert the anger and justice of Almighty God, asks for mercy and pardon: "Have mercy on me, O God! according to the multitude of thy tender mercies." It is thus that he cries out and implores that pardon and mercy, which washes and purges so that no stain or soil may remain: "Wash me yet more from my iniquity." And why? because he has confessed his sins and acknowledges the enormity of his offences: "Because I know my iniquity" (Ps. 50:3–5 [Ps. 51:1–3]). Why say "because"? asks St. Chrysostom. Because he acknowledges his fault, he wishes God to forgive him. Is that justice? Nevertheless, it is the royal penitent who speaks. It is true, O Lord, that the confession of my sins is an easy atonement; but You are content with this, I do not offer any other, and I have no other way open to be reconciled with You. Pardon my sins, because I acknowledge and confess them.

Confession is a fountain of grace. What does the devil do — he who is the mortal enemy of our salvation? He sees that confession is a pure fountain, and he seeks to poison its waters, by the bad use he tempts us to make use of it, or by the hardness of heart he instills in our mind not to go to confession at all. And in this way he acts as did Holofernes in the city of Bethulia, who broke all the conduits and drained the fountains in order that the Israelites should die of thirst. It is thus that the devil tries to dry up the canals of the sacrament, whence flows the Precious Blood of Jesus Christ. He also gives us a disgust for confession and makes us turn away from it. He whispers that there is great danger of using this sacrament badly. He suggests the disadvantage of performing the act badly. He tells us not to approach too often; he does not tell us to make frequent good confessions, but he persuades us that we may sometimes go to keep up appearances, or out of human respect, but he does not say that frequent confession is good, if it be accompanied with a good and pious motive.

In addition to the grace that is attached to the sacrament to prevent our falling back, what power has not a prudent confessor on those souls who are resolved to be under his direction? What will he not do when he knows how to win their confidence, and what pains will he not be compelled to take to secure the perseverance and salvation of the souls entrusted to his guidance? What injustices in trade will he not try to rectify, and what foolish engagements will he not break off? What zealous care will he not take to root out the most violent passions? What resentments will he not stifle? What reconciliations will he not effect when he sees any family disagreements? He will be the medium of making souls unselfish; he will cause many to renounce usury and avarice and will persuade others to make restitution for ill-gotten goods. This is what a good director can do, and what a zealous confessor aims to do.

We must also add that frequent confession is a powerful curb on the conscience and fosters the duty of the holy fear of God, so that a man has not an idea of returning to sin when he thinks of the pain and shame of confessing it. This thought produces nearly the same effect as the preparation for death, for it makes us remember that we ought to appear in the tribunal of penance, as if we should be summoned to stand before God to be judged.

What more can be said? The sweet use of confession redeems a soul from sins, and so invigorates the will that the most violent temptations are successfully resisted. How different the fate of those who shake off the yoke of confession, or who go to confession but very seldom, or those who abandon themselves to all kinds of disorderly sins!

— Fr. Louis Bourdaloue (1632–1704), *Sermon on Confession*

∞

If you love the beauty of your soul, says St. Bernard, cherish confession. It is that which re-ornaments it and renews all the traces of beauty that had been tarnished by sin. But why? one may ask. What does God want with a verbal declaration? Does He not read our hearts? Does He not see all that passes? Ah! says the saint, He demands this confession, not but that He knows better than we do, for He sees the innermost recesses of our consciences, but that He may be able to forgive us. It is sufficient to lay bare all our wounds, that He may cure them; it is sufficient to accuse ourselves, that we may be excused; it is sufficient that we should condemn ourselves in order to be absolved. Can confession offer more advantageous blessings?

— Fr. Masson

Holy Communion

Except you eat the flesh of the Son of man, and drink
his blood, you shall not have life in you.

—John 6:54 (RSV = John 6:53)

It is the opinion of St. Thomas and of all subsequent theologians that venial sins are remitted by the power of the sacrament of Holy Communion,
if received in a state of grace. Pope Innocent goes further than this, for
he assures us that a fervent Communion will prevent us from falling into
mortal sin, inasmuch as it enables us to keep in a state of grace; because,
says the saintly doctor, as corporeal nourishment strengthens the system
and renews fresh vigor in the body, so in like manner the constant use
of the spiritual food, Holy Communion, imparts a strength of will that
before was weakened by sensuality or by venial sins.

To this may be added that, as habitual venial sin decreases the fervor
of charity, therefore, in order to renew and rekindle our devotion, nothing is more beneficial, no cure more certain, than the devout reception
of Holy Communion. It is a daily remedy against our daily infirmities,
so says St. Ambrose.

St. Bernard says: If there be any among you who has experienced a
change of heart and will; if you have no innate desire for or delight in the
things of this world; if anger, envy, sensuality, or any other vice should
be deadened in you; if these do not tempt you, or if they do not disturb
your mind or conscience, do not be vainglorious in these victories, but

return thanks to Jesus in His sacrament of love. "Because the virtue of this sacrament will work within you," continues the saint. It is the strength and power of this adorable sacrament that has metamorphosed many a worldly man into a fervent servant of God.

To those who, after Holy Communion, fall soon into mortal sin, I implore them to consider with what zeal the holy Fathers have inveighed against such relapses, and in what terms they speak of the awful consequences resulting therefrom.

To return after receiving Communion to your former state of sin, is, they say, to profane the temple of the Holy Spirit, to dishonor the Mystical Body of Jesus Christ. It is to follow the example of Judas, to betray Jesus and to deliver Him up to His enemies.

The Body of Christ has been entrusted to you, says St. Athanasius. You are His temple, and He dwells within you. What do I say? You have become a member of His Body; treat Him with respectful love, and do not betray Him as Judas did.

In many passages, St. Chrysostom has displayed his eloquence, when he strongly recommended purity of life, after the reception of Holy Communion, and when he represents to his flock the enormous sin committed by those who easily return to their former state of tepidity.

—Fr. Matthieu de Castillo, O.P. (1664–1720)

∽

O my divine Savior! how sorely grieved am I, when I think how unworthy I am, and how I have hitherto abused Thy excessive goodness. How often have I wandered from Thee, I who have been more debased, more ungrateful than the prodigal son.

But if I have imitated him in his folly, I, following his example, return to You, overwhelmed with shame, and I hope that You will receive me, with the same tenderness as his father received him. I could say indeed with more truth that I do not deserve to be treated as one of Your children; but I know Your tender heart, and since You have deigned to will that I should partake of the Bread of Angels, I dare to believe that Thou wilt look on me and receive me as one of Thy servants.

—Fr. Luke Vaubert, S.J. (1644–1716)

∞

We ask daily for bread, for fear that being deprived of it, and by not receiving it in Holy Communion, we should be deprived of the Mystical Body of Christ.

He who abstains from receiving Holy Communion, and separates himself from the Body of the Lord, has much reason to fear, for he withdraws himself, at the same time, from eternal salvation; for does not Christ say, "Unless you eat the flesh of the Son of man, you shall not have life in you" (John 6:54 [RSV = John 6:53])?

—St. Cyprian (ca. 200–258), *On the Lord's Prayer*

The Holy Eucharist as a Sacrifice

*And the altar shall be sanctified by my glory. I will sanc-
tify also the tabernacle of the testimony with the altar.*

—Exodus 29:43–44

The Mass is a sacrifice, that is to say, it is supreme worship, a real im-
molation, a public recognition of the sovereignty of God, and a sincere
protestation by some visible ceremonies of the intimate and necessary
dependence of our existence on a Superior Being, which can be but God
alone. For, my brethren, recollect that we believe that we are rendering
to the angels, martyrs, saints—to the Mother of God herself, raised in
dignity above the angels, and in merit above the saints—that we are
rendering, I say, a homage that has been reserved for them as an inheritance, and as a regal mark of adoration that is due to Him.

The Mass is a sacrifice instituted by Jesus Christ, says St. Cyril, having
an immutable priesthood, consecrated by an everlasting unction from all
ages. In erecting the New Law, He has established this sacrifice of His
Body and Blood—a precious monument of His infinite love for men.

It was on that fatal night, when He was to be delivered up to His
enemies, that He offered Himself to His Father under the species of bread
and wine, being both together, says St. Paulinus, both the priest of His
victim and the victim of His priesthood; then enjoining His Apostles,
and those priests who legitimately succeeded them, to do the same, even
to the consummation of the world.

∞

There is, then, in the Church a divine sacrifice, which the Council of Trent has designated as the highest work of God:

- *divine in its beginning*, God alone by His almighty power being capable of changing the bread and wine into the Body and Blood of Jesus Christ
- *divine in its midst*, God alone becoming man, in order to be a victim fit to appease the anger of a sovereign majesty
- *divine in its end*, God alone being able to be the object of those everlasting testimonies and of that divine oblation
- *divine in its duration*, as the prophet Daniel had predicted

It is not composed, as formerly, of many victims, but of only one, which is perpetuated on our altars, which is multiplied without being divided, which is sacrificed without dying and eaten without being consumed, since it is the immortal and impassible body of Jesus Christ.

It is the same God who speaks through His prophet Malachi. Listen to Him with docility and respect: "For from the rising of the sun even to the going down, my name is great among the Gentiles. I see in every place altars whereon is offered to my name a clean offering" (Mal. 1:11).

What, then, is that victim that the Lord so honors as to attract His attention and complacency, which is so pleasing through its purity and innocence? Is it that of animals, whose impure and coarse blood would render it far from agreeable? Can it be our works, wherein malice is so often mingled, where flesh and blood have a share, where concupiscence is almost always mixed up with secret vanities or petty interests? Can it be our prayers, which are but too often accompanied with distractions, disgust, impatience, and self-love?

No, doubtless.

This glorious sacrifice is that of the Mass, which is offered up in every quarter of the globe for the propitiation and satisfaction of our sins; this oblation is of itself so pure and holy that neither the unworthiness of him who offers it up, nor the irreverence of those who assist at it, can in the least degree deprive it of its holiness.

We all meet in the church to give a public testimony of our faith and piety, and the visible sacrifice that is offered at the Mass is the sign of the invisible sacrifice; so, says St. Augustine, modesty and a devout posture of the body ought to be the sign of our devotion and interior reverence. It is there we go to confess Jesus Christ before men, so that He may acknowledge us before His Heavenly Father. Where is it that we ought to give outward signs of that respectful fear, but in the presence of that Divine Majesty of God, residing in the tabernacles of His Church? Our sole occupation should consist in adoring God, and acquitting ourselves well, in all our religious duties to Him to whom we are so indebted.

Besides, we are obliged to give edification to all the faithful; and if we are at all times, and in all places, expected to show a good example, surely it is in the church during the celebration of the divine mysteries that we should do so.

Nevertheless, how many profanations and irreverences are daily committed during Holy Mass? How many attend carelessly and thoughtlessly, although God bids us tremble when we place our feet on the threshold of those venerable piles, wherein religion and its mysteries are set apart for worship?

Many enter the church thinking only of useless trifles, foolish appointments, or frivolous amusements; they look out for a Mass that they suspect will be a short one, as if they begrudged the short half hour they give to Jesus every week.

Many wait to attend the latest Mass, in order that they may be more intimate and friendly with those who are equally undevout and lazy. They let the priest go away, or, perhaps better to say, they leave Jesus as if they had taken no heed of His sacrifice. And, far from having any feeling of devotion, they have deprived those who had, by the distractions they have given them.

—Bishop Esprit Fléchier (1632–1710)

∞

The Holy Eucharist as a Sacrament

Verily, thou art a hidden God,
the God of Israel, the Savior.

—Isaiah 45:15

The Blessed Sacrament is a mystery of daily repetition, of ordinary familiarity. We are coming across our Lord continually. Either we are calling Him from heaven ourselves, if we be priests; or we are witnessing that unspeakable mystery; or we are feeding on Him and seeing our fellow creatures do so also; or we are gazing at Him in His veils, or receiving His benedictions, or making our devotions at His tabernacle door.

Yet what is our habitual behavior to Him in this mystery? We are orthodox in faith, doubtless. Every word of that queen of councils, the blessed and glorious assembly of Trent, is more precious to us than a mine of gold. But have the intensity of our love, the breathlessness of our reverence, the earnestness of our prayers, the overbearing momentum of our faith, the speechlessness of our yearning desires been all they should have been, or half they would have been, if we had but corresponded to the grace that He was giving us each time?

There is no sign of lukewarmness more unerring than becoming thoughtless about the Blessed Sacrament and letting it grow common to us without our feeling it. Even though the disciples on the road to Emmaus did not know Jesus until He vanished from their sight, at least their hearts, they knew not why, burned within them as they walked and talked to Him by the way. Yet how often have we been at the tabernacle door, feeling neither His presence nor our own miseries more than a beggar sleeping in the sun at a rich man's gate?

True it is that the Blessed Sacrament is not a mystery of distance or of terror, but one of most dear familiarity. Yet the only true test of our loving familiarity is the depth of our joyous fear.

∞

Yet, alas! whenever we read or hear of some of the great things concerning the Blessed Sacrament, does it not often flash upon us that our conduct is not in keeping with our creed? And, looking back on a long sad line of indifferent Communions, distracted Masses, and careless visits to the tabernacle, are we not sometimes startled into saying, "Do I really believe all this?"

How many of us might simplify our spiritual lives, and so make great progress, if we would only look to the Blessed Sacrament, to our feelings and conduct toward it, and its impression upon us, as the index of our spiritual condition? We are always trying to awaken ourselves with new things, new books, new prayers, new confraternities, new states of prayer; and our forbearing Lord runs after us and keeps blessing us in our changeableness, and humoring us in our fickle weakness. How much better would it be to keep to our old things, to hold fast by Him, and to warm ourselves only at the tabernacle fire!

—Fr. Frederick William Faber (1814–1863),
The Blessed Sacrament

∞

Moses, desirous of making the Israelites understand how great was the happiness they possessed in being the chosen people of God, said to them: There never was a nation, however illustrious it may have been, who had gods so communicative, as is our God, who communicates Himself to us (see Deut. 4:7).

What shall we say to Christians when their loving and all-merciful God, not content with dwelling among us in our churches and visiting us in our homes, has further willed to dwell in the interior of our souls and to repose in our hearts as in a temple, where we can familiarly confer with Him and expose all our wants?

It was an incomparable joy for the Mother of God to have carried Jesus within her. Has not the Christian the happiness of also carrying Him within him?

St. Elizabeth esteemed herself happy when the Mother of God came to visit her, and the Lord Himself is willing to come and dwell in the interior of our souls! Mary Magdalen had the advantage of kissing His feet, and we have the opportunity of embracing Him and of receiving His caresses! After that, what heart would not be inflamed with love for a God who so familiarly communicates with men? Should this not induce us to offer to Him our fervent prayers, our fondest love?

Have we not indeed reason to reproach ourselves with coldness and ingratitude, when we think of the wondrous love that God has shown to men in this adorable sacrament?

As this God of love gives Himself entirely to us in the Eucharist, we ought to give ourselves entirely to Him. But alas! how very far we are from loving Him as He has loved us in this divine mystery. He has loved us to excess, He has loved us without reserve, He has given Himself to us whole and entire, He has spared nothing to show us His love; nevertheless, it is this same God whom we love with so much coldness and with so much reserve.

We give Him as little of our heart as we possibly can, and often give Him nothing at all; although that would not be a sin, still it would be indeed an act of a great ingratitude and greater meanness.

—Fr. John Garnier, S.J. (1612–1684), Sermon

∞

The soul must be in an utter swoon, if it be not roused and enlivened by the Holy Eucharist.

The Holy Eucharist as a Sacrament

We do not expose those whom we encourage to fight against persecution, or leave them devoid of help or even unarmed. But we fortify them with the protection of the Body and Blood of Christ, our Savior. For is it not true that the Holy Eucharist raises the faithful above themselves, and from its efficacy, a worldly man becomes a heavenly man?

—St. Cyprian (ca. 200–258), *Epistles*

∞

Matrimony

*This is a great sacrament, but I
speak in Christ and in the church.*

—Ephesians 5:32

Marriage may be said to be the nursery of mankind. From that are drawn daily new plants, in place of others that have withered and died away through length of time. This is a metempsychosis full of mystery, but is much more honorable and advantageous to mankind than that which some philosophers have imagined, who would revivify men from beasts and beasts from men.

Marriage shows that men are in some way immortal, for a father dies without dying, for he lives again in his son and in all his descendants. It is a fountain of life that ever flows and is never exhausted.

Death is an abyss in which all men are engulfed, as rivers are lost in the ocean; but because that spring may never cease to flow, for one who dies, many are often brought to life.

Without marriage, death, which spares no one, would ruin whole cities; whole provinces would be desolate. As nothing could check its violence, a century, and perchance much less, would suffice to hurry all men to the grave. But God, who does not wish His work to perish before the number of the elect is filled up, has made Himself the Patron and Protector of marriages, as He has been the first Founder of them; the same care that He has taken to preserve the world has induced Him to take in hand the marriages contracted therein, and which are the means of maintaining it.

That is the reason the world is daily replenished with inhabitants, why new cities and towns become populated, why states and kingdoms flourish.

Could He, I say, have found a more effectual method to maintain and preserve so great a work?

The strokes of death are continually at work but do not annihilate, because the fruitfulness of marriage wards off every blow, and the grand design of God to refill heaven with His elect is effected by this means. I call it the grand design of God, because it is the climax of all others, and to which all aspire and tend, as lines do to the center. This grand design could not be carried out in the order that God has willed to establish it without marriage, and this is the reason He has willed to be its Author since the creation of the world.

Marriage is the primary bond of everyday life; it is the foundation and support of all human relations; it is the beginning of every union. Everyone should acknowledge it as the rock from which they have sprung. It is an agreement as old as the world itself, and its Author is no other than God.

The Gnostics, who have been the most shameless heretics that hell has ever produced, have rejected it as a bad and detestable thing. But when we read in the book of Genesis that God was the Author of marriage, and when we read in the New Testament that God the Son honored it by His presence, we should detest those infamous heretics who have disapproved of it. It was not the honor and respect that they bore to the virtue of purity that made them speak, but the license of libertinism, which prompted them to keep as many women as they could seduce.

The Apostle's counsel to live single is not blaming or condemning the marriage state—for that can be condemned only by persons who have not a just appreciation of the works of God—but to teach us that it is not obligatory, and that we may increase in merit by renouncing one state of life by embracing another still more perfect.

The Church, which is ever guided by the Holy Spirit in all her ceremonies, retains a custom in all marriages that teaches those who receive this sacrament the affection that they should have for each other. It directs the priest to bless a ring, presenting it first to the husband in order that, by receiving it, he may encircle her in his heart and shut out all other loves. Then he places it on the wife's hand, in order that she may equally have no other affection for any man than the one God has given her for a husband. This ring is a seal that should have a double intent on the hearts of the married couple, the first being to preserve inviolate sworn conjugal love, the second is not to allow an entry for any strange love.

Confidence is the result of a tried fidelity and a constant esteem. If this be necessary for all who are engaged in any kind of commerce whatsoever, what partnership can be more complete than marriage?

Concord, says St. Chrysostom, constitutes the maximum of the happiness and blessing of a married life. And if the husband can place his entire confidence in a good and virtuous wife, they will be as one body, one flesh.

—Fr. Francis Cordier (d. 1695), *La Sainte Famille*

Part 5

∞

The World and Sin

∞

The World and Its Dangers

If any man love the world, the charity of the Father is not in him.

—1 John 2:15

Wondrous thing! the world is full of trouble, and we do not tire of loving it! What would it be were it always quiet? You attach yourself to this world, deformed and ugly as it is; what would it be were it always agreeable? You draw away your hand from the thorns of this world; what would it be if you had but to gather flowers?

Take care, the wind is violent, the tempest is terrible; each one has his own danger, for each one is tossed about with his own passions. Would you wish to know how to save yourself from this tempestuous sea? Love God, and you will walk upon its waters; you will tread underfoot the pride of the world, and you will be saved. On the contrary, if you love the world, you will be engulfed, for the world knows only how to shipwreck a soul; it knows not how to save it.

—St. Augustine (354–430), Sermons 76 and 108

∞

Would you know what happened to the great St. Benedict when he was in an ecstasy of prayer? He felt himself raised above himself; the heavens opened, and from an exterior darkness there came a kind of wondrous light, and the world was mirrored before him, and he, by divine permission, was allowed to view the world, and it showed him at a glance the nothingness and deformity of all human things.

Whether God had narrowed within the ray both heaven and earth, or whether He had enlarged His heart and mind, says St. Gregory, he sees revolutions and vicissitudes here below, creatures forced against their will to feed on vanity, and all the universe subjected to the covetousness of men. He sees, under cover of this celestial light, those grandeurs that are esteemed so highly gradually decrease. He sees ambition, which takes so firm a hold on man, sink and fade away; that universal hypocrisy of the age, which elevates vice and makes virtue look contemptible, where counterfeit miseries are cherished, where wretched pleasures are sought after. He sees a crowd of frivolous desires, hopes ill founded, unjust hatreds, irregulated loves; he sees the wanton extravagance of our pleasures, the inutility of our occupations, the instability of our fortunes, the emptiness of our wishes, the littleness of our interests. Ah! how mean and contemptible did the world appear to him! No wonder he despised it and retired from it for evermore.

— Bishop Esprit Fléchier (1632–1710), *Panegyric on St. Benedict*

∞

Pleasure is a feeling of joy that dwells in the soul during the existence of a blessing that is acknowledged as such.

Now, this pleasure is only perfect so long as the blessing that causes it is sustained. An imaginary blessing could not know a real pleasure. Its enchantments vanish in time; its illusions are soon dispelled. When the gratification of a blessing is deadened or exhausted, the mind and heart feel a void, and reason discovers, sooner or later, the depths of its nothingness, and at last bitter is the bitterness where passion anticipates, but does not realize so much pleasure.

From that proceed those involuntary anxieties and vexations that all the joys of the world, however harmless, cannot drive away. From that arise those adversities, those little crosses, that put the most good humored out of temper and makes them say with truth that worldly happiness is a myth.

As God alone can fill our heart, it is He who can satisfy our desires. Other objects amuse for a while, but they make our consciences uneasy, and, finally, they weary and disgust.

God alone can satisfy a soul, calm its anxieties, its suspicions, its fears, and every trouble that stirs within our hearts. Whenever I tried to fill up the aching void in my heart, said St. Augustine, I found that nothing equaled the happiness I felt in trying to do my duty in serving God.

What are the miseries that worldlings have to endure? Alas! everything seems to conspire to make them groan without being allowed to complain. Continuous and fatiguing cares inseparable from their state of life; ambition, jealousy, self-interest, inexhaustible anxieties; the uneasiness of a busy life, the fears of failure, the varied tempers of those in their employ—all of whom must be humored—a hundred vexing accidents they are liable to, and which can rarely be prevented, the bad weather they cannot avoid, a station of life that must at all risks be kept up, worry of competition, the malice of the envious, a heart ever agitated, an uneasy mind and conscience.

What! Does it require all these things to make a man unhappy? All such as these are nevertheless to be found united in the men who battle with the world.

—Fr. Croiset, S.J. (b. ca. 1650), *Réflexions Spirituelles*

The World and Its Maxims

*All that is in the world, is the concupiscence of the flesh,
the concupiscence of the eyes, and the pride of life.*

—1 John 2:16

The world that encompasses us is full of snares. One cannot dwell in it even for a short time without danger. You open your eyes, and the guard you thought you had over self is dispelled. You lend your ear to public discussions, and your attachment to party spirit breaks out. You walk in places strewn with flowerbeds and flowers, and your thoughts wander on joys. You taste delicacies that are offered to you, and the poison of sensuality is hid therein. You extend your hand, and it is enough to cause an embrace.

Ah! who can walk with a firm unshaken step in the midst of the passions of the world, amidst its seductive charms? Let us, then, think and meditate on the words of Job, "The life of man on earth is a continual warfare" (Job 7:1).

—St. Ambrose (340–397)

The world—it is that raging sea, on which are tossed to and fro vessels containing a crowd of sinners whose cares and projects depend on the fortunes or misfortunes of life; whose aim seems to be to build palaces on sand; whose hopes are fixed on the fleeting enjoyments of this life, who seek for joys and pleasures that are a thousand times more fatiguing than they are worth.

The world is a monstrous assemblage of party spirits who revile each other and regard each other with contempt, envy, and jealousy, devoid of honor and fair dealing. The world is a temporal kingdom that knows not Jesus Christ, where He Himself declares that He is not, and for which He does not wish to pray (see John 8:23; 17:9, 14, 16; 18:36). The world is that mass of wicked men and impious libertines who refuse to believe in the truths of the gospel, because they wage war with their vices, because they confute the Savior's maxims, despise His mysteries, ignore His precepts, and profane His sacraments. In short, the world is the majority who follow its maxims.

It is this world that you have to hate in your baptism and that you are taught to confute, condemn, and wage war against.

This world, then, is the enemy of the Cross and of the gospel of Jesus Christ, and ought therefore to be with you an object of horror that you ought to sacrifice to the interests of your salvation.

The first use we make of our free will is the choice of dangerous pleasures. The first temptation is that of our passions, and our reason believes only on the wreck of our innocence. All the land is infected through the wickedness of those who dwell on it. One no longer sees, says a prophet, the existence of truth or charity. Mercy is not there, and the knowledge of God is uncared for; all have overthrown the obstacles that preserved their innocence in their hearts.

Blasphemy, lying, injustice, adultery, homicide, perfidy, and other horrible crimes have inundated the land, says a prophet. Blood has tasted blood, the father scandalizes his child, the brother lays snares for his brother, and the husband seeks for a divorce.

Among men there are no ties but self-interest, passion, ill-humor, and caprice. Crime is common among the noble and great; virtue is meant only for the simpleminded; piety is the lot of few; hatreds are eternal, and an enemy is never looked upon as a brother.

Thence arise those resentments one against another; the purest virtue is not safe from slander; lawsuits and vexatious actions, and the meetings of friends and relations, are no longer public censures on public morals.

Gambling of every kind has become either shameful trafficking in shares or that blind infatuation that often ends in the ruin of families, and almost always causes the loss of the immortal soul.

Those innocent bonds of society, family meetings, are now only attractions for the indulgence of intemperance. Balls, theaters, and music-halls have become schools of impurity, and the present age is so refined in luxury that the carrying on of shameful intrigues soon soil the soul in ways of which our forefathers were not conscious.

—Fr. Jean Baptiste Massillon (1663–1742),
On the Small Number of the Elect

∞

The world is more dangerous when it flatters us than when it ill-treats us; we should be more careful of trusting it when it invites us to love it than when it admonishes us and compels us to despise it.

The chains that bind us to the world are pleasing to look at but hard to bear. The harm they inflict is certain; the pleasure they promise very doubtful. Those who wear them are ever busy but never exempt from dread.

They who follow the maxims of the world, experience nothing but misery, and the flattering expectation of happiness is delusive and vain.

Would you wish not to be an enemy of God? Do not be a friend of the world.

—St. Augustine (354–430), *Epistles*

The World and Its Duties

Fear God and keep His commandments; for this is all man.
—Ecclesiastes 12:13

There are still even now, through the mercy of God, many persons who live a Christian-like life, who keep God's commandments, and who do not willfully fail in any one of their duties. And if you do not know this, I am not astonished at it, since Elijah thought that he was left alone when God said to him, "I have left me seven thousand men that have not bowed their knees to Baal" (3 Kings 19:18 [RSV = 1 Kings 19:18]).

This example ought to convince us that there are still some among us who keep themselves unspotted from the world and who imitate the early Christians.

As for you, my brothers, if you have not as yet reached to that pitch of perfection, begin at least with the wish to aspire to perfection, cut off all inclination to do evil, resist the torrent of example, and do not think of doing any good unless you set to work in a right and lawful way.

We see that St. John the Baptist at first recommends the publicans and soldiers to be content with their pay. His zeal would have willingly led him to raise them to a high degree of perfection; but, they not being fit for much, he contented himself with giving them this simple advice, for fear that, by proposing something higher, they would not have been able to attain to a lower degree of perfection, much less to that height of virtue of which they were not capable.

It is thus that in the world there are different degrees of virtue; as among those who are consecrated to the service of God, in the religious state, there are novices, others more advanced, and others who reach to an eminent degree of sanctity.

—St. John Chrysostom (ca. 349–407), Homily on Matthew 6

∞

You are married; Moses was married, too. What, then, should prevent you from retiring every day, as he did, to confer with Almighty God on the important affair of your salvation and to pray for His grace? You have children; the mother of the Maccabees had seven of them, and that did not prevent her from being holy, and, when called upon, she preferred the love of God to that of her offspring. You are noble, and are required to keep up a certain splendor in the world. David, Joshua, and Ezekiel were no less noble; the government of states and the guidance of underlings did not hinder them from continually consulting God through prayer; they kept themselves humble in the midst of their grandeur, and they resided with their court without being infected by its vices.

You are a judge; that obliges you to practice virtue so much the more. That was just the case with the matchless Samuel. Follow his example, and on your bench you will be reproachless, and your position will afford opportunities of practicing the most heroic virtues. You are rich; Abraham perhaps was richer than you are. Well, like him, be the father of orphans, the entertainer of strangers, the defender and feeder of the needy, and your riches will help you to become a great saint.

You are poor, and your poverty brings on you illnesses and cares. Look at poor Lazarus; his poverty sanctified him, and he is placed on Abraham's bosom. You are a workman, and you are compelled to toil all the day, and part of the night, to support your family. St. Joseph, the glorious husband of Mary—was he not a workman? And, in the exercise of his trade, through his incomparable virtues, he is now one of the highest saints in heaven. You have joined the army; call to mind that brave officer of whom the Gospel speaks, who went to war as you do; and nevertheless you see that he was so full of faith, zeal, and charity, that the Son of God admired him and appeared to be surprised (see Matt. 8:5–13).

The inference that St. Chrysostom draws from this, is, to prove that, in whatever condition we may be, we can always observe the law of God.

God has given to all states and professions of life a help and steady support when He promulgated His law. Keep this law in your heart, and it will strengthen your steps, however slippery may be the path on which you walk. Amidst the worry of a family, the cares of business, and even the trouble and danger of war, the inviolate love of that law will keep your heart in peace, and there will be no scandal that can stop you. Would you live piously in your state of life? When you see the trickery and deceit that are practiced in high places, the corruption so common in law courts, the usual trickeries in trade, exclaim with David: "Withdraw from me all those that work iniquity" (Ps. 6:9 [RSV = Ps. 6:8]).

The Son of God, who is the Supreme Judge, elevates the vilest conditions in His own supernatural way and gives to all a sufficiency of sanctification. Thus, whether you are a gentleman, a judge, a soldier, a merchant, or a workman, you are something more than all these, since you are a Christian, and that is the foremost and noblest of your qualities.

This is what Tertullian has said: It matters little what you may be or what profession you exercise, since, if you are a Christian, you are no longer of this world.

—Fr. Claude Texier, S.J. (1610–1687), *Lenten Discourses*

∞

The World, Its Honors, and Its Dignities

A most severe judgment shall be for them that bear rule.
—Wisdom 6:6

The great and noble have to breathe an atmosphere of sensuality. Born and bred in idleness and effeminacy, they nourish within a hidden fire for all kinds of food that only feeds an ever-increasing appetite.

The world does not outwardly exhibit its attractions to the great; it simply offers them to their desires and delivers them over to their own keeping, so to speak, despoiled of all the difficulties that repulse and frighten others.

There are few, doubtless, who have not sometimes cherished the passions of avarice, vengeance, or ambition; these passions blind those who possess them. Now, before a person who has no influence or power, with but little money or property, could find the means to gratify his passions, the danger he would have to encounter, the precautions he would have to take: all these in time will open his eyes and calm the agitated heart. On the other hand, a powerful and rich noble, who, having within his reach all that can satisfy his wishes, has no sooner conceived a base design than he puts it into execution, finding everything in readiness for him.

But what! must those who are in high places and have plenty to spare despair of their salvation? Certainly not; but they must work with fear and perseverance. They must, by fervent and constant prayer, try to draw down from heaven that immense help that they stand so much in need of, in order to avoid the snares that surround them, and, by the frequentation of the sacraments, they must never cease to fortify themselves against the attacks of such formidable enemies.

Moreover, the noble are necessarily compelled, as they often are, to be richly dressed, to live in grand houses, expected to give luxurious dinners, to take part in the vain pleasures of worldlings. They should, I say, situated as they are, take especial care not to go beyond the mark that necessity and custom require.

When you act in this way, you will be able to say that if you run any risk, it is the providence of God that has placed you in the position in which you are, and that it is through the goodness of God that you have been able to avoid its dangers.

Yes, the high and mighty should anticipate a more rigorous punishment than ordinary mortals. Says Wisdom 6:9: "A greater punishment is ready for the mightier."

Why? In the first place, on account of their ingratitude to God, who has loaded them with temporal blessings, which He has kept back from the rest of mankind; for not having found in them that thanksgiving that such blessings well deserved. Secondly, they will suffer much more than those who have endured misery during this life because those who have so suffered have, by the hardships they have patiently endured, expiated the greater part of their sins; while the rich and noble, who have always lived in luxury and plenty, not having paid any debt of justice to a merciful God, will find themselves accountable and indebted for everything. In the third place, as there is nothing to hinder them from following the bent of their vicious inclinations, they the more easily and the more readily fall into sin; consequently, the quality and quantity of their transgressions will far exceed those committed by persons in the middle class of life.

In addition to that, they will not only be accountable for their own sins, but they will be answerable for those committed by others, whether from their neglect of those under their care, or whether, by their pernicious example, they may have introduced, encouraged, or authorized habits of vanity and vice.

But consider what thrones and mansions God will prepare for those who, by the practice of heroic virtues, sustain and even increase their merit in the midst of a corrupt court! What praises will not He reserve for those who have practiced humility in the midst of honors and dignities, a spirit of poverty in places where riches abound, an aversion for pleasure where pleasure is ever sought, an inviolate purity in an infected atmosphere, in a world that is full of tempting snares, a persecuting world, a world that sneers at virtue and, in a word, glories in incontinency.

—St. Claude de la Colombière (1641–1682)

༖

The honors paid to the wicked only hasten their ruin.

The power of the wicked is likened, in Holy Scripture, to the flowers of the field; because no sooner does worldly splendor outshine other lights than it fades and perishes; no sooner has it reached its height than down it falls.

—St. Gregory (ca. 540–604), Moral 7

∞

Mortal Sin

*Flee from sins as from the face of a serpent. The teeth
thereof are the teeth of a lion, killing the soul of man.*

—Sirach 21:2–3

Sin is a monster conceived in the darkness of error and born amidst the
malice of deceit. "Error and darkness are created with sinners; and they
that glory in evil things grow old in evil" (Sir. 11:16). God alone has the
light to pierce into that gloomy abyss, in order to discover sin as it is. It is
the Uncreated Spirit, says St. Paul, who, immersed in the depths of the
Divinity, can penetrate into the mire of the malice of sin. And as there is
but the immense capacity of the knowledge of God, who can comprehend
what He is and the honor that is due to Him, so there is only His perfect
intelligence that can form a true estimate of the enormity of mortal sin.
We can well say with St. Ignatius the Martyr that sin is a cursed child of
Satan, who transforms us into so many devils, as the grace of God is a seed
of the Divinity, which makes us participators of the divine essence. We
can say with St. Denis that it is a deprivation of beauty, life, and reason;
with St. Augustine, that it is a universal overthrowing of mankind; with
Tertullian, that it is a detestable preference of the devil to the sovereign
majesty of God; with St. Anselm, that it is a sacrilegious robbery of the
scepter and crown of God; and finally, with St. Paul, that it is a renewal
of the Crucifixion of Jesus.

We say, however, that mortal sin is the entire extermination of grace, the death of the soul, the corruption of human nature, the horror of heaven, and the desolation of the land. But after having said all this, after having compared it to the most detestable and pernicious of earthly things, after having exhausted all the terms that eloquence can command, we are obliged to confess that we have given but a faint idea of that boundless evil that is the cause of every evil, and whose malice is beyond the comprehension of angels and of men.

I am well aware that Holy Scripture teaches us that the sinner drinks in iniquity like water; but I learn also from the prophet Ezekiel that he drinks a deadly poison that tears his very entrails and kills him. That the sinner flatters his vices willingly, that he idolizes his guilty passions — these are the serpents that cruelly bite him.

"Flee from sins as from the face of a serpent." Yes, mortal sins are furious lions whose cruel teeth kill the soul. "The teeth thereof are the teeth of a lion, killing the souls of men" (Sir. 21:2–3).

Yes, that property unjustly acquired, those adulteries, those inordinate pleasures, in a word, all those iniquitous deeds are, at the judgment tribunal of God, nothing else but a double-edged sword with which the distracted sinner kills his soul and body — his soul by the loss of grace, and his body by depriving it of the right of a glorious resurrection. "All iniquity is like a two-edged sword, there is no remedy for the wound thereof" (Sir. 21:4).

In fact, if we have no faith on this subject, here is an evident proof of it. Every reasonable man fears the death of his body, says St. Augustine, but scarcely anyone fears the death of his soul. People work, perspire, and fret themselves to prolong a life that must soon end; and they wish to do nothing to avoid sin, that is to say, to lose a life whose nature is immortal.

What did I say? Not wish to prevent the loss of his soul! Alas! the number of these madmen who sharpen the sword that gives the death blow to their souls is incalculable. Who will give me the feelings of the saints, as well as their words! I hear a St. Cyprian exclaim indignantly:

What! if the news of the death of a parent or a dear friend reached you, you would weep and sigh bitterly; you would outwardly manifest your grief. O hard-hearted sinner, I tell you from God that that slander, that black calumny, that infamous deed has killed your soul, and you appear to think nothing of it.

—Fr. Claude Texier, S.J. (1610–1687), Lenten sermon

∞

If the Almighty had never visibly punished the enemies of the Faith, men might have imagined that God was indifferent to what was going on in the world. And if God should punish every sinner during his lifetime, one might have thought that the effect of divine justice exercised here below would lead to the belief that there was no future state, and all would be annihilated, according as the human race disappears.

What God has done at different times against the wicked is the testimony of what He will do someday against all those who have so abused His patience.

If the sinner wishes to ponder on his condition, let him recall to mind Sennacherib, Pharaoh, Antiochus, and many others who have been struck by God's all-powerful arm. History does not tell us how many more, perhaps much guiltier, have finished their career in an awful manner; but divine justice is ever the same, and if it has been delayed during life, it has overtaken them when they have ceased to breathe.

Reason is here in accordance with religion. The words of the prophet against Sennacherib is a divine oracle, but a revelation of light is sufficient to discover this truth.

O unjust man! O thou who sheddest the blood of thy equals! thou shalt one day be crushed with the weight of thine iniquity. Thou layest waste to all the land, and thou in thy turn shalt be laid low. Thou despiseth all laws, and thou in thy turn shalt be covered with confusion.

—Fr. William Francis Berthier, S.J. (1704–1782), *On Isaiah*

∽

Look at the havoc that hail and storm spread around our gardens and orchards; look at the rot fast spreading among the cattle; look at the winds and hurricane that toss the ships at sea. This is only but a feeble image of the ravages of sin in a soul.

Mortal sin destroys the merits of good works, corrupts every faculty of the mind, and leads the sinner on to certain death.

—St. Cyprian (ca. 200–258), *De Lapsis*, 5

Venial Sin

He that is unjust in that which is little,
is unjust also in that which is greater.

—Luke 16:10

The same God who is offended with mortal sin—a God infinitely great and loving, the God to whom we are indebted for everything, and who has so often prevented us from falling into mortal sin—this same God, I say, is offended by venial sin.

It is true that it may be a trifling fault, but this selfsame venial sin becomes in a way infinite when it is committed against infinite goodness and majesty.

I know full well that the faults that a subject can commit against his king are not always equally bad, but it is certain that he will not overlook faults, however trifling they may be. To make an attempt upon his life would, I grant, be the blackest of crimes, but to injure him purposely, by word or intention, would deserve a severe punishment.

We would call that child who would kill his own father an unnatural monster; but he who has cherished the thought of injuring him, or of raising his hand against him, would he not be held in abhorrence by all the world? O my God, how blind we are! These examples make us shudder, but we are not moved when we look into our own consciences and try to persuade ourselves that we are not so bad as they.

Let me, O Lord, constantly meditate on those parables that represent to us Your blessings and Your Majesty.

What is a king, what is the greatest monarch on the earth, in comparison with Thee, my God?

Everyone knows that when one gives way to any bad habit, it becomes daily more and more difficult to overcome, and that at last it quite gains the upper hand.

It is in this way that all the most wicked of men, are lost—not one of them ever commencing with a great crime. It is certain that if they attended to the first twinge of their conscience, they might still have been innocent; but when once they have paid no attention to inward warnings, it becomes morally impossible to arrest its downward progress.

This is the way of the devil, who would not be satisfied if he did not deprive the sinner of the grace of God, never tempts him to begin by the commission of a grievous offense at first.

He is content, if he can feed the vanity of that young girl by inspiring her with a love of dress, and displaying the last new fashions, because he knows well she will not fail to go further, and even without his interference she will at last come to a bad end.

A person who simply wishes to abstain from mortal sin has not a very great desire to avoid it. It is an idle fancy to suppose that that plan of life that never fails to attend to great essential things without taking the trouble of taking precaution to avoid lesser evils can be sufficient to ensure perseverance in the love of God. However venial my sins may appear to me, O Lord, they are attached to Thee, although they do not kill my soul. I am always in need of Thy Precious Blood to avert Thy justice, and they will never be remitted, unless a just proportion be kept between the evil and the remedy, the satisfaction and the injury. It is true that a sprinkling of holy water, taken with a feeling of true devotion, is sufficient to wash away the stains; that an alms distributed to the poor can, in the sight of God, discharge many a small debt; that a fervent prayer can obtain a cure of my sins, and all that are called sacramental remedies can help to staunch my wounds; but all sufficient as these remedies may be, they would be inefficacious if they were not mingled with the wounds of our Savior and supported by His merits.

It is necessary that that drop of holy water should be mingled with the tears He has shed over our miseries; that that alms should be united to the immense love that led Him to shed His Blood for our redemption, as says the Apostle; that that prayer be in union with those He addressed to His Father in our favor.

—St. Claude de la Colombière (1641–1682)

∞

I acknowledge, O my God, that it is only by a constant and wearisome practice of little duties that I can prove, exercise, and fortify my virtue for great occasions. I will henceforth be faithful to Thee in little things. It is only thus that I can store up a treasure of merits for heaven.

What should I do? What could I suffer for You, O Lord, if I waited for great opportunities?

Alas! fatal experience has taught me but too often that the lightest venial fault diminishes the horror of sin; that it strengthens in my soul an attachment to evil; that it is easy to fall when venial sins are disregarded.

—Fr. Paul Segneri, S.J. (1624–1694), *Meditations*

∞

Habitual Sin

*I say unto you, that whosoever
committeth sin, is the servant of sin.*

—John 8:34

You tell me that it is useless for me to try, for my bad habit has too strong a hold upon me. But I say: Watch over yourself, and you will soon be corrected. The more inveterate the habit is, the more it deserves your attention.

The tongue is a very quick and dangerous member: be, then, more attentive to restrain its volubility. If you try today, it will be easier to restrain it tomorrow. If your victory is not complete tomorrow, you will find that, by the efforts you made yesterday, your task is less difficult.

Vice expires in three days. We shall soon reap the fruit and rejoice at the great advantage we have gained by being delivered from so sad an evil.

I know full well that it is difficult to break off a sinful habit, for I have experienced it, but, through the holy fear of God, I have conquered the habit of swearing. When I read and meditated on His law, I was seized with fear. I fought manfully against my bad habit. I invoked the Lord in whom I trusted, and He gave me the aid I prayed for, and soon nothing appeared to me more easy than to refrain from swearing.

—St. Augustine (354–430), Sermon 307

Habitual Sin

∞

When we begin to offend Almighty God, when the sin has not taken deep root, we can easily tear it out, just as it would happen to newly planted trees. But when the earth has nourished its roots, little by little, they grow gradually and insensibly, they multiply their branches, they spread quickly and become so deeply rooted that nothing but a tempestuous wind can break the tree or root it up.

Ah! such is the frightful state of the sinner. At the beginning, conversion is easy, his inclinations for evil, his attachment to sins, are not so strong, nor so numerous, nor so rooted within; but after years of continuous perseverance, his affection for sin is increased, his longings are multiplied, and his attachments become rooted. And nothing but the mighty stroke of God's all-powerful arm can break his stony heart.

—Fr. Jacques Biroat (d. 1666), Lenten discourse

∞

Habitual sin may be justly called the highest point of sin, since it causes the loss of the fear of God, and begets a contempt for His holy law. A sinful act, often reiterated, becomes a habit, habit engenders necessity, necessity becomes impossibility, impossibility is the mother of despair, and despair finishes its work and seals its own damnation.

—St. Bernard (1091–1153), *On Consideratio*

Occasions of Sin

And such of them as shall flee shall escape.
—Ezekiel 7:16

It is a delusion to fancy that an occasion is necessary when it is purely voluntary.

What is more usual in the world than to make excuses for a pretended necessity, merely because everyone considers it to be the right sort of thing to do, and because self-love prompts us to acquiesce in any imaginary engagement?

I am, says one, in a position of life, such as rank or station, that renders it impossible for me to avoid seeing, or being seen, paying or receiving visits. How, then, should I occupy my time?

I am, says another, in an office, in a post of great responsibility, and it is really necessary for me to enter into particulars, however hazardous they may be for my salvation, however dangerous they may be for the purity of my conscience.

I grant all this. You must appear in society; you should have recreations and ought not to be prevented from mixing in company. But is there not something over and above these amenities and rules? If your rank, condition, or position in the world should compel you to pay visits, however honorable or decorous they may be, what necessity is there for prolonging such visits? Why receive at your house people of all ages of different sexes? Why engage in every party of pleasure, promenade, or play? It is that you wish to shine above others, to show yourself off on every occasion, and thus you make amusement the chief occupation of your life.

What necessity is there that if you must belong to a club or society, you should select the one most scandalous and worldly, one that only flatters vanity and engenders effeminacy? Why, of all theaters, should you select those where the most sensual exhibitions are given? What necessity is there, that you should always be in the company of those whom you wish to please or who please you? What necessity is there for encouraging the acquaintance of dissolute libertines, who unfortunately know no better and are capable only of persuading you to join them in their evil course of life?

Would you wish to be shown the danger that you are in, and the consequent misery that must result from these proximate occasions of sin?

They are only vain terrors, say you, that a confessor or a director would wish to depict.

What! you do not call those clandestine interviews, unknown even to father or mother, a proximate occasion of sin? Those appointed meetings when the passions are so violent, and virtue is so weak, that it yields at last to the tempter? You do not call those free and easy conversations a proximate occasion of sin, where intrigues are openly discussed, where the heart, more than the mouth, suggests many an expression capable of poisoning every sense of right? You do not call that an occasion of sin, when you write and receive letters wherein the heart is freely opened? You do not call that a proximate occasion of sin, that secret conversation with a creature, and you do not deem it to be a guilty occasion to remain under the same roof with the object of your passionate love? You are deceived. Withdraw from them and separate.

Separation, divorce; an entire separation, an immediate divorce; leave the guilty object, and withdraw from him.

If you do not do this, you break the commandment of God and complete your condemnation.

—Fr. Jean Baptiste Massillon (1663–1742),
From a sermon on this subject

My Daily Visit with the Saints

∞

You inwardly reproach me, O Lord, for having, like unto St. Peter, rashly exposed myself to danger, notwithstanding Your threats and prohibition, and notwithstanding the proper sense I should have had of my own weakness, with which You have often been willing to inspire me.

Relying on my own strength, I foolishly thought that those interviews, those occasions that have so often proved to be fatal, would not have injured me. I continued to associate with companions who were corrupt, slanderous, and impious, and I fancied that I could throw myself into flames without being burned.

Now, O my Savior, I will follow the example of St. Peter, and will fly, cost what it may, from the dangerous society of those who sought my ruin. I will avoid every occasion of sin and will weep bitterly for my poor soul, my tarnished innocence.

—Bishop Jacques Bénigne Bossuet (1627–1704)

Frequent Relapses

And the state of that man is made worse than the first.

—Matthew 12:45

The chief misfortune that accompanies a relapse is to withdraw God from us and to exhaust, as it were, His mercy, which although infinite in itself, still cannot be carried beyond bounds with regard to ourselves, and to the distribution of those special graces, as also those extraordinary helps on which our conversion depends.

"For three crimes of Damascus, and for four, I will not convert it" (Amos 1:3). For the three first crimes of Damascus, said the Lord, through one of His prophets—the three first crimes I have endured and have willingly forgotten them, but for the fourth, I shall not allow my justice and my anger to be passed by—why that? Because I was withdrawn from those wicked ones who had angered me by their infidelities.

Besides, from the moment that God withdraws His help, it is not to be wondered at that penitence should become difficult, and that this difficulty should increase in proportion to the length of the withdrawal. Why? Because God alone can fill our hearts with the sense of His divine presence and diffuse the unction of His Holy Spirit, which can alone make our penances easy, and in the end make us love Him.

Can you find a more beautiful illustration of this than that of the man so famed in the Old Testament, the invincible Samson? A guilty passion had blinded him; but the blindness into which he had fallen was not such to deprive him of that strength with which God had so singularly and so miraculously endowed him. The stranger to whom he was so attached had frequently attempted, by binding his limbs, to deliver him up to the Philistines; but he had always found the means to break his bands and recover his liberty. Hence he flattered himself that he would always be able to free himself from her treachery, and he said to himself: I will go forth, as I did before (Judg. 16:20).

At last, that perfidious woman so cleverly employed her fascinating ways, that she cut off that fatal hair, in which, by a secret mystery, all his strength was centered. The news was soon conveyed to the Philistines. They surrounded him unawares and fell upon him in great numbers. He wished to be relieved, as he formerly had been, but he knew not that God had withdrawn His help from him: "not knowing that the Lord was departed from him" (Judg. 16:20).

Here, my dear brethren, you have the picture of a soul in that unhappy and miserable state that usually succeeds to a willful relapse into sin.

On awaking from your deep sleep of indifference and reflecting on your misery, you will say with Samson: "I will go forth as I did before." I will break my chains. I will make a vigorous effort, and I will free myself from a guilty passion that has so long enchained me.

But you do not consider that God retires from you, and that in proportion as He retires, you are deprived of His aid; that penance then becomes a heavy burden, an insupportable yoke; and, whereas heretofore, it was a source of comfort to you, it now creates horror and disgust in your mind; for your frequent relapses have separated you from God and have placed an almost insurmountable barrier between you and your God: "Not knowing that the Lord was departed from you."

In truth, is it credible that a man should have had a firm determination to renounce his sin and then soon afterward, cowardly and unresistingly (his sin being always before him), fall again into the same grievous sin? Ah, said St. Bernard, there is nothing stronger than our free will: everything submits to it; everything obeys it. There is no difficulty that it will not remove, no opposition that it will not surmount, and what appeared otherwise impossible, becomes easy, when undertaken in earnest.

Now, this is true, in a particular manner, with reference to sin; for however depraved we may have been after all, we sin only because we have the will to commit sin. And if we do not will to sin, it is indisputable that we do not commit sin. In this way, our free will preserves a kind of sovereignty over itself and participates in some measure in the divine omnipotence, as, in what regards sin, the will does only what it wishes to do; and it has simply to consent in order to overcome the power of not doing it. I am, then, inclined to think that in reality it has not the wish to resist and renounce sin, when I see plainly that the subsequent wish is to resist but feebly, and in the end it fails to renounce sin altogether.

This is the argument of St. Bernard, who cannot be suspected of Pelagianism, since he always acknowledges the efficacy of the grace of Jesus Christ and is easily reconciled with what St. Paul said of himself when he complained, "I do not that good which I will; but the evil which I hate, that I do" (Rom. 7:15), because by that, he understood and meant the involuntary motions of his heart; whereas St. Bernard speaks of the free consent that is given to sin.

—Fr. Louis Bourdaloue (1632–1704), *Dominicale*

∞

Final Impenitence

You shall seek me, and ye shall not find me,
and you will die in your sins.

—John 7:34; 8:21

I called and you rejected me; I also in my turn will laugh you to scorn. This is, at the same time, a reproach and a threat that God makes to sinners.

I have waited, says He to them, until the time you asked me for; I have permitted you to satiate those youthful passions that you alleged as an excuse; I have allowed the fire of your passions to die out; I could have left you at the very moment you abandoned me.

Nevertheless, I pitied you and took compassion on your weakness. I delayed, and even tolerated, your long-continued neglect. I have even followed you to the last great feast, as you requested me to do. I hoped that you would return to me, that you would do something for your own salvation; nevertheless you have not fulfilled your promises.

My preachers have spoken with all that zeal that my glory and your salvation have inspired in them. The ministers of penance have waited for you in the confessional. The treasures of my grace, and those of my Church, have been ever opened for sinners. In a word, I have waited for you to work out my justice.

But what has been the result, what the success of my patience? It has been iniquity. One day of penance and years of sin; a confession hurriedly, slovenly made, and a thousand relapses during the rest of your life—some trifling alms after a thousand injustices. You have despised my grace, my warnings, my threats. "I also in my time will laugh you to scorn."

That which keeps back the conversion of so many sinners is that they want to wait for their conversion until they are free from all hindrances, from businesses that occupy them whole time. When I have settled that lawsuit, says one; when I shall be free from all the cares of my numerous engagements, says another; when I shall have restored order and peace in my family, when I shall have provided for my children, when I shall have put by enough for the wants and comforts of my old age, then I will think of being good and of doing penance. This is how worldly people act. You wish to wait, in order that you may be free from every obstacle, free from all temporal anxieties.

Ah! you deceive yourselves, blind sinners. You will never reach to that freedom of mind, to that disengagement from everything; for you will always be slaves of habits that drag you down, and that will grow stronger in you more and more.

Well, if you wish to emerge from the darkness in which you are, do not delay one single moment when the voice of God calls you.

Although you may be still attached to the good things of this world, although you may cling to the corruptions of the age, although you may be slaves of a vice that tyrannizes over you, listen to Jesus Christ, who speaks to you, and when you hear His voice, arise from sin, as did Lazarus from the grave. Without that, you will perhaps never, never be converted.

A change from bad to good is not effected in a moment. How great a change, then, must that be, from a bad life to a good death!

You know that the grace of a deathbed repentance is the most extraordinary of all graces; and still you think that you have a right to expect it—you who have brought yourself to be most unworthy of so great a grace; unworthy by that career of callous indifference of which you know all the baseness; unworthy by the knowledge of inspirations from heaven, which you have so many times misused; unworthy by the neglect of those blessed inward warnings from above; unworthy by that false and deceitful security you have cherished, and which is the climax of all your sins.

I ask you, if there ever was a sinner who ought to expect from God the grace of conversion, would it be a sinner of your grade, and if there is much to fear for one sinner, ought you not to fear that the curse of heaven would descend upon you, and that you would be rejected as a criminal too guilty to merit forgiveness?

—Fr. Jean Baptiste Massillon (1663–1742)

∞

A man, when he is at death's door, is like unto a city besieged and vigorously stormed by the enemy. Every civil function is suspended; courts of justice, schools, business, fine arts are all suspended during that calamity. Everyone runs to the ramparts to share in the common danger. So a person, the citadel of whose heart is besieged with the pains of death, to make use of the prophet's expressions, thinks only of his pain. His soul is entirely at the mercy of those who torture the most. It is then that it must strive its utmost to drive away an enemy, ready to make itself master of the place. During this temptation, it no longer sees or hears; it only feels the pain. In that dread hour one hardly dares to call its attention to many important affairs; nevertheless it is the time reserved expressly for the only great affair, for an affair on which hangs an eternity.

Woe to me! if I am so badly advised as to use my soul thus. Woe to me! if I delay to the last moment of my life that which should have been the occupation of my life.

—St. Claude de la Colombière (1641–1682)

∞

Do not, I implore you, delay your conversion to God, for you know not the day appointed to carry you off.

Final Impenitence

You tell me that God has given to some when they have reached extreme old age His grace to be converted. Does it follow from this that He will grant you the same favor? Perhaps He will grant it. Why add "perhaps"? Because it has sometimes happened. What! Does the question of your salvation depend on a perhaps?

— St. John Chrysostom (ca. 349–407), *Epistle ad Theodore*

Part 6

∞

Vices We Should Flee From

On Ambition

They much preferred the glory of man
to the glory of God.

—John 12:43

Of the chastisements inflicted by Almighty God on the ambitious man, there is no instance more terrible than the fate and punishment of Nebuchadnezzar. The king ceased to be a prince and, at the same time, lost his reason and his crown.

We read in the book of Daniel: "But when his heart was lifted up, and his spirit hardened with pride, he was put down from the throne of his kingdom, and his glory was taken away" (Dan. 5:20).

He lost his speech and was forced to bellow like the oxen and eat grass, and from the highest rank he was reduced to the lowest pitch of misery. He was driven from a palace wherein he formerly was idolized, and therein was a sight never before witnessed in any palace of a king. The magnificent buildings that had been the unfortunate source of his pride could serve him only as a humiliating retreat; the majesty that all obeyed tremblingly was in the twinkling of an eye deprived of every mark of honor.

One sought for Nebuchadnezzar in vain. His children no longer knew their father; his subjects no longer recognized their king.

—Fr. Vincent Houdry, S.J. (1630–1729)

My Daily Visit with the Saints

∞

Ambition is a passion that prompts men to raise themselves higher than their due. It is ever unjust, and insatiability becomes a part of its character.

What vice is more hurtful to repose! Disdainful and discontented, it despises all that is lowly and recognizes no equal. No vice is more hideous! Ambition seeks only its aim—no exertion and labor is too difficult, provided it accomplishes its object. All roads to advancement appear to the ambitious man to be level. Ambition is his idol, and to this he sacrifices duty, friendship, and gratitude and scorns every law, human and divine. No passion is more hardhearted, more irreligious. What scheme does not the ambitious man resort to, to attain his object? Intrigues, quarrels, intercession, base flattery—all are made use of. The ambitious play many parts—now a friend, now a suppliant, but rarely that of an honest man, and still more seldom, that of a Christian man.

Conscience is disregarded, religion unheeded, and passion reigns supreme in the ambitious heart. From this arise failures, total disregard of morality, and all that is sacred.

Ambition upsets, so to speak, the economy of providence. Opposed as it is to its designs, it follows and pursues its own plans and projects. It selects positions, procures dignities, seizes hold of the foremost place, seeks to displace others, and yearns to be higher, higher still.

The life of an ambitious man is spent in sighing after an imaginary fortune, a phantom of glory. His present state of life displeases him if he sees an opportunity of obtaining a higher position, and which he flatters himself he has the ability to fill. To secure this, what measures will he not take, and to what meanness will he not resort?

One might say that the majority of mankind seem to imitate those rash children of Noah who busied themselves in erecting a tower that would reach to heaven.

Christian virtue is the only object worthy of ambition. God alone can satisfy our heart, and that heart must be centered in Him alone.

—Fr. Croiset, S.J. (b. ca. 1650)

∞

Anger

*Whosoever is angry with his brother, shall
deserve to be condemned by the judgment.*

—Matthew 5:22

Those persons who are subject to the furious passion of anger are compared in Holy Writ to beasts, because they imitate their malignity; and those who are in the habit of committing all kinds of crime are rightly placed in the category of those ferocious and carnivorous animals who bear a natural enmity to man.

Quickness of temper, ill-natured, inconsiderate words, violence, calumnies, reproaches, injuries, blows, and all other disorders are the result and fruit of anger. It is that vice that sharpens the swords with which men kill each other, that causes brothers no longer to recognize their own flesh and blood, that leads parents and children to stifle the best feelings that nature implants in them.

A passionate man does not even know himself. He respects neither age, virtue, nor kindred; he forgets benefits and is not moved by aught that is most sacred among men.

Anger is a momentary madness. Those who are prone to it neglect themselves for the sake of revenge and often thereby expose themselves to all sorts of danger.

The remembrance of wrongs that may have been inflicted on them is like a needle that continually pricks them; their excited minds know no rest until they have caused some great grief or until they have inflicted some injury on those who may have offended them, when what they wish to do often recoils upon themselves, and this is frequently the case.

—St. Basil (ca. 329–379)

∞

Do you not know that when one flies into a passion, trifling things appear insupportable, and what is the least injurious becomes magnified and appears to be an insulting outrage? That which we look upon as a little word has often caused murders and ruined entire cities.

Thus, when we love someone, the most disagreeable task appears to be light and easy; in like manner, when we cherish hate, the lightest things appear to be insupportable. Although the word or words may have been uttered without intention of hurting the feelings, we harbor the thought that it must proceed from a heart that is poisoned against us. St. Paul says, "Let not the sun go down on your anger" (Eph. 4:26). He fears that the night, finding the offended person alone, may fester the wound. During the day the work and bustle of the world causes his anger to slumber, but when the night has come, he is alone, and he broods over his fancied injuries, and his troubled soul becomes excited, and passionate anger resumes its sway.

St. Paul, foreseeing this evil, wishes him to be reconciled before the sun goes down, in order that the devil may not have the opportunity of rekindling his anger and thus make it turn to hate.

—St. John Chrysostom (ca. 349–407)

∞

If a man cannot help feeling angry, in spite of himself, he can at least try to mitigate his wrath.

Against that unhappy feeling of anger, we should oppose, by that gentlest of all virtues, patience. For if anger exceeds its proper limit, it opens in the soul a wound that allows itself to be led away, it deadens every proper feeling, thickens the tongue, disturbs the eye, and, in fact, revolutionizes the whole frame.

Therefore, in dealing with an angry man, resist him if you can, and if you cannot, yield to him.

Do you wish to know how to act when you have received an insult? Do not return evil for evil; pay no attention to malicious reports; neither be wicked because others are wicked. The pagans have often quoted a remark made by one of their philosophers and which is certainly deserving of praise. His servant having greatly displeased him by an act of gross injustice, he said to him: "Go, wretched man, how severely would I punish you, were I not in a passion!"

David acted in a similar way. He restrained his anger when he felt tempted to revenge; he so thoroughly had mastered his passions that he did not answer a single word to the insults they heaped upon him.

—St. Ambrose (340–397), *De Officiis*

Avarice

Let your life be exempt from avarice;
be content with what you have.

—Hebrews 13:5

There is nothing crueler, nothing more infamous than the usury, so common among men.

The usurer traffics on the misfortunes of others; he enriches himself on their poverty, and then he demands his compound interest, as if they were under a great obligation to him.

He is heartless to his creditor but is afraid of appearing so. When he pretends that he has every inclination to oblige, he crushes him the more and reduces him to the last extremity. He offers one hand, and with the other pushes him down the precipice.

He offers to assist the shipwrecked, and instead of guiding them safely into port, he steers them among the reefs and rocks. Where your treasure is, there is your heart, says our Savior. Perhaps you may have avoided many evils arising from avarice; but still if you cherish an attachment to this odious vice, it will be of little use, for you will still be a slave, free as you fancy yourself to be. And you will fall from the height of heaven to that spot wherein your gold is hidden, and your thoughts will still complacently dwell on money, gains, usury, and dishonest commerce.

What is more miserable than such a state?

Avarice

There is not a sadder tyranny than that of a man who is a willing subject to this furious tyrant, destroying all that is good in him, namely, the nobility of his soul.

So long as you have a heart basely attached to gains and riches, whatsoever truths may be told you, or whatsoever advice may be given to you, to secure your salvation—all will be useless.

Avarice is an incurable malady, an ever-burning fire, a tyranny that extends far and wide; for he who in this life is the slave of money is loaded with heavy chains and destined to carry far heavier chains in the life to come.

— St. John Chrysostom (ca. 349–407), *De Avaritia*

∞

It is that insatiable greed for gold and the goods of this world that engenders all those crying injustices—all those double-dealings in trade and companies, those infidelities to promises, that all-devouring rapacity that, heedless of the widow and orphans, violate the most sacred laws merely to satisfy the cravings of a vast cupidity.

From avarice arises that desire of establishing the status of your own family and of building up a name and reputation at the expense of the holy commandments of God and His Church.

From that proceed those forced sacrifices of unloved children to occupations for which they may have a distaste, merely for the sake of aggrandizing those for whom they have a greater love—that bold usurpation of the poor, by depriving them, so to speak, of the inheritance of Jesus Christ.

It is a sin of which a man can very seldom be cured without the help of an especial grace.

When a vice is not sufficiently strong of itself to be satisfied, it generally calls in the assistance of another vice near at hand; for instance, vengeance is satiated when blood is spilled. Misfortune cures us of pride and ambition; sensuality dies out with our strength and health; but avarice alone increases with our age.

Ambition feeds avarice, pleasure flatters it, and the old man used up by sensuality becomes eager for money, and so hoards something daily for the end of a journey, which, alas for him! is so near at hand.

One look of our Savior touched the heart of Peter; a word converted Paul; the incredulous Thomas became a firm believer as soon as he touched the wounds and side of his Lord and Master; but neither look nor word nor touch did the avaricious Judas heed.

Ah! my brother, if a little limpid stream were near, and that was sufficient to satisfy your thirst, why seek for one as wide as an ocean, which will only make you thirstier? If you have sufficient for your wants, why seek for more?

A man who is in heart a miser has plenty, and yet has it not. He has enough, because he is already rich and amasses daily. He has it not, for with all his gold he yearns for more; he lives as if he had nothing, and at last he dies poor. His gold is as nothing, and he dies poorer than the poorest beggar.

Jesus Christ came down from heaven to cure this dreadful vice. To drive away avarice, He elevates the love of poverty to the highest rank, and to effect this, He who is the Lord and Master of all riches on earth preferred to be born in a stable, to pass His early days in a carpenter's workshop, and then die naked on a cross, in order to establish a religion, poor and pure, in the midst of a coarse and cruel world.

—Fr. Jean Baptiste Massillon (1663–1742)

∞

Atheism and Unbelief

I am the first, and I am the last, and beside me there is no God.

—Isaiah 44:6

If I asked an atheist how I can be convinced that he is alive (for, indeed, I cannot see the soul that dwells within him), he would answer that he acts, he speaks, he walks, and that consequently he is a living being. But it is possible to move, walk, and even speak by mechanism, and I see nothing that persuades me that he has within himself a principle that of its nature can control or instill such an animation. At least I may obstinately require proofs from him of that interior source that belies him.

The intelligence, reflection, and freedom that accompany these exterior signs of life, he replies, leave no doubt that the source from which they spring must be the soul.

I agree and am forced to agree with him.

In admitting creation, why, then, does he not adore the Creator?

O fool! let him acknowledge that Supreme Being, whose wisdom and power shine so visibly in the world.

Holy Scripture makes no distinction between the atheist, and the madman and fool; they are nevertheless led by a very different way. The fool thinks what he says, and says what he thinks; the thoughts and words of the atheist do not agree. His opinions give the lie to his words, and his words give the lie to his opinions. In his heart he denies the Divinity.

I am wrong.

My Daily Visit with the Saints

I should say he would wish to deny it. He, however, cannot succeed in this, for he dares not publish his opinion, because he does not understand it. Every effort he makes to fly from the fear of God (who is a witness of all his deeds) ends only in a vague, confused idea of a belief that startles him in spite of himself.

O madman! to wish to force his reason, to lose his reasoning faculties.

It must be madness to battle against a truth that has been accepted at all times and in all places. There is a Divinity, and this is what all have agreed upon; a God has been acknowledged, and Him they have adored.

This conviction is not the result of education, for education differs in all parts of the globe. It is not the commerce that has spread from one nation to another, for all nations have not been able to agree on this point, without the help of a mutual intelligence. Questions of policy have not been able to produce it, for governments so opposed to each other, so different in manners and customs, could not possibly come to terms. Princes and subjects could not have been able to combat with the impressions, naturally formed in all kinds of intelligences.

Is it study that has given it birth? Certainly not! On this point, the grossest ignorance does not yield to good breeding or knowledge. In favor of a Divinity, I do not ask, said Tertullian, for the testimony of a soul in established schools, in well-stored libraries, or in first-rate colleges; I appeal to a simple and savage soul; I invoke the soul itself, such as it comes from the hands of its Creator. If any person has been the first to discover or make known the existence of that Supreme Being, tell me the land from which he has sprung, and the nation that has published it to the whole world. Point out the time, and the age that has first heard it. The birth of a truth so startling, so important, could not have failed to have been noticed.

Perhaps it may be said, in opposition to this, that idolatry has reigned, that empires and kingdoms have adored different gods; I know it, and I maintain only to establish a universal knowledge and recognition of the Divinity.

Atheism and Unbelief

If there be under heaven an atheist, he must acknowledge that idolatry destroys itself, and that his ridicule is only equal to his error. But reason alone cannot compass all the perfections of the Divinity, of which it is struck with wonder, and which it cannot ignore.

All men yearn after a happiness that they naturally aim at acquiring; but without the assistance of faith, how could they agree as to its quality and essence? To an ordinary intelligent mind, how difficult it would prove to act in opposition to an opinion that is universally recognized! And yet would not that very difficulty be a convincing proof of the truth he would deny?

One could scarcely imagine a man to be more wicked than he who coolly and deliberately resolves to riot in the commission of the most abominable vices. And yet a man who makes it his study and profession, and who piques himself upon it to deny the existence of a Supreme Being, is such a man. It is neither chance, nor delusion, nor reflection, nor knowledge, nor even debauchery that has led him into that frightful error; it is his will only.

We are born ignorant, weak, inconstant, inclined to evil; but we come into this world, with all the prejudices that wage war against atheism.

If it is possible to be an atheist, it is because the will to be one is there. It is undoubtedly true that such a wish arises from debauchery, but such a will is in itself a lewdness of the most detestable kind. One does not plunge himself by degrees into the lowest depths of vice; as soon as he affirms that there is no God, he casts himself suddenly into the abyss.

—St. Augustine (354–430), *On Psalm 73*

∽

God cannot be seen; He is far too bright for us. Neither can we understand Him; He is far beyond our comprehension. He is not sufficiently valued, because He is out of the reach of our senses. This is why we should worthily estimate the perfection of His being, when we say that He is inestimable.

My Daily Visit with the Saints

If I know not myself, if I know neither the nature nor the essence of my soul, if I cannot give a reason of what is in me, how shall I dare to lift up my eyes in order to understand God, who is the beginning and end of all things, and who is Himself without beginning and end?

—St. Cyprian (ca. 200–258), *De Idolorum Vanitate*

∞

Blasphemy

A man that sweareth much shall be filled with iniq-
uity, and a scourge shall not depart from his house.

—Sirach 23:12 (RSV = Sir. 23:11)

All oaths are forbidden, except when absolutely necessary; and it is breaking the commandment that God has made, not only by taking His sacred
name in vain, but by dishonoring Him by blasphemies, impious jests,
oaths uttered on trifling occasions, and frequent and habitual swearing,
uttered through wicked malice or through useless, frivolous promises,
confirmed on oath.

We acknowledge the holiness of the name of God by faith, and it is
by faith that we know that perjury dishonors Him. With regard to this
precept, every oath, every curse, every kind of swearing is against this
precept and is opposed to the respect due to the holy name of God; for
"holy and terrible is his name" (Ps. 110:9 [RSV = Ps. 111:9]). But where
are the men and traders of the world who obey this commandment? Alas!
many swear of their own accord, without a thought, without reflection,
and very many through habit.

Let us take care to avoid the use of oaths in our temporal affairs; for
it is an abuse of religion and is taking a mercenary view of God.

The abuse of swearing arises either from a bold defiance of Him who forbids it, or from the malice of those who make use of it, or from thoughtless-
ness and irreverence. Religion, honesty, and honor would remedy all this.

Nothing would be so contrary to the Spirit of God and to the doctrine of Jesus Christ as the making use of oaths in the church, because it would be the occasion of perjury, would lay snares for the weak and the ignorant, and sometimes would place the name and truths of God in the hands of the wicked.

—*La Morale Chrétienne*

∞

I beseech you, my brothers, to be ever on your guard against the habit of swearing and blaspheming.

If a slave dares to pronounce the name of his master, he does it but seldom, and then only with respect. Therefore, is it not a shocking impiety to speak with contempt and irreverence of the name of the Master of angels and seraphim? People handle the book of the Gospel with a religious fear, and then only with clean hands, and yet your rash tongue would inconsiderately profane the name of the Divine Author of the Gospel.

Would you wish to know with what respect, fear, and wonder the choirs of the angels pronounce the adorable name? Listen to the prophet Isaiah: "I saw the Lord sitting upon a throne high and elevated: upon it stood the seraphim ... and they cried one to another and said, Holy, holy, holy, the Lord God of hosts, all the earth is full of his glory" (Isa. 6:1–3).

See with what terror they are seized, even while they praise and glorify Him. As for you, my brethren, you know how cold and indifferent are the prayers you say, and you know how frequently you blaspheme a name so majestic, so sacred, and how you try to make excuses for the bad habit you have contracted. It is easy, yes, I say, it is easy, with a little care, attention, and reflection, to leave off this vicious habit.

Since we have fallen, my brethren, into this sin of blasphemy, I conjure you, in the name of our Lord, to rebuke openly these blasphemers. When you meet with such who publicly sin in this respect, correct them by word of mouth.

Blasphemy

∞

Do you remember that it was a false oath that overturned the house, temples, and walls of Jerusalem, and from a superb city, it became a mass of ruins? Neither the sacred vessels nor the sanctuary could stay the vengeance of a God, justly angered against a violator of His Word.

Sedecias did not receive a more favored treatment than Jerusalem. Flight did not save him from his enemies. This prince, escaping secretly, was pursued and taken by the Assyrians, who led him to their king. The king, after asking him the reason of his perfidy, not only caused his children to be killed, but deprived him of his sight and sent him back to Babylon, loaded with iron chains.

Would you know the reason why? It was that the barbarians who inhabited the country adjoining Persia should know, by this terrible example, that the breach of an oath is punishable.

—St. John Chrysostom (ca. 349–407), Seventh Homily

∞

Calumny and Slander

The tongue is a fire, a world of iniquity;
it is an unquiet evil, full of deadly poison.

—James 3:6, 8

Scripture, in giving us a portrait of a slanderer, represents him as a terrible and formidable man: "A man full of tongue is terrible in his city, and he that is rash in his word shall be hateful" (Sir. 9:25). In fact, he is formidable in a city, formidable in a community, formidable in private houses, formidable among the rich, and also among the poor. He is formidable in a city, because he creates factions and parties; in a community, because he disturbs its interior peace and union; in private dwellings, because he introduces coolness and enmities; among the rich, because he abuses the confidence they place in him, in order to work the destruction of those whom they may dislike; among the poor, because he urges them on to quarrel one with another. How many families have been estranged through a petty slander! How many friendships have been severed by a scandalous joke! How many hearts lacerated by indiscreet reports!

What is it that daily occasions so many open and declared ruptures? Is it not an offensive expression that was totally uncalled for?

What is it that causes duels (now so wisely forbidden by laws human and divine)? Is it not often only a stinging remark that is not credited but that, according to the false honor of the world, could not go unpunished?

Calumny and Slander

Although other vices generally increase in virulence with time, still there are certain states and conditions of life that retard or stop their growth; it may be by the grace of vocation, or by a firm resolution to conquer bad habits, or by a withdrawal from occasions of sin, or it may be by a kind of necessity. Avarice, for instance, is less liable to be rooted in the heart of a religious; ambition is rarely to be found among the poor and the lowly; there have been maidens in the Christian world who have immediately overcome all temptations of the flesh; but as for slander, it exercises its sway over every class.

It is the vice of the adult, of the young, of sovereigns, of the learned and the ignorant; it is the vice of the court, of the city, of the lawyer, of the soldier, of the young and the old. Shall I say it? And yet I cannot draw the line here. No, my brethren, I must say it with all respect; it is the vice of priests as well as of laymen, of the religious bodies as well as the seculars, of the devotee as well as, perhaps more than, that of the wicked.

Recollect, however, I do not say it is the vice of the truly devout, thank God! True piety is exempt from every vice, and to attribute a single fault to such a one would be an insult to God and throw discredit on the worship due to Him. But those who profess devotion have their besetting sins like unto all, and you know if slander and calumny are not among the most usual. Besides that, it is a sin that tempts the most devout, a sin that nullifies the gifts of grace, a sin that corrupts their minds while their bodies remain chaste, a sin that sadly shipwrecks their souls, even after having avoided the most criminal perils, and the fiercest passions. In fine, it is a sin that is the cause of the loss of many a pious soul and that dishonors devotion.

—Fr. Louis Bourdaloue (1632–1704), *Dominicale*

∞

Look at that clever calumniator! He begins by fetching a deep sigh, he affects to be humble, and puts on a modest look, and with a voice choking with sobs, tries to gloss over the slander that is on the tip of his tongue.

One would fancy that he expressly assumed a calm and easy demeanor; for when he speaks against his brother, it is in a tender and compassionate tone. I am really hurt, says he, to find that our brother has fallen into such a sin; you all know how much I love him and how often I have tried to correct him. It is not today that I have noticed his failing; for I should always be on my guard to speak of others, but others have spoken of it too. It would be in vain to disguise the fact; it is only too true, and with tears in my eyes I tell it to you. This poor unfortunate brother has talent, but it must be confessed that he is very guilty, and however great may be our friendship for him, it is impossible to excuse him.

—St. Bernard (1091–1153), Sermon 24 on the Song of Songs

∞

To commit a murder, besides not having the person in your power, there are many measures and precautions to take. A favorable opportunity must be waited for, and a place must be selected before we can put so damnable a design into execution. More than this, the pistols may misfire, blows may not be sufficient, and all wounds are not mortal.

But to deprive a man of his reputation and honor, one word is sufficient. By finding out the most sensitive part of his honor, you may tarnish his reputation. By telling it to all who know him, you may easily take away his character for honor and integrity. To do this, however, no time is required, for scarcely have you complacently cherished the wish to calumniate him than the sin is effected.

—St. John Chrysostom (ca. 349–407)

∞

Discord and Lawsuits

He that studieth discords, loveth quarrels.

—Proverbs 17:19

Quarrels, enmities, and law proceedings do not very often cease among people who are at variance with others: these kinds of disputes are for the most part hereditary in some families; they continue and pass from generation to generation. They communicate their differences and aversion to their children; they speak of them in their presence; they tell them of the injuries they pretend to have received from those with whom they have been at variance.

Such a one, they say, is a declared enemy of our house; his sole object is to injure us; we have always had some disagreements together; it is a long time since we went to law, and our suit is not as yet ended. Young children, susceptible as they ever are, listen attentively, soon share in their parents' dislikes; they enter into the passionate feelings of their fathers; they suck in with their milk, so to speak, their parents' corrupt inclinations, and scarcely have they arrived to man's estate than they have imbibed, through those bad discourses, dispositions that will lead them to perdition.

It is thus that enmities multiply and become lasting; they descend from father to son, from generation to generation, and a wretched, miserable misunderstanding, although small at its birth, grows and grows, and descends by degrees to the end of ages. Time even does not finish it, but it continues still in an unhappy eternity.

—Fr. Jean Lejeune (1592–1672), *Sermons*, volume 5

∞

As the Son of God censures and condemns the dissensions and animosities that are permanent among men, so is it His intention to recommend peace and concord. This is what the Holy Spirit teaches us through the mouth of the royal prophet: Seek peace, and do not weary in its pursuit (see Ps. 33:15 [RSV = Ps. 34:14]). The Apostle in like manner in his epistle to the Romans: "If it be possible, my brethren, as much as is in you, having peace with all men" (Rom. 12:18).

St. Chrysostom weighs those words "If it be possible," for, says he, it sometimes happens that it is not possible to be at peace with certain persons and on certain occasions—for instance, when there is a question of upholding Christian piety and truth, which is sought to be vilified. The Apostle says: "Do your duty in the sight of all men, not revenging yourselves, so that you may give no countenance to discord or iniquity"; but if piety and devotion be attacked, if anyone should infringe the rules, leave peace to defend the truth and keep it unto death, so that you may ever maintain charity inviolate toward those with whom you may have been at variance. You will not treat him as an enemy, but you must speak to him in a friendly way, tell him of his fault in a mild and charitable manner, and explain the truth as it is; for this must be the meaning of those words "As much as in you, having peace with all men." Show him that you are a sincere friend, taking care, however, that you do not disguise the truth.

The glorious St. Gregory of Nazianzen, seeing that the assembled bishops of the city of Constantinople were vexed and troubled at his being elected bishop, which dignity the saint had accepted only through compulsion, not only, for the sake of peace, willingly sent in his resignation, but also beseeched and entreated the emperor Theodosius to allow him to refuse the offered charge. "I ask of you," said he, "to grant me one favor: this is to lighten and relieve me from the weight of the work with which I am loaded. You have triumphed over savage enemies, but your glory and the grand trophy of your empire is to establish peace and concord among the bishops. In their councils they are disunited; the only means of reuniting them is a resignation. The Church's ship is disturbed, rocking fearfully; since it is on my account that this storm has arisen, throw me overboard and there soon will be a calm."

The emperor and his councilors, knowing the eminent virtue and the profound learning of this holy prelate, were so surprised at this request so touchingly delivered that it was with extreme reluctance that they agreed to accept his resignation.

—*Homélies Morales*

∞

In order to avoid dissensions, we should be ever on our guard, more especially with those who drive us to argue with them, with those who vex and irritate us, and who say things likely to excite us to anger. When we find ourselves in company with quarrelsome, eccentric individuals, people who openly and unblushingly say the most shocking things, difficult to put up with, we should take refuge in silence, and the wisest plan is not to reply to people whose behavior is so preposterous.

Those who insult us and treat us contumeliously are eager for a spiteful sarcastic reply. The silence we then affect disheartens them, and they cannot avoid showing their vexation. They do all they can to provoke us and to elicit a reply, but the best way to baffle them is to say nothing, to refuse to argue with them, and to leave them to chew the cud of their hasty anger. This method of bringing down their pride disarms them.

—St. Ambrose (340–397), *Offices*, chapter 5

∞

Effeminacy and Sensuality

*Many walk, of whom I have told you often (and now tell you
weeping), that they are enemies of the cross of Christ: whose end is
destruction, whose God is their belly, and whose glory is in their shame.*

—Philippians 3:18–19

It is a very dangerous error to fall into, to imagine that in leading an effeminate and indolent life, one does not stray into the broad road that
leads to perdition. This is as much as to say that you cannot be positively
wicked if you do not give way to excess, and that it is not going to perdition if you go on slowly, or step by step. If you examine your conscience,
you would soon see that in leading such a life, you are not walking on
that narrow path on which our Savior bids you enter.

As you would not like to confess that you are in the broad path, you
must as readily acknowledge that you are not of the number of those who
daily take up their cross and practice austerities that accompany those
who walk in the narrow path.

From this it follows that we imagine that there must be a third road
of which Jesus Christ does not make mention, and that it is in this said
third path that we can securely walk, without giving ourselves too much
trouble, to reach the gates of heaven.

Perhaps you may have never thought of this third road that we have
just mentioned, but it is a fact that you naturally love an easy and indolent life. You wish to enjoy all its attractions, to have all your own way,

without being troubled with sufferings, or with contradictions, and in that state of mind, if you were compelled to make a choice of the two paths, you would say that you would choose neither the one nor the other. You have no desire to go by the narrow path, because you have a horror of trouble and constraint, and you do not wish to go by the broad path, for you dread the loss of your soul.

What would you then? Which road do you intend to take? How do you purpose living?

If you dare to be candid, you would make this sincere avowal: that you seek for liberty to enjoy the pleasures of this life, without the fear of losing your soul for all eternity, and you seek for a path that would conduct you to eternal bliss without suffering all the pains and labors that we have to endure, before we reach the end of our journey.

This, then, is what you seek for, and what you lay claim to. But where is this path? Where shall we find it on this side of the grave?

Two paths are spoken of in Holy Writ: one on which we find thorns and crosses—these we flee from; the other leads to perdition, which we fain would avoid. Our Lord said "Strait is the way that leadeth to life" (Matt. 7:14). The Son of God does not say, "The way that leadeth to perfection," but "the way that leadeth to life," is strait.

He does not say that there is a strait way that leads to life, as if there were another; but He says positively, "The way that leads to life eternal is strait"; to teach us that whosoever wishes to enter heaven must resolve to enter in at the narrow gate. In many other chapters of St. Matthew and St. Luke He repeats the same thing.

Has He told us, even once, that there was a sweet and easy way to work out our salvation? If there were one, would He have been ignorant of it? If He had known it, would He have concealed it? Had He not known of it, how could He be called the true way, and the most excellent of all guides: "I am the way, the truth, and the life" (John 14:6)?

If after He had discovered it, He had concealed it from us, would we not have had a right to complain of His silence on so important a subject? Would we not have had reason to reproach Him, for having loaded us with a useless burden by conducting us along a rude and rugged path, strewn with flinty stones, bristling with thorns, to a terminus, when He might have led us through a smooth and even pathway all covered with flowers?

Remark then, how emphatically He speaks of the difficulties of the road, "How strait and narrow is the way!" Ah! once more, how narrow is the way that leadeth to eternal life!

If the effeminate and sensual life, which so many Christians lead, could pass through the narrow way, what need would there be for our Savior to say so emphatically, "How strait and narrow is the way"?

But note especially that our Savior speaks but of two ways—one narrow, the other broad. We cannot trace a vestige of the third; and as all the wicked march on the broad way, it evidently follows that all the elect, without exception, must go by the narrow way.

After that, what delusion, what blindness to imagine for a moment that we can work out our salvation by leading an effeminate, an indolent life!

—Fr. Haineuve, *The Broad Way That Leads to Perdition*

Envy and Jealousy

By the envy of the devil death came into the world,
and they follow him that are of his side.

—Wisdom 2:24–25

O! ye who are envious, let me tell you that however often you may seek for the opportunity of injuring him whom you hate, you will never be able to do him so much harm as you do harm to yourselves.

He whom you would pursue through the malice of your envy may probably escape, but you will never be able to fly from yourselves. Wherever you may be, your adversary is with you; your sin rankles within.

It must be a self-willed evil to persecute a person whom God has taken under the protection of His grace; it becomes an irremediable sin to hate a man whom God wishes to make happy.

Envy is as prolific as it is hurtful; it is the root of all evil, the source of endless disorder and misery, the cause of most sins that are committed. Envy gives birth to hatred and animosity. From it, avarice is begotten, for it sees with an evil eye honors and emoluments heaped upon a stranger and thinks that such honors should have been, by right, bestowed upon himself. From envy, comes contempt of God and of the salutary precepts of our Savior.

The envious man is cruel, proud, unfaithful, impatient, and quarrelsome; and, what is strange, when this vice gains the mastery, he is no longer master of himself, and he is unable to correct his many faults.

If the bond of peace is broken, if the rights of fraternal charity are vio-lated, if truth is altered or disguised, it is often envy that hurries him on to crime.

What happiness can such a man enjoy in this world? To be envi-ous or jealous of another, because such a one is virtuous and happy, is to hate in him the graces and blessings that God has showered down upon him.

Does he not punish himself when he sees the success and welfare of others? Does he not draw down upon himself tortures, from which there is no respite? Are not his thoughts, his mind, constantly on the rack?

He pitilessly punishes himself, and, in his heart, performs the same cruel office that Divine Justice reserves for the chastisement of the great-est criminal.

—St. Cyprian (ca. 200–258), *De Zelo*

∞

O! envious man, you injure yourself more than he whom you would injure, and the sword with which you wound will recoil and wound you.

What harm did Cain do to Abel? Contrary to his intention, he did him the greatest good, for he caused him to pass to a better and a blessed life, and he himself was plunged into an abyss of woe. In what did Esau injure Jacob? Did not his envy prevent him from being enriched in the place in which he lived; and, losing the inheritance and the blessing of his father, did he not die a miserable death? What harm did the brothers of Joseph do to him? Their envy went so far as to wish to shed his blood. Were they not driven to the last extremity and well-nigh perishing with hunger, while their brother reigned all through Egypt?

It is ever thus: the more you envy your brother, the greater good you confer upon him. God, who sees all, takes the cause of the in-nocent in hand, and, irritated by the injury you inflict, deigns to raise him whom you wish to lower, and will punish you to the full extent of your crime.

Envy and Jealousy

If God usually punishes those who rejoice at the misfortunes of their enemies, how much more will He punish those who, excited by envy, seek to do an injury to those who have never injured them?

—St. John Chrysostom (ca. 349–407), Sermon 40

∞

Envy is a gnawing pain that springs from the success and prosperity of another; and this is the reason why the envious are never exempt from trouble and vexation. If an abundant harvest fills the granaries of a neighbor, if success crowns his efforts, the envious man is chagrined and sad. If one man can boast of prudence, talent, and eloquence; if another is rich, and is very liberal to the poor, if good works are praised by all around, the envious man is shocked and grieved.

The envious, however, dare not speak; although envy makes them counterfeit gladness, their hearts are sore within. If you ask him what vexes him, he dare not tell the reason. It is not really the happiness of his friend that annoys him; nor is it his gaiety that makes him sad, nor is he sorry to see his friend prosper; but it is that he is persuaded that the prosperity of others is the cause of his misery.

This is what the envious would be forced to acknowledge, if they spoke the truth sincerely. But because they dare not confess so shameful a sin, they, in secret, feed a sore that tortures them and eats away their rest.

As the shadow ever accompanies the pedestrian when walking in the sun, so envy throws its shadow on those who are successful in the world.

—St. Basil (ca. 329–379), De Invidia

∞

Flattery

It is better to be rebuked by a wise man, than
to be deceived with flattery of fools.

—Ecclesiastes 7:6

Sins that flatter us are always the most dangerous, because they please our self-love, and they favor the inclination and humor of sinners. It is on this account that there are few who distrust it, and fewer still who guard against it. It is somewhat difficult to look upon a vice as an enemy that so well knows how to flatter the disorderly passions and the corrupt inclinations of our nature.

St. Jerome says that flattery is always cunning and insidious; and indeed flattery is the most accommodating of vices. It is flattery that agreeably harmonizes with the feelings and inclinations of men, whether they are good or bad, just or unjust, solely to humor them, while the poison works within. It does the contrary of what the Apostle did; it is all to all, corrupting and seducing those who put their trust in it; and not only does it enter into the inclination of sinners, but it advises them ever to follow the disorderly motions of their pernicious passions and interests for their own gratification. It praises with affected applause the vicious and criminal actions of the rich and powerful.

But the malice of such pernicious complacencies goes still further, when it prefers to attack the good and just and censure their virtues, notwithstanding the curse that this draws down: "He that justifieth the wicked, and he that condemneth the just, both are abominable before God" (Prov. 17:15).

If you wish to know the evil effects of flattery, details could easily be given; but it may be said, in general terms, that through this detestable flattery, truth is betrayed, minds are seduced, the most upright hearts and intentions are corrupted. It inspires a contempt for virtue, and a relish for vice. It prevents sinners from being converted and confirms them in habitual sin; and, to complete their ultimate loss, says St. Augustine, it induces them to take a delight in bad actions, which they hear so praised.

Of all interested men, he who is the most selfish is the flatterer, because, although his praises cost nothing, still he does not give his applauses for nothing. It is of little consequence what profit he gains, as long as he can extract usurious interest therefrom. For if he approves of the vices of others, it is so that they should not condemn his own. It is indifferent to him if he flatters that which is good or that which is bad, as long as he sees a prospect of gaining something by it. If he employs his artifices to please the rich and noble, he does it with the hope of securing their favors or of obtaining their patronage. If he bestows his praises on all sorts of people, he does it with the idea of receiving something in return, or to obtain something he has in view. And thus it is that flatterers corrupt and seduce us.

To shield ourselves from one vice, we must take care not to fall into another, and for fear of being taken for a selfish flatterer, we must not in any way be cynical or churlish. Those saints who have respectfully praised one another were not flatterers. They have taught us that we should esteem, praise, and love virtue and virtuous persons, says St. Augustine.

The majority of good Catholics, being humble and timid, need to be encouraged to continue to be good, by a just meed of praise that their virtue deserves, and we should be convinced that there is no less injustice in refusing praises to those who deserve them than to flatter those whose wicked conduct has rendered them unworthy.

My Daily Visit with the Saints

This right medium consists chiefly in three things. The first is never to praise wicked and vicious persons, nor to approve of their bad conduct, but rather to keep silent. If pressed to give your opinion, declare frankly and without exaggeration in what such and such a deed may be approved of. The second is never to praise anyone except for things that really deserve praise, and to do this with all sincerity. The third is to be sparing of praise of good people, in their presence, but to honor and praise them highly when absent, when an opportunity occurs, and when we can do so without affectation.

Thus we should destroy flattery, and untruth, and we should, at the same time, perform acts of justice and charity.

—*Guerre Aux Vices*

∞

St. Basil remarks that vices and virtues are so alike in color that it is not always easy to discern the difference. Prodigality, for example, has somewhat an air of magnificence; rashness imitates, by its fits and starts, the generous impulses of valor; hypocrisy has some outward resemblance to the exterior signs of devotion. This it is that gives rise to the abuse of this resemblance, and by two classes of persons—namely, the envious and the flatterers. The flatterer takes vices for virtues, and the envious, on the contrary, takes virtues for vices. The flatterer, to shield the vices of the great, gives them the color of virtues, and the envious, to obscure the luster of virtues, gives them the color of vices. If you are prodigal, the flatterer will say that you are magnificent; if you are generous, the envious will say that you are a prodigal. If you are rash, the flatterer will say that you are brave; if you are really courageous, the envious will say that you are rash.

What does the flatterer mean by such false praises, but to aggrandize himself and build up his fortune? What do the envious mean, but to destroy that of others?

—St. Basil (ca. 329–379)

Flattery

∞

Nothing so corrupts the heart and mind as flattery, for the flatterer's tongue does more harm than the persecutor's sword. We are dragged downward by an evil that is inherent within us, we feel favorably toward those who flatter us, and although in our reply we show, or pretend to show, that we are unworthy of their praise, we nevertheless receive the flattering praise with a secret joy and pleasure.

—St. Jerome (ca. 347–420), Epistle 121

∾

Gambling

The people sat down to eat and drink, and then rose up to play.

—Exodus 32:6

It is undoubtedly true that all immoderate amusements are sins; and I am of the opinion that there is not one, from whatever way we look at it, from which you may not find many irregularities arising. Why? Well, we shall see. Pleasures and amusements are determined by the result.

In reference to work, when it is finished, they may be looked upon as relaxations; with regard to any heavy labor we may have to perform, then such recreations may be considered as preparations. They are then allowable, so far as they are necessary, either to refresh your mind, or to give you additional strength.

Such is the extent. All that extends beyond is against God's view of them, and consequently forbidden.

Now, who does not often see that the gaieties of the world are neither preceded by work, nor followed by hard labor? They are sought for, for the love of the amusements alone, with no other view than that of tasting their sweetness, or with the idea of leading an easy, agreeable life, thus employing their whole time immoderately, or without stint; consequently, it is this excess that makes it so culpable and, as it were, reverses the order of Providence.

I acknowledge that there are certain games that are innocent, provided that they are not carried to excess. Recreation is necessary for the mind as well as for the body; the one, to avoid too great a strain upon the brain; the other, to relieve constant fatigues.

But gambling, playing the whole day, and stealing away the hours of night when repose and sleep are needed, amusements that are the sole occupation when they ought to occupy the least portion of our time here on earth; in a word, gaieties that we notice in high life, all such as these, I condemn. And have I not a right to condemn them? In them, I do not find the intentions of God; they are not even the teachings of nature. I do not ask you if you live as Christians, but as men.

Amusements so paltry, so evanescent, were not made for the purpose of clouding the intellect of a reasonable man.

—Fr. Jaques Giroust (1624–1689), Advent sermon

∞

You love gambling. It is this that destroys the conscience, this inordinate love of play. It is a mania that is no longer an amusement, but a business, a profession, a traffic, without stint or measure; and, if I may dare to say so, it is a mania, a madness, that drags you down from one abyss to another deeper still. From this passion arise those innumerable sins of which they are the consequence. From that mania arise neglect of your duties, misrule of home, pernicious example you give to your children. From that proceed the squandering away of your property, those unworthy meannesses, and, if I may use the term, those trickeries that proceed from a greediness of gain. From this mania arise quarrels, oaths, swearing, and despair when all is lost. From that proceed those shameful resources that you fancy that you are forced to have recourse to. Lastly, from this proceeds that dishonesty to seek for any excuse to supply yourself with funds to carry on the sinful game.

One excess brings on another. Excess in the time employed in play is attended by excess in the sums played for. To play but seldom, yet when you do play, to hazard much, or to hazard a little but play continually, are two excesses, both of which are forbidden by the law of God. But over and above these two excesses, there is a third, which is to play often, and every time you play, to venture a large sum. Do not, however, mistake my meaning when I say play in which you hazard a large sum. I speak not only of the great and the rich, but of all in general, and each in particular, conformably to their means and station in life. What is nothing for one is much for another. One may easily bear what would hurt another; and what for the former would be a small loss might have fatal consequences for the latter.

Nevertheless, men will play; and it is a rule of life, a rule to which they unalterably adhere; so that no consideration can draw them from it. Cost what it will, they will go on; and for what purpose?

O my brethren, cut off this love of play. It is far easier to give it up entirely than to try to retrench it or leave it off by degrees. Quit it once for all, and make a public avowal of it.

—Fr. Louis Bourdaloue (1632–1704)

∞

Hardness of Heart

With desolation is all the land made desolate; be-cause there is none that considereth in the heart.

—Jeremiah 12:11

St. Augustine compares the blindness of a soul to a man who is asleep. When our eyes are shut during sleep, we are blind; nevertheless, we see something, for although our eyes are shut, our imagination is at work. We dream that we are very rich; we fancy that we are living in the lap of luxury. In a word, we picture to our mind strange events. This is our case. We do not see things in the right light; we do not hear the mute language that ought to lead us up to God. No! Our imagination conjures up fantastic phantoms.

We thought to have found true happiness in the wealth and riches of this world, and they have vanished. We sought for earthly joys, and these pleasures have become insipid.

When our soul is preparing to leave the body, then our eyes will be opened, and we shall then feel and know our terrible darkness.

—Bishop Jules Mascaron (1634–1705)

∞

St. Augustine remarks that we are all born blind, because we are all born in sin. We are all born blind, and the dimness of our sight is the universal scar that original sin has imprinted on every heart, stifling the light of heaven in its birth, and surrounding the aurora of life in the darkness of death.

Sin, which we inherit from our birth, leads us into an obscure night, deprives us of the sight of the Sovereign Good, and fills us with errors and illusions. This blindness is so much the more to be deplored, because it grows with our growth, and being an original curse, it becomes free and voluntary in its growth; so much so, that our malice makes a personal crime out of a hereditary punishment, and thus, it corrupts every stream that flows from so poisonous a source.

It is the characteristic of sin to overshadow every action, whether it be the banishment of grace, which is the light of the soul, or whether it blinds the understanding, thus rendering it incapable of receiving the light of the Holy Spirit, who abandons the sinner, and leaves him exposed to all kinds of dangers and misfortunes.

O! unhappy darkness, exclaims St. Augustine, in which I have lived. O! frightful blindness, which has hindered me from enjoying the light of heaven. O! deplorable ignorance, which has hidden the beauty and infinite goodness of God. O! beauty ever ancient, beauty ever new, more brilliant than the light of the sun, would that I had known and loved you sooner! Ah! why cannot I hide the many days and years in which I lived? O! that I could blot them out with my tears!

—Fr. Nouet, S.J. (1605–1680), *Meditations*

∞

Hardness of heart leads to sad results. Light blinds or dazzles a hardened heart; it does not enlighten it. The just punishments of God, which weigh heavily on it, only make it rebellious, and do not subdue it. The scourge that God inflicts on it overwhelms but does not humble it; miracles astonish but do not convert it.

Would you wish to know the sure marks of hardness of heart? St. Bernard will give them to us. A hardened heart, he says, is a heart unbroken by remorse, unsoftened by devotion, and unmoved by prayer. It yields to no threats, which only harden it the more; it is unmindful of all the blessings of God, and unfaithful to grace. It blushes not at things most shameful, heeds no danger, has no love for brethren, no fear of God.

It forgets the past, neglects the present, and cares not for the future. It forgets its duty, and finally forgets itself. There is the picture of a hardened heart.

How frightful! How terrible!

Is it your heart? If you have not all the marks, do you not, on examination, recognize some few like unto them?

—Fr. Nepoue, *Reflections*

Hypocrisy

The hope of the hypocrite shall perish: his folly shall not
please him, and his trust shall be like the spider's web.

—Job 8:13–14

The Pharisees were, as the Gospel represents, of a mortified exterior and piqued themselves on a strict observance of the laws; and relying on that, they were filled with a self-satisfied opinion of their own merit.

On this principle, they looked upon themselves as perfect and irreproachable. They took pains to keep themselves aloof from others and believed themselves to be better than their brethren.

In their ordinary devotions, they fasted only to show that they had fasted, and disfigured their features so as to attract the notice of the unsuspecting multitude.

Under the pretext of practicing austerity, they assumed a studied appearance of a well-governed life.

Thus, without any other title than a sanctimonious regularity, they thought that they were entitled to occupy the foremost places in all festivals and assemblies. These are the marks of a false devotion and hypocrisy; and to these our Savior alluded.

There are some who are willing to practice Christian virtue, but at the same time, they wish to gain the credit. Some who do not like to be unnoticed, but wish to make a show, and to be different from others, affect humility and do not associate with all.

Whence comes it, that singularity is so sought after? Because it is that which excites admiration, which is the charm of vanity.

If there is anything out of the way, it is there that they seek for it. And even in their penances they wish to attract notice, unlike St. Augustine, who, when he was meditating his conversion, wished to keep it secret, lest the world might think that his former wickedness was only a pretense to show off his present virtue.

A parade of regularity and mortification induces them to usurp a certain kind of superiority that neither God nor man gives them. For after that, they set themselves up as censors of all the world, and they, like the Pharisees, consider themselves worthy of the highest places in the Church and state. They unscrupulously meddle with everything; and, what is more dangerous, under the pretense of piety, they are not aware of their own failings, and so degenerate into an ambition more criminal than that with which the Son of God reproached the Pharisees.

—Fr. Louis Bourdaloue (1632–1704)

∞

If you wish to know the difference between a hypocrite and a just man, between showy and solid piety, between human motives and Christian motives—here are some marks.

Human virtue seeks for witnesses who praise, and its wish is to appear to be, rather than to be. True piety loves to be hidden, contented with being seen by God, and with the witness of its own conscience. Worldly goodness is full of presumption; there is no accident that it thinks cannot be repaired, no obstacle that cannot be overcome. True virtue is ever mistrustful of self; it is never rash and is always anxious to avoid occasions of sin, or to fly from the presence of objects that may have been the cause of former falls.

Human virtue is proud, overbearing, and contemptuous; it knows not what it is to yield, to be humble, or to obey; it looks down disdainfully on those who have no merit; it examines with a critical malignant eye those who are reputed to be good, and turning to itself, it is flattered at possessing something out of the ordinary way. True piety is humble and submissive, glad to be surpassed by others; and if there be any rigor to exercise, it is against itself; and if there be any indulgence, or consideration to bestow, it is given to others.

Human goodness is interested; self-interest is the main motive of all its actions, so that if there is no fortune to gain, no glory to establish, no reputation to preserve, such goodness remains inactive, so long as self is not disturbed. True virtue makes a man thoroughly disinterested in his reputation, in his worldly goods, in the contempt that others display, in the praises that are showered down upon him.

Finally, human virtue is fostered by pride, is constant through obstinacy, liberal through vanity, honest through interest, affable and mild through policy, and even humble through a refinement of self-love.

All these false and imposing pretensions to virtue, not having God in view, are like those empty titles that nobles, who having sold their lands, still preserve their title and coats of arms.

Those people whom the world believed to be so generous, so faithful, so affable, so patient, so honest, so sincere are like handsome mausoleums, on the outside of which are depicted representations of every virtue, and inside you find a frightful corruption.

—*Dictionnaire Moral*

∞

Idleness and Sloth

Why stand you here all the day idle?
—Matthew 20:6

There is, says Holy Writ, a great occupation, imposed not on anyone in particular, but on everyone, and a heavy yoke that all the children of Adam are compelled to bear. But where are these children? Is there no exception to this universal law? "From him that sitteth on a throne of glory, unto him that is humbled in earth and ashes" (Sir. 40:3). The children of Adam include everybody, from royalty to the meanest beggar, "from him that weareth purple and beareth the crown, even to him that is covered with rough linen" (Sir. 40:4). This sentence excludes no one; princes and grandees of the world are included with miserable wretches and with slaves.

In fact, my dear brother, whoever you may be, I ask you what dispenses you from work? Is it because you are high in the world, as if your grandeur could wipe out the stain of your origin, or exempt you from that universal curse that God has pronounced on the whole human race—namely, to eat your bread with the sweat of your brow?

But tell me—that high rank, that noble birth, that distinguished position that you make so much of: Are they higher than kings and sovereign pontiffs?

Listen to the words of St. Bernard when he wrote to Pope Eugenius: "I beseech you, with all the respect I owe to your Holiness, not to consider that you are raised above all the world, but take care that you are born to work, aye, even more than others; and if you wish to be exempt, you must first of all wipe out the stain of original sin, which the luster of your purple and your tiara can never hide."

Consider, then, that a man who is born a slave, clothed in the livery of sin, must think only of work, and endure great fatigue, in order that he may better his condition in this world.

There is no condition of life among men where idleness may not become a sin, and the higher the position, idleness and sloth are the guiltier. For instance, a young man of high connection who remains idle in youth, without a wish to cultivate his mind by learning and to acquire such a knowledge requisite to prepare him for a post; when, through influence, he may be appointed to a responsible position, how will he acquit himself? God will not give him an infused science, for that would be a miracle. What will he do then? Why, he will be ignorant of the duties of his profession; and if, for example, he becomes to be a judge, he will judge badly.

Even if he has the good intention of administering justice, he cannot do so, from the want of legal knowledge, and he will be responsible for all the losses and injury that parties may have suffered. In addition to this, it is not just and right that he should learn experience at the expense of others; and however good his intention may be, a poor man may perchance lose a lawsuit that will deprive him of all his property. On this I cannot say too much, for if he be judge, he has another kind of idleness to battle with: he will not take the trouble to examine into matters, for he loves his pleasures more than the careful examination of right and wrong.

I would never finish, if I were to run through every condition of life. I could say that through idleness and sloth it has happened that preachers and directors of souls have acquitted themselves so badly that their sloth has produced frightful disorders in the functions of their ministry.

I could also say much on the negligence of mothers, a negligence that is the cause of the confusion we often notice in households; for when the mistress of the house is fond of frequenting theaters and balls, what are the servants doing, and what will become of the children?

Instead of that, if she attended to her home duties, all would go well; her servants would do their duty, her children would be instructed and would not be brought up, as they often unfortunately are, in idleness and sloth.

—Fr. Louis Bourdaloue (1632–1704), Lenten sermon

∝⊗

Ignorance

For some have not the knowledge of God:
I speak it to your shame.

—1 Corinthians 15:34

If one could not sin through ignorance, it would be wrong, says St. Bernard, to blame the persecutors of the Apostles and the martyrs, since those persecutors did not believe that they committed wrong by so cruelly putting them to death; on the contrary, they considered that they rendered a great service to their gods by massacring their enemies.

It would also have been of little use that Jesus, hanging on the Cross, should have prayed for His murderers, since, not knowing what they did, they were free from sin, and even, according to St. Paul, had they known the King of Glory, they would not have nailed Him to the Cross.

See, then, concludes this Father, into what a profound ignorance those were plunged who believed that they could sin through ignorance. From this, we must always understand that a voluntary culpable ignorance arises from a wanton negligence of being instructed.

According to the teaching of St. Thomas, we have two rules for our conduct and actions—namely, the law of God and our own conscience.

Now, it is not enough, in order to constitute a good action, that it should be conformable to one of these rules; it suffices to render it bad if it is opposed to one of these two rules. Thus, one is not exempt from sin, continues this saintly Doctor, when it violates any precept of the law, even if it follows the judgment of a false conscience.

And in this same sense St. Augustine says that people take for good that which is in itself bad, and that to persevere in this erroneous belief, they are not free from sin, since this false persuasion is in itself a sin. And if you wish to know why this error and ignorance is a sin, because one has not been willing, or has neglected to know the law; for if one is in invincible ignorance, then that ignorance and that error, being involuntary, would no longer be sin.

One cannot excuse from sin those heretics who live among Catholics, although they doubt not the truth of their own religion, and although they think that they are in the right path, because they have every means of clearing up their doubts, and opportunities are not wanting to disabuse them, if they really wished to be instructed in the Faith. But holding to an obstinacy joined to prejudice, convenience, and advantages that they find in the state of life in which they have been reared, or which they may have embraced through debauchery, or through error, they persist in their culpable ignorance.

Thus, when such as these, in their fancied security, blaspheme against the true religion that they look upon as false; when they cry it down; when they pettily persecute the defenders of it, or revile them by cruel calumny, and inflict on them outrage and insult, they are not exempt from sin, although they may have, through ignorance, been driven to excess, and by this means called to their aid a false zeal that is so opposed to the law of God. This ignorance will never excuse them of all these crimes, since it is an inexcusable sin to be a heretic and not to take every means in their power to undeceive themselves.

We must, however, remark, that the care required by some who plead ignorance as an excuse does not apply to others, who need a more search-ing inquiry into the truth. If it depended only on some trivial point, such as if a certain day was a feast day or a fast day, a competent authority can be applied to; and if there be some mistake, it can be easily or readily explained. But when it refers to a matter of equity, such as if a contract is usurious or not; or if it be permitted to expose to public view engravings or pictures of scandalous nudities, then we ought not to be content with consulting anyone who may be of our own opinion.

When one has on hand an important lawsuit, does he not apply to the ablest lawyer? Or when we are seized with a dangerous illness, do we not seek the advice of the most experienced and cleverest physician?

Can anyone, then, look upon the laws of God, and the precepts of the Church, as simply an invincible ignorance, when they can be so easily explained, by simply taking the same pains they employ in temporal affairs?

To act otherwise, is simply to show a manifest indifference for their eternal salvation.

—Fr. Pierre de la Font (d. ca. 1700),
Sixth Sunday after Pentecost

∞

Immodest Attire

The attire of the body, and the laughter of the teeth,
and the gait of the woman, show what she is.

—See Sirach 19:27

From whom do those women attract notice — women who are of the world most worldly — women whose vanity leads them to employ every artifice to attract remark and win esteem? Is it from the good and pious? Oh no! for they look upon them with horror, seeing that they dishonor Jesus Christ and ruin His religion. Is it from clever people? No, for they regard them with indignation, seeing that by their vain display they are eager to astonish, and take them by surprise. Is it from rakes and libertines they seek esteem? From these, doubtless, they would rather fly than seek. Oh, if they only knew how they speak of them, how coarsely they criticize them, their confusion would be equal to their pride.

You show yourselves in public, you worldlings, with all that furniture of vanity. You do not even spare the temple of the living God, whose sanctity should not be violated by your luxuries, for the church was not built for the display of all such vanities. We should appear therein richly clothed with grace and virtue, not decked out with gold and jewels. Nevertheless, you attend church dressed out as if you were going to a ball, or like actresses on the stage, so careful are you to be noticed, or rather to be laughed at, by those who see you.

My Daily Visit with the Saints

When the divine service is over, and all are returning homeward, your vanities and follies are the theme of their conversation; they forget the important instructions left us by St. Paul and the prophets and can talk only of the value of your beautiful dresses and of the luster of your jewelry.

Tell us, I entreat, what are the useful advantages to be drawn from these precious stones and from these costly dresses? You tell me that you are satisfied with yourself and that you take delight in that magnificence. But alas! I ask what benefit you derive from your vanities, and they tell me of only the harm they do.

There is nothing more deplorable than to be ever running after frivolous fashions, to take a pleasure in studying them. Shameful and shocking must that slavery be when its golden chains are enjoyed.

How can a Christian female apply herself as she ought, to any exercise of devotion or solid piety? How can she despise the follies of the age if she encourages a taste for finery? In time she will experience so great a distaste for prayer that she will not like to hear it named.

You will perhaps reply that you have made yourself admired by all who saw you. But this is an additional misfortune, that these costly trinkets should have gone so far as to feed your growing vanity and pride!

Is it not an evil most grievous to be overwhelmed with cares so vain and restless, to neglect the beauty of the soul and the love of one's salvation; to fill oneself with pride, vanity, and conceit; to be, as it were, intoxicated with the love of the world; willingly to give up going to those sacred places where your thoughts should be raised to God; to have no fear of prostituting the dignity of your soul, and subject that soul to things so base and so unworthy?

You will perchance reply that when you frequent assemblies and promenades, everyone turns around to look at you. It is for that very reason that you should shrink from gaudy attire, in order that you should not expose yourself to the gaze of every man, that you should not give anyone an opportunity for making scandalous remarks.

Not one of those who gaze upon you will hold you in the esteem you imagine you have secured. You will be the laughingstock of everyone, and people will set you down as a vain ambitious woman, as one who wishes to be admired, as one absorbed in the love and vanities of the world.

—St. John Chrysostom (ca. 349–407)

∞

Do you not tremble, ye gay and worldly women, at the thought that, when our Lord and Savior shall come to judge the living and the dead, He will bid you leave His presence forevermore, and that He will thus reproach you?

"Depart from me, you are not my work, and I cannot trace the least resemblance to your former self. The paint, powder, false curls, and other vain appliances have so altered and disguised you, that I cannot recognize that you once belonged to me. You will not be able to see me, disguised as you are by face, eyes, and features, so utterly spoiled and disguised by my enemy the devil. You have followed him; you have selected the brilliant hues of the serpent's skin; it is from your enemy you have learned and kept those embellishments and fineries; you will be with him forever and forever. My kingdom is not for such as you, and no part of it can you ever share with me."

—St. Cyprian (ca. 200–258), *De Habitu Virginum*

∞

Impurity

*When concupiscence hath conceived, it bringeth forth
sin: when it is completed, it begetteth death.*

—James 1:15

You will sometimes meet with old men whose gravity and age give them
an appearance of severity, who are modest in society, and who are much
esteemed for their apparent goodness, but who secretly and heartily indulge
in every sort of vice, which they carefully conceal from human eyes. In their
imagination, they picture objects that they delight in; the idea flatters them
and leads them to indulge in indelicate pleasures, unseen and unnoticed.

These sins are committed in the heart and will there remain hidden
until the coming of our Lord, who will bring to light every dark mystery
and will expose to the whole world the secrets of the heart.

We must, then, particularly watch over our thoughts, for deeds that
spring from our free will require time, assistance, and opportunity, but the
workings of the brain are active in a moment, without trouble, without
hindrance, without waiting for opportunity.

—St. Basil (ca. 329–379)

∞

Not only is this passion a sin, but it is the epitome of every sin; it includes
sins of the eye, sins of word, sins of thought, sins of desire.

Impurity

As for sins of deed, who would dare to paint them? I have no wish to place so foul a sight before you. Property, riches, talent, and heart will be, and on every possible opportunity are, all employed in its service.

Desires are fondly cherished, when deeds cannot satisfy.

A lascivious man is a man of sin, because he disseminates sin wheresoever he may be; in every place, in public, in private, in intrigues, and so forth.

The evils that impurity causes to those who indulge in this vice are numberless; it spares nothing; it undermines the health, and youth is soon succeeded by a peevish, dissolute, premature old age.

There is no trouble they will not undertake, no constitution they will not sacrifice, no amount of money they will not squander away. Have they ruined their prospects in life? To indulge in luxury and continue to satisfy their lustful desires, they will seek to find means at any price.

This vice is not content with being the cause of ruin of families, but it haunts them in their dreams.

From this arise jealousies, divorces, and sad estrangements. From this succeed assassination, murder, poison, conspiracy, and all felonious plots, to supplant a dangerous rival, or get rid of a jealous accomplice.

Meditate for a while on the scourges and punishments that God has inflicted on this sin. Holy Scripture is content to threaten other vices, but see how it inveighs against and casts a thunderbolt on this.

The Deluge, was it not a punishment? The burning of a whole city, was it not the result of a just vengeance?

If this sin was the reason why God repented of having created man, and made Him resolve to annihilate him, how can you look upon it as a pardonable sin?

The waters spread over the surface of the earth, flames consume Sodom — do not these teach you that God is the defender of purity, the avenger of incontinence?

Is it that such sins should have become less enormous, that God the Son deigned to be born of the Virgin Mary? Ah! place before you the thought of St. Augustine.

"What! shall I purchase torments without end, for a vain and transient pleasure? Pleasures will pass away, but eternity will never pass away; pleasures vanish, but the penalty remains."

—Fr. Vincent Houdry, S.J. (1630–1729)

∞

God, speaking to Noah, told him that His spirit would not dwell in man, because he was only flesh. Nevertheless, I hear that the unchaste allege this as a reason for making this sin excusable—human weakness, which is only flesh; but I say that, for this reason, immodesty and impurity will be punished by God.

It is for that that all should be more cautious and be not without fear. It is for that that one ought to seek for the help of that grace that God has promised to all. It is for that that man, being so weak and frail, should ever have recourse to prayer, to occasional retreats, and to fly from all occasions of sin. It is for that that you should not rashly expose yourself to temptation, or be found frequenting dangerous places, where there are immodest eyes upon you. And this for fear of losing the grace of the Holy Spirit, who departs from the impure.

—Fr. Charles de la Rue (1643–1725)

∞

Ingratitude

Were not ten made clean? and where are the nine?
There is no one found to return and give
glory to God, but this stranger.

—Luke 17:17–18

It would be a monstrous ingratitude to receive daily many blessings of the Divine Goodness and not to acknowledge your gratitude, if not in deeds, at any rate, in words and canticles.

Besides that, if this gratitude is due to Him, it is no less advantageous to ourselves. God has no need of us, but we have every need of Him.

The thanksgiving we offer to Him adds nothing to what He is, but it helps us to love Him more and to repose a greater confidence in Him.

For if the remembrance of benefits we have received from men induces us to love them more, there can be no doubt that, meditating on the graces that Almighty God has showered upon us, we should naturally feel more desire to love Him, more prompt to obey Him.

—St. John Chrysostom (ca. 349–407)

∞

We ought to imitate the liberality of the soil, which repays with usurious interest the smallest seed that is sown therein. Holy Scripture compares an ungrateful person to a field or vine that remains barren if not carefully cultivated; on the other hand, a grateful man is like a fruitful field that increases in value a hundredfold.

It is thus that we must act toward those from whom we have received benefits, and not be like the ungrateful and avaricious land, which retains the seed. It is not everyone who has the power of doing good, but we can always show our gratitude, for ingratitude is an unpardonable vice.

—St. Ambrose (340–397)

∞

St. Bernard, pondering on the many graces that God had bestowed upon him, and of His immense love for us all, cries out: "O Lord, I have nothing to give you in return for so many blessings I have received from Your merciful goodness. When I look upon my own nothingness, I am so confused that I dare not raise my eyes, but when I consider that You are rich in Yourself, that You have no need of me, and that You seek for my heart and not my riches: ah! I am quite consoled. When I see in the Gospel that a poor woman who drops two little pieces of money in the poor box receives from Your lips more praises than do those rich Pharisees who place therein large sums, I begin to hope.

"I have only two small pieces, and these are my heart and my body. You are the Master of the latter; take Thou possession of the former. I give it to You; it is Yours on the principle of justice, love, and gratitude."

A faithful and truly grateful soul ought to imitate the conduct of that prince mentioned in the book of Esther, where it is said that he wrote down, and kept an account of all the services his brave followers had done for him during his reign, in order that, by reading them often, he was forced to acknowledge them.

This is what a faithful soul should do, in order to remind Him of the many graces and favors God has bestowed upon him, during the whole course of his life. Ah! what would such a soul do? Would it not read over the list with care, and ponder on it every day?

Ingratitude

See, here is the time when, by an especial grace, I was called to fulfill duties in the Church or in the world. Here are so many favors received; here so many holy inspirations; here, so many good works; here, so many averted dangers; in a word, here are so many benefits received. Think of them, O my soul, and never forget them, and say with the prophet: "I will bless my God for ever and ever, and I will never cease to sing His praise" (see Ps. 144). The last thought, when I retire to rest, will be to thank God, and the first prayer on awaking shall be to bless Him.

If we closely examine the conduct of the greater portion of sinners, we would be easily convinced that there are gifts and blessings of God that are made use of for the purpose of adding to their sins. If God has given extra beauty to that woman, to what use does she devote it? Alas! to idolize her body and to draw around her a crowd of admirers. If God has given health and strength to that man, of what use are they to him? For he destroys them both with debauchery and vice. If to another has been given the gift of knowledge and science, does he not use them to disseminate his erroneous opinions, or to impugn the dogmas of our holy mother the Church? If to another, fortune and riches, are not these squandered away in pleasure or ambition?

And thus it is with other gifts, which are all received from heaven.

—Fr. Louis Bourdaloue (1632–1704)

∞

Intemperance

Woe to you that rise up early in the morning
to follow drunkenness, and to drink till the
evening, to be inflamed with wine.

—Isaiah 5:11

A reasonable man eats in order to give strength to his body, lest its weak-ness might have an effect on his mind; but those who are addicted to intemperance eat even to clouding their intellect and ruining their body. They eat merely for the sake of eating. There are some people whose body is of no use to the intellect (unlike the saints, who complained of having a body, which occasioned so much trouble to the mind); such as these would like to be deprived of the qualms of conscience, in order to partake of the pleasures of beasts, pleasures they constantly seek and sigh for.

They do not eat to live, since nothing is so pernicious to health as excess in delicacies and made dishes, and nothing is so conducive to a healthy and long life as a frugal and well-regulated table.

Is it that we are slaves of our body, and that everything ought to be sacrificed to gratify that insatiable animal? One ought to take food as one would take remedies. Necessity ought to rule our inclination, so as to free us from the inconvenience of hunger, and not that concupiscence that lays a snare in the pleasure that follows, that solace that we seek for in eating and drinking.

Thus we do, for this single pleasure, what we ought to do through necessity; from this follows that we seek to deceive ourselves, persuading ourselves that we owe to our health what we give to the passion of intemperance.

—St. Claude de la Colombière (1641–1682), *Christian Reflections*

∞

All the Doctors of the Church tell us that the state of intoxication that deprives us of grace and reason at the same time is a mortal sin.

It is this that St. Augustine calls a great sin, a monster of crime; in fact, it is a brutal stupidity and a wanton blindness to sell (like another Esau) one's right to the inheritance of heaven, the hope of an eternal happiness, for the sake of some glasses of wine; rivaling that madman who sold his claim to the paternal estate for a few lentils, to satisfy his inordinate appetite.

But St. Paul expressly names it and places the vice of drunkenness on the list of those sins that are excluded from heaven. Do not be deceived, says he; do not flatter yourself that it is a venial sin: "Drunkards shall not possess the kingdom of heaven" (see 1 Cor. 6:10). In a former chapter he says that this kingdom and happiness that are destined for us are not intended for those who eat and drink. Those, therefore, who pamper their appetites, those who are slaves of intemperance, have no claim or right.

Drunkenness is the source of an infinite number of sins, but among those that are its boon companions the most universal is that of impurity. Take heed and avoid drinking to excess, says the Apostle (Eph. 5:18), because it infallibly enkindles the shocking vice of impurity. Again, it is St. Jerome who says that he who is always full of wine is easily led to the commission of shameful brutalities, and he confirms this truth by quoting the example of Lot. What more astounding than to see a man who was preserved in innocence in the center of the city of Sodom; he drinks a little too much wine and commits a frightful incest.

A man addicted to wine, says St. Chrysostom, is fit for nothing, for of what use is such a man? Would he be able to keep a secret? Two or three glasses of wine would make him so talkative that he would reveal everything. How could you confide an affair of importance to him? No! says the saint, such a man is useless; he is fit for nothing; he is a fool; he must be left to himself; he does not deserve a thought. This same Father represents the ugliness and infamy of this vice in such animated language that it strikes one with horror. How shameful is intoxication, he exclaims; can anyone imagine a man more despicable than he who is habitually tipsy? He lowers himself in the eyes of his servants; it makes him a laughingstock to his enemies, and even his friends put him down as a fool. All look upon him as an object deserving of the contempt and hatred of all.

If there be any here who are addicted to this vice, hear the words that the prophet Joel addresses to you on the part of God: "Awake, ye that are drunk, and weep and mourn, all ye that take delight in drinking sweet wine" (Joel 1:5). Arise from your negligence, at the sound of the threats of the anger of God; weep and send up your sighs to heaven, in order to avert His justice, which is ready to deliver the world from a useless burden and a scandal to all men.

Instead of drowning your intellect in wine, apply it to more serious work; avoid the impending misery, and henceforth lead a life worthier of a man and a Christian. Give up a habit that renders you unfit to associate with men. Detest a vice that is as odious as it is wicked; fly from the society of those who encourage and join you in those unworthy debaucheries, dissipations that will easily lead to the loss of honor, health, the life of your body, the loss of your soul, and eventually drag you to the gates of eternal perdition.

"Woe to you that rise early in the morning to follow drunkenness, and to drink till the evening, to be inflamed with wine," says the prophet Isaiah; and St. Paul says that such people have no other god but their belly, which is as much as to say that they are idolaters, for they make a god of their own body for no other purpose than that of satisfying an inordinate appetite, and thus idolizing their stomach (Phil. 3:19).

Intemperance

The misfortune of this kind of men is such that the Apostle with tears in his eyes can only deplore their blindness and look upon their misery as meriting God's vengeance.

—Fr. Vincent Houdry, S.J. (1630–1729)

∞

Excess in eating and drinking has killed many a man; frugality has killed no one. Immoderate use of wine has injured many a constitution; temperance has never done any harm. Many have died in the midst of banquets, and have soiled the very tables with their heated blood.

You invite your friends to a feast, and you lead them to death; you ask them to a merrymaking, and you conduct them to a tomb; you promise them the greatest delicacies, and you condemn them to the most exquisite tortures; you fill them with wines, and lo, it is their poison.

—St. Ambrose (340–397), *De Jejunia*

∞

Lying and Trickery

God hateth a deceitful witness that uttereth lies.

—Proverbs 6:16, 19

We have in the New Testament several examples of duplicity and trickery.

We see the dissimulation and pretended concern Herod the Ascalonite displayed to the Three Kings, when he asked them to return to Jerusalem and tell him where the Messiah was born, so that he might go and adore the newborn King. As he fully intended to murder the Infant Jesus, this lying deceiver will cause the name of Herod to be held in horror for all ages.

The second Herod, called the Tetrarch, was the successor of the first and was the governor when Jesus was sent to be tried. He was a man full of deceit, and our Lord gave him the name of the fox, to work his cunning and duplicity; and far from wishing to perform miracles before him, our Savior did not deign to answer him a word.

The most evident punishment that God has ever exercised on those who fail in sincerity, and use a lying deceit, was that of Ananias and Sapphira, related in the fifth chapter of the Acts of the Apostles. They sold their piece of land, and, by fraud, kept back part of the price of the land, contrary to the promise they had made to bring the whole. Their bad faith cost them their lives. They were masters of the money that they could have kept without injustice; but because they told untruths, and agreed together to tempt the Spirit of the Lord, they were punished for their deceit.

—Fr. Vincent Houdry, S.J. (1630–1729)

∞

One of the strongest reasons that can be urged against lying is the infamous consequences that accrue from such a habit.

A lie covers its author with confusion, and a man who has acquired the habit of telling falsehoods becomes in fact the universal horror of all who know him. Because a lie usually precedes many other vices, it makes use of candor and truth only through motives of avarice, pride, jealousy, impurity, impiety, or some other sin; consequently, these can only proceed from a mass of corruption.

These are the reasons why we have so bad an opinion of liars, and this is why the Holy Scripture describes the liar as a foul blot and an everlasting shame.

Now, you who cannot endure to be charged with practicing this vice; you who would expose your life and salvation, and would be impelled to wipe out the implied reproach with your blood if the law did not put a stop to your blind fury; you who blush and are ashamed that men should know what you cannot endure to be charged with; listen to and reflect on the threats and judgments of the God of truth, for He has so great a horror of lying and deceit that He has said that all who speak falsehood shall be lost.

It would take up too much space to give all the reasons that would induce us to give up lying and deceit. It is sufficient to know that the lie increases other greater sins, that it lessens the simplicity of virtue, and it scandalizes truth. Avarice is rendered more criminal when, in order to secure or purchase another person's property, it makes use of a false oath; pride is more sinful when it circulates false reports in order to gain the approbation of some, or to avoid some affront. Hatred is rendered more intense when it forges imaginary crimes in order to deprive the innocent of their honor. Heresy is more detestable when it designedly misinterprets the sense and meaning of Holy Scripture, the Fathers, and the precepts of the Church. Virtue loses its simplicity when deceit is introduced. Humility is not entirely innocent if it induces a man to lie in order to hide his perfection. Mercy becomes sinful if it excites a man to make use of a falsehood for the purpose of giving relief to the poor, or with the intention of checking the vices of his neighbor. Justice partakes of injustice when by use of an untruth, it ascertains the truth of an important fact.

Other virtues cannot possibly preserve their purity, however good the intention may be, if a lie or a deceit be made use of.

—Fr. Heliodore of Paris

∞

When the tongue says one thing, and the heart means another, this is deceit, and a lie.

If through humility you circulate a lie, if you had not committed a sin of lying before, you become, by lying, what you were not before, a sinner.

The sin of lying is not solely committed by word of mouth, but by deeds designedly carried out for the purpose of deceiving. It is a lie to call yourself a Christian when you do not practice the works of Jesus Christ.

—St. Augustine (354–430), *Enchiridon*

∞

The Prosperity of the Wicked

Why then do the wicked live? Are they
advanced and strengthened with riches?
Their houses are secure and peaceable,
and the rod of God is not upon them.

—Job 21:7–9

The continued prosperity of sinners is the greatest of all misfortunes for them. The less our Lord disturbs their torpor, the more He punishes them afterward. It is at that time that vicious habits increase in power day by day; it is then that they indulge themselves the more, that they delude themselves, that they are blinded more and more, to the important interests of their salvation.

But the mad multitude do not reason thus. According to the idea of the majority, the world is pleased when the greater part of common people are like princes through good fortune, although they would be poor, and the very reverse of pious; when theaters are thriving, although religion may be despised; when luxury attracts the notice of all, although Christian charity would be neglected; when the dissolute well-nigh exhaust the well-filled purse to satisfy their excessive wants, although the poor can find none to relieve their extremest need.

Nevertheless, if God permits these disorders to reign in the world, be sure that at that time, He is the more irritated against us. His most terrible vengeance is to leave for a while crimes unpunished.

If, on the contrary, He deprives us of every kind of luxurious pleasure, of good living, of theaters and other amusements, of the extravagance of the age, it is then He manifests to us His mercy.

—St. Augustine (354–430), Fifth Letter to Marcellinus

∞

Opportunities and all exterior things contribute to withdraw the prosperous man from the way of salvation, and these are for him so many obstacles, too difficult for a soul accustomed to effeminacy to surmount. Everything concurs to feed and cherish vices in his heart, more especially the most dangerous passions, and a crowd of objects fascinates his every sense.

Those miserable parasites of the fortune of a great man make a study of his weaknesses and neglect nothing that can give him pleasure; theaters, games, acquaintances, flatteries, intrigues cleverly begun, and as cleverly carried out—nothing is forgotten; each one seeks to take him by surprise, and each one glories when that success is gained.

These flatterers who gather round about him studiously contrive to bring fresh incentives to feed his passions. Thus everything concurs to make even the contented forget that there is a holy and a happy land that they ought to aspire to reach.

It is here, O Lord, that I adore Thy secret judgments; for, seeing on earth the good in trouble, and the wicked laden with the blessings of prosperity, the one in misery, the other in plenty, the one in poverty, the other in prosperity, it cannot be wondered at that I should be surprised at a sight that appears to be so contrary to Thy wise and just providence. When I see the splendidly garnished table of the proud rich man, while a poor Lazarus begs for the crumbs that fall from his table, and is even cruelly refused; when I see so many unworthy wretches superabundantly supplied with all that contributes to ease and comfort, while so many good and honest people are in want of even the necessaries of life, I confess to Thee, says the prophet, that my feet shake under me, and I am

The Prosperity of the Wicked

tempted to question Divine Providence for showing too much indulgence to the wicked, and too much harshness to the good, or that I should go so far as to accuse Thee of injustice.

For why, I say to myself, should that man who is only nominally a Christian, and a heathen in his manners and actions—why does he enjoy an easy life, a peace here on earth, while the faithful and pious man groans and sighs under the weight of his miseries? Why should everything smile on the rich unjust? The princely treasures are open only for him; every luxury shines for him; the hail and storm do not injure his lands; the earth, the sky, the elements, seem to contribute to the joy and pleasure of the sinner; while the good poor man dwells here on earth, helpless and unassisted. And while the former is well-nigh satiated with the best of everything, the good man sees himself alone and abandoned by all, despised by the world, and deprived of help.

Do not fall into the fatal error of believing that worldly prosperity may be a favor that God grants to His favored ones. God often, in His anger, gives riches and honors that are prayed for, and He grants them by punishing, says St. Augustine. He would have destined you to live a retired life in humility and lowliness, in order to lead you, by those means, to the height of glory. But you have obstinately rejected His merciful intentions; you have mapped out your own way of life, and, intoxicated with success, you have tried to subject His will to your own; you have made your own choice; He grants what you ask for, and He hears you in His anger. Riches, honors, dignities, fortune, grandeur, success, and robust health are yours for a time; all these, however, are given to you as a punishment.

—Fr. Jean Baptiste Massillon (1663–1742), Sermon on prosperity

∞

Rash Judgments

*Judge not, that you may not be judged: for, with
what judgment you judge, you shall be judged.*

—Matthew 7:1

"Judge not, and you shall not be judged," says the Savior of our souls: "Condemn not, and you shall not be condemned" (Luke 6:37). No, says the holy Apostle, "Judge not before the time, until the Lord come, who both will bring to light the hidden things of darkness, and will make manifest the counsels of the heart" (1 Cor. 4:5).

Oh, how displeasing are rash judgments to God! The judgments of the children of men are rash, because they are not the judges of one another and therefore usurp to themselves the office of our Lord. They are rash, because the principal malice of sin depends on the intent of the heart, which is an impenetrable secret to us. They are not only rash, but also impertinent, because everyone has enough to do to judge himself, without taking upon him to judge his neighbor.

It is as necessary that we should refrain from judging others, as that we be careful to judge ourselves. For as our Lord forbids the one, so the Apostle enjoins the other, saying that if we judged ourselves we should not be judged.

But, O good God! we act quite the contrary; for by judging our neighbor on every occasion, we do what is forbidden; and by not judging ourselves, we neglect to put into practice what we are strictly commanded.

Rash Judgments

We must apply remedies against rash judgments, according to their different causes. There are some hearts naturally so sour, bitter, and harsh, as to make everything bitter and sour that they receive, turning judgment, as the prophet Amos says, into wormwood, by only judging their neighbor with rigor and harshness.

Some judge rashly, not through harshness, but through pride; imagining that in the same proportion as they depress the honor of other men, they raise their own. "I am not as the rest of men," said the foolish Pharisee (Luke 18:11).

Others, to excuse themselves to themselves, and to assuage the remorse of their own consciences, willingly judge others to be guilty of the same kind of vice to which they themselves are addicted, or of some other as great, thinking that the multitude of offenders make the sin the less blamable.

Others judge through passion and prejudice, always thinking well of what they love, and ill of what they hate.

In fine, fear, ambition, and other such weaknesses of the mind frequently contribute toward the breeding of suspicious and rash judgments.

—St. Francis De Sales (1567–1622), *Introduction to the Devout Life*

∞

How dare we judge others? Circumstances are so varied that it is almost impossible that we should not make a mistake. It is the magistrate's duty to judge the guilty; our duty, as regards our neighbor, is ever to take the defensive side. Nothing shows the wisdom and truth of those words from Holy Writ, "Judge not, and you will not be judged"—"Condemn not, and you will not be condemned"—as the injustice and rashness of our judgments.

To judge, we must know the heart of the person accused, and this is a sanctuary reserved for God alone.

Ah! if we only knew our own shortcomings, we should rather accuse and judge ourselves.

—St. John of God (1495–1550)

∞

It is the ordinary custom of those who have not within them the Spirit of God, to be scandalized at the most virtuous and edifying of actions. This we see in the Gospel of St. Luke: "A sinner, knowing that Jesus sat at meat in the Pharisee's house, brought an alabaster box of ointment, and standing behind at His feet, she began to wash His feet with her tears." This woman outwardly displayed her love and respect; she threw herself at the feet of the Son of God, full of grief, incapable of fear, and pierced with a lively sorrow for having offended Him.

Such were the feelings with which our Lord had inspired her.

However, the Pharisee formed a rash judgment; for he said, "This man, if he were a prophet, would know surely who and what manner of woman this is that touched Him, that she is a sinner."

But the Savior, who knew her better, judged otherwise; for she had blotted out her iniquities by the abundance of her tears, by the excess of her love, and by her contrition.

This is an example that ought indeed to be consoling to those who, in actions that they have performed for the honor and glory of God, may have drawn upon themselves rash and false judgments, censure, and condemnation of others,

—Fr. Armand de Rancé (1626–1700), *Reflections*

∞

Rash judgment seldom hurts the one upon whom it falls, but the one who judges rashly cannot fail to injure himself.

There are two things we should guard against in forming rash judgments; the first is when it is uncertain from what motive such and such a thing may have been done; the second is when we cannot foresee what may one day be the state of that man who now appears to be either good or bad.

—St. Augustine (354–430), *On the Sermon on the Mount*

Scandal

*It must needs be that scandals come; but neverthe-
less woe to that man by whom the scandal cometh.*

—Matthew 18:7

Scandal is a diabolical sin, and the reason that St. Chrysostom gives us is conclusive enough. For (according to the Gospel) the particular characteristic of Satan is that he was a murderer from the beginning. And he has not only been a homicide, continues this holy Doctor, but because, from the beginning of the world, he has been the cause of souls being lost by seducing them, by drawing them into snares, by making them yield to temptation, by putting every obstacle in the way of their conversion.

Now, is not this the constant employment of the libertine, the vicious man, the man swayed by the spirit of debauchery, who seeks on all sides (if I may dare to use the expression) for an easy prey for his sensuality? What does he do besides, and in what is his scandalous life taken up? Is it not in deceiving and damaging souls, in taking advantage of their weakness, in imposing on their simplicity, in making the most of their imprudence, in flattering their vanity, in undermining their religion, in triumphing over their modesty, in dissipating their just fears, in rendering ineffectual all their good desires? Is it not in keeping them from the ways of God, when, touched with His grace, they become conscious of their misery, and sincerely desirous of recovering their innocence?

Are not these, O sinner, the deeds of darkness in which your infamous life is spent? Is it not then the employment of the devil in which you have been engaged?

You do, then, the office of the evil one, and all the more dangerously, because they whom you scandalize, being accustomed to be led by the senses, are the more exposed to your baneful insinuations, and more impressed by them, since you move among them a visible and incarnate demon. The devil was, of himself, a murderer from the beginning but is a murderer through you. It is you who are his deputy, who furnish him with weapons; you who carry on his work; you who, in his place, have become the tempter, the murderer of souls, by sacrificing these unfortunate victims to your passions and pleasures.

—Fr. Louis Bourdaloue (1632–1704), Advent sermon

∞

St. Cyprian, who lived in the third century, in explaining the reason why God permits that His own should be persecuted, gives us a picture of the manners and customs of his time. Later, St. Bellarmine, in his work On the Sighs of the Dove, *quotes the whole passage, and says: "Would to God that we had not reason to bewail the same scandalous practices in our time."*

Each one thinks only of enriching himself; and forgetting what the first Christians had done at the time of the Apostles, and what they ought always to do, they cherished so great a longing for riches that they fancied that they never could accumulate sufficient. There was no devotion in the priests, no faith in the ministers of the gospel, no regularity in their manners, no charity in their works.

The women painted their faces, the men knew how to change the color of their hair, and they quite made an art of dyeing. You could detect something approaching to lasciviousness in their eyes and looks, and so careful was their studied talk that they sought to impose on the simple, and tried to deceive each other.

Scandal

They swore not only unnecessarily, but falsely. They, with insupportable conceit, despised the orders of their superiors. They had no fear of slandering their neighbor, and they in their hearts cherished mortal hatreds.

Several prelates, who ought to have induced people to be pious by showing a good example, neglected their duty, quitted their dioceses, abandoned their flocks, and went into far-off countries in order to carry on a business that was mean and unworthy of them. They took no heed of the pressing wants of the few who were faithful. Their only endeavor was to amass riches, to deprive others of their lands, and to multiply their wealth by usury.

—St. Cyprian (ca. 200–258)

∞

There is nothing that St. Augustine deplores more, in his *Confessions*, than the misery of the bad example he had followed when a youth. He was naturally inclined to be good, he had even received a sufficiently good education, and he confesses, without flattery or vanity, in a book in which he seeks his own confusion, that he would have never committed the atrocities of a dissipated, ill-regulated life, had it not been for the bad example that his companions had given him. Here are the words he uses: "O friendship, worse than the cruelest enmity, which seduced my mind, and dragged me on to sin—'Let us go'—'Let us do'—still dinning incessantly in my ears so vividly, that it is shameful to have some shame for acting so ill."

We have, in the words and experience of this glorious saint, an example and an evident proof of the boldness and impudence that ever accompany scandal.

—Fr. Vincent Houdry, S.J. (1630–1729)

∞

Self-Love

He that loveth his life, shall lose it;
and he that hateth his life in this world,
keepeth it unto life eternal.

—John 12:25

Original sin gave birth to the tyrannical empire of love of self, and it so poisons an ill-regulated mind that it loves naught else but self, and even ignores God.

St. Thomas says that this false love is the root of every sin committed from the beginning of the world, and that it is the source and cause of all that is most miserable. This is very true, since it is sinful self-love alone that makes us desire all inordinate affections for the enjoyments here below and makes us forget God and the observance of His commandments.

Every kind of misery we see in the world springs from the root that ripens on this infectious tree. From this arises that anxiety that men manifest for their own affairs, and for that negligence of all that appertains to God. From that comes that delicacy on all points of honor, while they think little of God's honor.

It is this that so interests them in all that is for their worldly advantage and makes them so indifferent to the service due to God.

No work is deemed too difficult, if it be for their temporal welfare, while for God they take no pains. The loss of a slight temporal advantage drives them nearly wild; but they have no thought of losing their immortal souls. The love of pleasure fosters a distaste for all that is good; in fine, they labor incessantly for success in this life, and never prepare for the life to come.

—Venerable Louis de Grenada (1505–1588), *Meditations*, 6

∞

The difference between self-love and charity is shown by the movements and workings of each.

- Self-love shows that it neglects nothing that may reflect on itself; on the good it has done, it wishes to be secretly admired and hears others praised with contempt. Charity praises and admires virtue in others, as something out of the common; and if it be reflected on itself, it looks upon itself as an object worthy of the vengeance of heaven.

- Self-love is violent, impetuous, fantastical, and imperious; it wishes to command and to be obeyed. In the place of this, charity, according to the Apostle, is mild and meek; it yields easily to others and waits with patience for success, which, if not obtained, blesses those who persecute it.

- Self-love is always wrapped up in self. If it go out of the way to do some virtuous action, it does it to draw down praises that it may receive or, at any rate, hopes to receive.

- Self-love looks after its own interest, does nothing but what may accrue to its advantage; instead of that, charity does not seek its own, but looks only to God's interest.

- Self-love is singular; it wishes for out-of-the-way things, particular devotions, and loves and seeks for distinction; whereas charity flies from all kinds of singularity and wishes for nothing particular.

- Self-love in devotion seeks for sweetness, and when that fails, feels discouraged; but charity seeks for the will of God alone, and on this will it depends.

We must watch continually over ourselves, and over every movement of the will, to repress a number of selfish frailties that, on examination, will be found to be as minute as they are continuous.

There are so many petty interests that center in self, even among those who are pious, that it is incumbent upon us to be ever on our guard. There are so many little meannesses that overshadow our best actions that, if encouraged, will diminish merit and be the cause of attempting much but advancing very slowly.

Men, for the most part, flatter themselves that they seek God alone, but they search for Him through the medium of self; and they prefer ease and reputation, and thereby encourage secret pride and self-love.

—Fr. Camaret

∞

Two loves: one good, the other bad; one sweet, the other bitter. The two cannot agree or dwell together in a sinner's heart. It is this, therefore: if anyone loves anything but Thee, O Lord, Thy love is not in him.

Doubtless it is a grand and wholesome doctrine how to guard against that self-love that is so capable of being your ruin, and with what hatred you should hate yourself if you wish to escape from eternal punishment. If you love yourself with an inordinate love, then you should hate yourself indeed; if you cherish a proper hatred of yourself, then you have a proper love of yourself.

Do not then love yourself in this life, lest you lose your soul in the life to come.

—St. Augustine (354–430), On John 1:4

∞

Theaters

He that loveth danger shall perish in it.

—Sirach 3:27

St. Augustine confesses that the affection he had for shows and theaters had been the cause of his continued indulgence in sensuality, and that he always came away more unchaste than when he entered, because, he says, what one sees or what one hears excites bad thoughts, seduces the mind, and corrupts the heart.

St. Cyprian affirms that theaters are a school of impurity and a place wherein modesty is prostituted.

Salvian, Bishop of Marseilles, says that in his time it was the custom in the sacrament of Baptism to make an extra renunciation, namely, a promise to avoid going to theaters.

St. Chrysostom wishes that all would fly from theaters as from a plague.

Minutius Felix inveighs against dangerous pastimes in an Apology he published in defense of the Christians.

— Archbishop François Fénelon (1651–1715),
Christian Instruction for the Education of Young Ladies

∞

Although balls and dancing are recreations, in their own nature, indifferent, yet, according to the ordinary manner in which they are conducted, they preponderate very much on the side of evil and are, in consequence, extremely dangerous. Being generally carried on in the darkness and obscurity of night, it is by no means surprising that several vicious circumstances should obtain easy admittance, since the subject is of itself so susceptible of evil. The amateurs of these diversions, by sitting up late at night, disable themselves from discharging their duty to God, on the morning of the day following.

Is it not, then, a kind of madness to exchange the day for the night, light for darkness, and good works for criminal fooleries? Everyone strives who shall carry most vanity to the ball; and vanity is so congenial to evil affections as well as to dangerous familiarities, that both are easily engendered by dancing.

These idle recreations are ordinarily very dangerous; they chase away the spirit of devotion and leave the soul in a languishing condition; they cool the fervor of charity and excite a thousand evil affections in the soul, and therefore they are not to be used but with the greatest caution.

Physicians say that after mushrooms we must drink good wine; and I say that after dancing it is necessary to refresh our souls with good and holy considerations, to prevent the baneful effects of these dangerous impressions that the vain pleasure taken in dancing may have left in our minds. But what considerations?

- Consider that during the time you were at the ball, innumerable souls were burning in the flames of hell, for the sins they had committed in dancing, or were occasioned by their dances.
- Consider that many religious and devout persons, of both sexes, were, at that very time, in the presence of God, singing His praises, and contemplating His beauty. Ah! how much more profitably was their time employed than yours!
- Consider that, while you were dancing, many souls departed out of this world in great anguish and that thousands and thousands of men and women then suffered great pains in their beds, in hospitals, in the streets, by the gout, the stone, or burning fevers. Alas! they had no rest, and will you have no compassion for

them? And do you not think that you shall one day groan, as they did, while others shall dance, as you did?

* Consider that our Blessed Savior, His Virgin Mother, the angels and saints beheld you at the ball. Ah! how greatly did they pity you, seeing your heart pleased with so vain an amusement and taken up with such childish toys.

* Consider that, alas! while you were there, time was passing away, and death was approaching nearer: behold how he mocks you, and invites you to his dance, in which the groans of your friends shall serve for the music, and where you shall make but one step from this life to the next. The dance of death is, alas! the true pastime of mortals, since by it we instantly pass from the vain amusements of this world to the eternal pains or pleasures of the next.

I have set you down these little considerations. God will suggest to you many more to the like effect, provided you fear Him.

—St. Francis de Sales (1567–1622), *Introduction to the Devout Life*

Theft and Larceny

Woe to him that heapeth together that which is not his own.

—Habakkuk 2:6

It is seldom indeed that larceny and injustice can be separated from avarice; at any rate, the wrong inflicted on one's neighbor is the same. This is what the prophet Hosea insinuates when he says that theft has spread like a deluge among men (see Hos. 4:2).

No need, my brethren, to confine thieves to the woods and forests; they are to be found everywhere. And however infamous this vice may be, there are very many in the world who, although looked upon as honest, respectable men, are quite as guilty.

It is very true that when we hear, as we often do, of highwaymen and housebreakers breaking into houses and carrying off all they can, respectable men are not to be found in their company; but when it has been shown that there are many kinds of larceny that the world does not consider as shameful—nay, even some are looked upon as honorable—you must then be convinced that the prophet is right, when he says, that theft is spread among men like a deluge.

If it is absolutely impossible that those who have acquired riches through defrauding another of his property can be saved without making restitution, when they have the power to do so, it is also, on the other hand, almost impossible that they could do so if they are possessed with a vicious self-interested passion.

Theft and Larceny

One may say that this kind of impossibility is to be found in the moral actions of men, where there are so many difficulties that hinder them from putting them into execution, where there are so many obstacles to overcome, and where miracles of graces are needed to induce us to make extraordinary efforts.

Experience has shown us that the restitution of stolen property should be placed in the ranks of impossibilities of this kind, since out of the incalculable number of persons who have been unjust enough to defraud, very few indeed have been found who have been just and honorable enough to restore it. Almost all the restitutions that are made consist of some crowns that a servant may have stolen from his master; but, for those thieves who retain large sums of others' property, those moneylenders whose riches consist of accumulations of usurious interest, those masters of chicanery who have cunningly obtained, through favor, friends, or court influence, property that was not theirs; to gentry, such as these, it would be useless to speak of restitution; it would be a recommendation to which they would not willingly listen.

That shows that there is a species of secret impossibility in an act of justice that, in practice, we find so rare.

It is not, say you, our intention to die holding the property of another person; it is our intention to return it through our will, but not now. What if you die without making your last will—what will happen then? And if your will is not properly drawn up or not properly attested, your heirs may easily upset the will, or fail to carry out your intentions; what will become of you then? And even if all this should not occur, do you not see that by deferring to make restitution, which you could now do, you render it most difficult, since not only would you be compelled to pay the principal, but it would be incumbent on you to make some satisfaction for the injury caused by your delay?

You cannot keep for long those ill-gotten goods; they will be the cause of an unhappiness that will last forever. Notwithstanding you hold it now, you must, when you die, leave that money that you cannot now give up, and you will then be compelled to do necessarily and fruitlessly what you could now do, willingly and meritoriously. Ah! would it not be much better to make a willing restitution now than to make it at the hour of death, when, perchance, you may do it with regret, through constraint, and without reward? Would it not be better, says St. Bernard, to despise those benefits with honor and with an interior conscientious satisfaction than to lose them and part with them all with a great but useless grief? Would it not be far more prudent to give them up willingly for the love of Christ than to leave them behind you, whether you like it or not?

I tell you now, beseechingly, since it is for the salvation of your soul: Return what you owe. Ah! have some compassion on yourself. Restore to that tradesman, to that workman, to that servant what you owe them; make some reparation to that poor widow whose pittance you have kept back; repair the injury you have inflicted on that poor family by the sale of worthless shares; in a word, give up property that does not belong to you. Pay what you owe.

I say this now, beseechingly, but recollect that death will one day sternly say, "Depart, wretched man; leave a house which is not legitimately yours; leave behind thee monies that you cannot carry away with you."

—Fr. Jean Lejeune (1592–1672), *Sur le Larcin*

∞

Vainglory

Let us not be made desirous of vainglory,
provoking one another.

—Galatians 5:26

The yearning after glory is a strange passion. It displays itself in a hundred ways. Some wish to be honored, some wish to be in regal power, some aspire to be rich, and others sigh to be strong and robust.

This tyrannical passion, passing still further on, induces some to seek for glory by their almsdeeds, others by their fasts and mortifications, some by their ostentatious prayers, others by their learning and science; so various are the forms of this monster vice.

One need not be astonished that men seek after the emoluments and grandeur of this world, but what is more astonishing (and more blamable) is that anyone can be found who is proud and vain of his good works, of his fasts, of his prayers, and of his alms. I confess that I am pierced to the heart when I see such holy actions tarnished by secret vanity. I feel as much grieved as I should be if I heard of an illustrious princess, of whom much was expected, giving herself up to all sorts of debauchery and vice.

Men soon find that there is no one more importunate than he who, filled with vainglory, praises himself, gives himself airs, and places on his head a wreath of incense. He is laughed at for his vanity, and the more they notice that he boasts of himself, the more they endeavor to humiliate him.

In fact, the more you try to attract the praise of the world by your own vanity and vainglory, the more will people either avoid you or laugh at you. Thus it happens that the result is contrary to our expectations; we are eager for the world to praise us and to exclaim, "What a good man! How charitable he is!" But people will say, "What a vain man! How easy to see that he wishes to please men, rather than please God!"

If, on the other hand, you hide the good you do, it is then that God will praise you; He even will not allow any holy action to remain long concealed. You may try to suppress the performance of good deeds, but He will take care to make them known, aye, better known than you could possibly have intended.

You see, then, that there is nothing more antagonistic to glory and honor when you seek to do good merely for the purpose of being seen, known, and admired.

It is the way of doing quite the contrary to what you intended, since, instead of showing off your goodness, you will only cause your vanity to be known to all men, and punished by Almighty God.

This vice seems, as it were, to smother all our reasoning faculties, so much so that one would say that he who is a slave to vainglory had lost his senses.

You would look upon that man as a madman who, being short of stature, would really believe that he was growing so tall that he would soon be able to look down on the highest mountain. After this extravagance, you would need no further proof of his insanity.

So in like manner, when you see a man who considers himself to be above all his fellow creatures, and would be offended were he compelled to mix with the common herd of men, you would seek for no other proof of his madness.

He is even more ridiculous than those who have lost the use of reason, for he voluntarily reduces himself to that pitiable state of extravagant folly.

—St. John Chrysostom (ca. 349–407), Homily 58 on St. Matthew

Vainglory

∞

Public approbation has but little effect on a man who has acted from good and conscientious motives; such a man merits as much again as he seems to have disregarded before.

Those who seek with too much eagerness for the esteem and applause of the world receive during this life the reward of their good works but merit nothing for eternity. This is a maxim drawn from Holy Scripture.

I tell you, however, that all those alms that are given to create a sensation are not meritorious; that those who, with a flourish of trumpets, proclaim to the world the good they have done have already received their reward; and even those who make a parade of their fasts and mortifications lose all the merit by vain ostentation.

Our Savior teaches us to do good by stealth. It is God, not men, we ought to study to please. The reward that men can give us is frivolous and transient, but God reserves for us an infinite reward, an eternal recompense.

—St. Ambrose (340–397), *De Officiis*, 1

∞

All the saints admonish us to be on our guard against vainglory, because, say they, it is a cunning thief that often steals from us our best actions and that insinuates itself so secretly that it has struck its blow even before we have perceived it. St. Gregory says that vainglory is like a robber who first craftily insinuates himself into the company of a traveler, pretending to go the same way as he does, and afterward robs and kills him when he is least upon his guard, and when he thinks himself most secure.

I confess [says the saint in the last chapter of his *Morals*] that when I go about to examine my own intention, even while I am writing this, I think that I have no other will than to please God; but, notwithstanding, while I am not upon my guard, I find that a certain desire of pleasing men intermixes itself, and methinks I feel some vain satisfaction for having performed it well. How it comes to pass I know not, but I perceive that, while I go on, what I do is not so free from dust and chaff as it was in the beginning. For I know that I began it at first, with the sole view of pleasing God; but now I perceive other considerations mixing themselves, which render my intention less upright and pure than it was.

What sufficiently demonstrates the deformity of the vice is that the saints and divines rank it among those sins ordinarily called mortal, or which are more properly styled capital sins; because they are, as it were, the head and source of all others.

—Fr. Alphonse Rodriguez, S.J. (1526–1616), *On Mortification*

∞

Our Bad Passions

For this cause God delivered them
up to shameful affections.

—Romans 1:26

Pagan philosophers all agree that wisdom consists in a tranquility of the soul, which it enjoys when the sensual appetites are entirely subdued. It is then that there are no violent passions to trouble the peace of the soul by inordinate desires or by darkening the understanding, which is sure to be the case when they are in agitation; for the peculiar property of passion is to blind the reason and diminish within us the liberty of our free will.

But when the passions are lulled, the understanding has purer lights to know what is right, and the will has freer liberty to embrace what is correct and good.

Now, God wishes to find this peace and quietude in our heart, in order that He may dwell therein, and wills to infuse wisdom within us and to bestow His graces upon us. The mortification of our passions and the control of our appetites are the only means of obtaining that peace and of securing that tranquility.

One can obtain peace only by going to war; if you do not wish to battle with your passions, to curb your inordinate desires, to gain a victory over self, you will never obtain that peace; and you will never be master of yourself if you are not the conqueror.

It must be reckoned as a certain truth that the intemperateness of our appetites and the perverse inclinations of our flesh are the greatest obstacles we have, not only to our salvation, but, still more, to our progress in virtue.

What has often been said is that the flesh is our greatest enemy, because, in fact, from that spring all our bad passions, all our disorders and our falls. "From whence are wars and contentions among you?" says the Apostle James. "Are they not hence from your concupiscences, which war in your members?" (James 4:1).

Sensuality, concupiscence, and the unruliness of self-love are the cause of all our wars in our members, of all the sins, of all the imperfections we commit, and consequently are the greatest hindrance we meet with in our way of perfection and salvation.

From whence it is easy to see that real mortification consists in repairing the disorder of our passions, that is to say, by overcoming the evil propensities of our passions and the obstinacy of our self-love.

— Fr. Alphonse Rodriguez, S.J. (1526–1616), *On Mortification*

∞

One can safely say that there is no virtue more recommended by Jesus Christ than the mortification of our passions.

A large portion of the Gospels tends to make us understand its necessity, and there is no truth more often repeated, more often expressed. You read therein of the cross, of sufferings, of death, of denying yourself, of hatred of self, of the violence we must use, of the narrow way whereon we must necessarily enter.

At one time, our Savior tells us, "He who wishes to come after me must deny himself, take up his cross, and follow me" (see Matt. 16:24); at another time, He assures us that since the preaching of St. John the Baptist — that is to say, since the promulgation of the New Law — the Kingdom of heaven is taken only by violence, and that only those who use violence can gain it (Matt. 11:12); at another time He tells us that the road that leads to life is narrow, and there are few who enter on it, and it is on that account, He exhorts us to enter thereon (Matt. 7:13–14).

Now, what does our Lord wish to infer from this necessity of carrying one's cross, of denying oneself, of entering into the narrow path, of doing violence? He points out the obligation we all have of repressing the bent of our natural inclinations, which, coming from a corrupt source, are always unruly, and of continually fighting against our passions, especially those that are the most dangerous, because they all usually lead to evil consequences.

If mortification is a remedy for past sins, it is a preservative against evils to come. We have, as children of Adam, received with our inherited original sin a strong repugnance to do good, a violent inclination to do that which is wrong; we cannot get rid of this inclination. Can we give in to this repugnance without falling into disorder? Neither can we safely resist without using violence, without incessantly battling with our bad passions, and is not this the chief exercise of Christian mortification?

We are all born proud, ambitious, choleric, vindictive, self-interested, sensual—this we are naturally. You see, then, that we must cease to be wicked if we wish to be Christians, if we are eager to work out our salvation.

To effect this, must we not always watch over ourselves, must we not ever be engaged in a spiritual combat, and, consequently, must we not practice continual mortification?

—Fr. F. Nepveu, S.J. (1639–1708), *Esprit du Christianisme*

∞

To mortify one passion, no matter how small, is a greater help in the spiritual life, than many abstinences, fasts, and disciplines.

—St. Philip Neri (1515–1595)

Part 7

∞

Virtues We Should Practice

∞

Almsdeeds

According to thy ability, be merciful.
If thou have much, give abundantly; if thou have
little, take care even so to bestow willingly a little.

—Tobit 4:8–9

Of the great advantage to be derived from almsgiving, and of the love that we ought to feel in bestowing, with liberality, every kind of help to the poor, there is nothing more impressive than the Gospel of St. Matthew, where the Apostle relates what our Savior will say, and do, on the last great day — the day of judgment.

The elect are ranged on the right, and the reprobate on the left. Jesus, fixing His eyes on the wicked on the left, will pronounce those terrible words: "Depart from me, you cursed, into everlasting fire which was prepared for the devil and his angels" (Matt. 25:41). And to justify this frightful sentence, He will add: "I was hungry, and you gave me nothing to eat; I was thirsty, and you gave me no drink; I was a stranger, and you had no wish to receive me; I was naked, and you clothed me not; I was sick, and you did not pay me a single visit. Go! ye accursed, depart from me" (see Matt. 25:42–43).

Listen and tremble, you who, far from protecting the widow and orphan, have unjustly oppressed them. You who are enriched with the spoils of the unfortunate; you who have heard, without being moved, their complaints and their groans; you who have even insulted their poverty; you who, by taking advantage of a bad season, have rendered the poor more miserable, by assisting in keeping up or by raising the price of necessaries, or by usurious interest, have drained their little savings; you, in fine, who have designedly shut up your bowels of compassion—come and hear the Supreme Judge pronounce the sentence of your condemnation: "Withdraw from me, ye accursed." And where are they to go, Lord? Into eternal fire. Why?

"Because," says the Lord, "I was hungry, and you gave me nothing to eat. I was ill, and in prison, and you have not visited me! I have suffered extreme want, in the persons of my poor, which you ought to have looked upon as my members, and you have not seen to this." It is thus that the Lord of Justice, on the day of wrath, in the presence of the whole world, will compel the merciless rich to seal their own condemnation.

Can one, after that, question the obligation of this precept, since the Supreme Judge seems to forget the other breaches of His laws, to condemn the sinner on this precept alone?

Fr. Vincent Houdry, S.J. (1630–1729)

∞

St. Chrysostom says that God, when He deigned to become Incarnate, was so united to poverty, with such an inexpressible union, that the poor is a tabernacle where God is hidden, in the same way as He is veiled in our ciboriums.

It is the poor who beg, but it is God who receives the alms; God is our debtor, and it is the Almighty who wishes to repay us. By this means, although He is invisible, He is still with us in the person of His poor. He receives the alms, and, in return, He loads us with His graces and blessings.

—St. John Chrysostom (ca. 349–407), Homily

∞

I cannot bring myself to believe that a professedly pious person, who is very guarded in giving alms, has the genuine spirit of inward repentance.

Almsdeeds

Now, in the present day, it is not uncommon to see pious people acting as if they really thought their piety in other respects was almost a dispensation from almsgiving. Others, again, when they give, give in ways that minister to their own humors, so that even in almsgiving, self-love shall find its account.

Moreover, generosity is not almsgiving. The quantity given must have reference to the means of the giver, but more to the amount of sacrifice and self-denial, which his alms entail upon him. Expensiveness is perhaps not a distinct sin in itself, though even that may be questioned; but it is the mother of many sins, and it is remarkably uncongenial to the spiritual life. Yet pious people are particularly given to be expensive, when they have the means.

An alms that does not put the giver to inconvenience is rather a kindness than an alms; and certainly the alms, which is to be a satisfactory evidence of inward repentance, ought to reach the point of causing some palpable inconvenience, of involving some solid self-denial.

—Fr. Frederick William Faber (1814–1863), *Spiritual Conferences*

∞

Keeping the Commandments

My son, keep my commandments, and thou shalt
live; and my law as the apple of thy eye.

—Proverbs 7:2

The word *Decalogue* signifies a law that comprises ten commandments, the purely excellent, the most just and the most conformable to the law of equity that could be given to the world, whether we consider the Author, who is God Himself; whether we look to their end, since they have for their aim, not a decaying or perishable benefit, but an eternity of happiness; whether, in fine, we consider the things they contain, since therein, there is no virtue that they do not command, no vice they do not forbid.

St. Augustine says that the Decalogue is an abridgment of every law.[3] He also says that in the New Law the commandments are less numerous, easier, and more beneficial.

The law of God—does it appear to us to be difficult? It is because we have so little love. The law of God, in all that it embraces, is sweet to him whose heart is full of charity. Love, says St. John, consists in keeping His commandments, and His commandments are not painful.

They are not painful when love induces us to keep them. If they should appear to be painful or laborious, it is that your heart is full of the love of the world, full of self-love, and destitute of the love of God.

[3] Q. 401, supp. Exodus.

Keeping the Commandments

St. Augustine makes our Savior speak and puts into His mouth the following words and complaints.

Avarice commands the hardest tasks; see what I command, and make the comparison.

Avarice induces men to cross the seas, to go into unknown, undiscovered countries, and a thousand perils are eagerly sought. Avarice is obeyed; all my commandments are set at nought. Is it not shameful that the world should have more authority than God? That they should plead difficulty when it is God who speaks, that they should daily surmount the most difficult obstacles, when it is a question of pleasing or getting on in the world?

It is a general principle, in all that God enjoins, that He asks and seeks first above all our hearts. Does not God command us to give alms? He wishes, however, that we should do these acts of charity from a pure motive, that is to say, from the heart; and He Himself says that He loves the cheerful giver. God asks us for good works, exterior homage, proofs of our entire dependence on Him as His creatures. He gives us to understand that if these good works do not proceed from the heart, He will reject such gifts and class us with those hypocrites who honor Him with their lips while their hearts are far from Him.

Those, then, are displeasing to God who in their heart disown actions that they consider they are obliged to perform through a natural human benevolence, or through a love of display. Those, again, who indulge in murmuring, grumbling, and in seeking for excuses do not obey the commandments as they ought.

—Fr. Lambert (d. 1836), *Ecclesiastical Discourses*

∞

Conscience

Our glory is this, the testimony of our conscience.

—2 Corinthians 1:12

At the very moment we commit a sin, we feel within a remorse of conscience, and this is the reproach for the sin committed. Now, I say that this remorse is a grace; for what is a grace? How many are ignorant of it, or rather how many ignore it, although it is received every day? Grace, say the theologians, is a help that God gives to man, in order that he may act upon it, and so merit heaven; and if he be a sinner, in order that he may work out his salvation by penance.

Now, all this perfectly tallies with that synderesis, that is to say, with that remorse of conscience, that grows within us after sin. For it is certain that God is the Author of it, that it is solely through love that He excites it in us, and that He uses it as a means of working out our conversion.

Whence comes the conclusion that this remorse has all the qualities of a genuine grace? For there is nothing more certain than that God is the source from which it arises, since the Scripture declares the same thing to us in a thousand places.

Yes, it is I, says the Almighty speaking to a sinner, it is I who will reproach you for the enormity of your sin. When, after committing it, your conscience disturbs you, attribute your disquiet to me, and do not seek elsewhere from which comes this remorse. A hundred times, after having yielded to temptation, you would try to conceal from yourself your cowardice; you would wish to turn away your eyes, so as not to see your sin; and you fancy that I shall do the same and fall in with your notions; but you deceive yourself: "Thou thoughtest unjustly, that I was as thyself"; for being your Lord and your God, I will always be your accuser, and as often as you shall commit an offense against me, I will, whether you will or not, lay before you your iniquity and the horror I have of sin. "I will reprove thee, and set them before thy face" (Ps. 49:21 [RSV = Ps. 50:21]).

You see, Christians, that God is the principal Author of remorse of conscience. But what motive has He for this? I have said that it is through love, through a miracle of His goodness, an effusion of His mercy.

Does He not explain Himself to the same purpose to His beloved disciple in Revelation? "Those whom I love, I rebuke and chastise [see Rev. 3:19]; and it is by chastising them that I show my love for them." But what occasion for other testimony than the word of our Savior, when He announced to His Apostles the coming of the Holy Spirit: "When He shall come, He will reprove the world of sin" (John 16:8, KJV). And by whom will it be reproved? "By the Spirit of truth, which I shall send for that purpose." And what does He mean by the Spirit of truth? The substantial love of the Father and the Son, the Divine Person, who is charity itself. Observe, then, dear brethren, that it is the love of God that reproves when we are sinners: "He will reprove the world of sin." And now, is there the least room to doubt that the remorse of our conscience is not a grace?

It is not an external, but an internal grace, as it is in the very bottom of our souls that this gnawing worm of remorse is found. Wherefore the Apostle of the Gentiles tells us that God "hath sent forth the Spirit of His Son into our hearts, crying out" (Gal. 4:6). This Divine Spirit (as St. Augustine observes) cries out, not after the manner of a preacher, who speaks to us and reproaches us with the viciousness of our life: for not all the preachers in the world have it in their power to probe the conscience; and, however their words may strike the ear, they are far from reaching the human heart. But the Spirit of God, the better to be heard by us, holds, as I may say, His place in the center of us; and from thence (says

St. Augustine) He incessantly cries out, in opposition to our passions, censures our pleasures, and condemns our sins. Ah! Christians, can we carry our ingratitude to that pitch, as to think the contradiction of the Holy Spirit an importunate rigor, and not confess that it is a gift of His grace, a mercy on the sinner, a help of salvation, and a favorable means of bringing him back to God? Can we be so blind as to suppose the sting that pains us an insupportable pain, and wish to be rid of it?

No, my Lord, we will never entertain such dangerous notions; and as we are assured that it is Your Spirit, the Divine Comforter, who infuses these salutary remorses within us, we will always receive them as benefactions from Thy hand and, far from complaining, will think only of giving fresh proofs of our love and gratitude, by our fidelity.

—Fr. Louis Bourdaloue (1632–1704), From his sermons

∞

When God will be your judge, He will require no better witness than your own conscience.

—St. Augustine (354–430), On Psalm 37

∞

The Conversion of Sinners

If you seek the Lord your God you will find Him,
provided always you seek with all your heart,
and in the bitter tribulation of your soul.

—Deuteronomy 4:29

It is an error to maintain that the tears our Lord shed dispense us from shedding our own, for tears are indispensably necessary, principally those that St. Augustine calls the tears of the heart, since by these is commenced our spiritual conversion.

The conversion of Magdalene began with tears. She wept more for herself than she did for her brother Lazarus. It was through contrition that David expiated his sins, for he wept night and day, and watered his couch with his tears. It was by that that St. Peter blotted out his crime, for it is written that he went out and wept bitterly.

When one begs pardon for a fault, he may fail of convincing others of his sincerity, for words are not always the true interpreters of the heart; but with respect to tears, they have less cunning, and are far more eloquent, because they disclose the soul's deepest sorrow.

In this consists true penance, an index of an abiding sorrow for having offended God, which then prompts us to do our utmost to satisfy His justice.

For it is of little worth to acknowledge our sins (the wicked, the hypocrite, often see their crimes but are not sufficiently aware of their enormity), but we must also feel an inward grief, a salutary compunction of heart, and that bitterness of soul that the Apostle calls sadness unto God. From these arise our sighs, our wish to cover our head with ashes, our dejected look that make one strike the breast, that suggest the discipline and the hair shirt; that sorrow from which proceed deep regrets for the past, fear for the future, and anguish for the present; that sadness that complains like the dove and that makes tears supply the place of food, according to the expression of David (Ps. 41:4 [RSV = Ps. 42:3]).

Infallible are the marks of repentance when the feelings are so acute that it pierces the wounded conscience; not only does it rend our hearts within, but outwardly, it escapes in sighs and tears.

Thus the royal prophet tells us that he bedewed his bed with his tears; thus also, the sinner in the Gospel washed the feet of Jesus and mingled with the ointment the tears of a breaking heart.

See how efficacious is the remedy of such happy tears, so different from our ordinary worldly weepings.

In vain you weep when you are overwhelmed with debt and when you are pressed hard by creditors. In vain you weep when you are lying on a bed of sickness, racked, perchance, with pains. In vain you weep for a dear one dead. Rivers of tears will not blot out such griefs.

But O! marvelous virtue of the tears of penance! They cancel debt; they cure your sickness; they restore you to life. And provided that you weep from the heart, behold you will be transformed into new creatures, and you will begin to lead a life of heavenly spirituality.

—Fr. Louis Bourdaloue (1632–1704)

∞

Scripture speaks of a converted man as a new man, because, in fact, it produces a wonderful renewal in a regenerated creature. He is no longer himself, he is another man, another being; everything is changed. He cannot recognize the past; on whatever side you look, you find a new man. He has other eyes, eyes so full of renewed faith that they penetrate unto heaven; they now perceive the celestial light of truth, and the beauty of holiness and sanctity, and fathom the unseen and distant future. He has other ears, ears attentive and obedient, that take pleasure in hearing the Word of God, and they listen to the oracles of heaven.

He has another taste, by which he relishes spiritual delights; he has far better feelings than he had before. He has a horror of sin and a fear of offending God; his anger is zeal for the glory of God; his joy is the peace of his conscience; his love, a love for God and his neighbor; his hatred, his former love of self; his hope, the search for heavenly things; his occupations are in good works; his recreation the praises of God; his life a continual practice of piety. You would say that his nature was totally altered and changed.

This change of grace is not the work of a single day. When the strong arm of grace takes possession of a heart, it progresses with difficulty. A house built on a rock does not overturn with the first gust of wind; the devil, in quiet possession of a soul, does not yield to the first effort to drive him away.

In the same way, grace of conversion is not suddenly established in a heart; its progress is slow, almost imperceptible; it is only by degrees that the work is perfected. We must first fight against our dominant passions, the dire enemies of our salvation.

—Fr. Vincent Houdry, S.J. (1630–1729)

∞

The Employment of Time

Therefore, while we have time, let us work good to all men.

—Galatians 6:10

God allows us ample time to do good: "I gave her a time that she might do penance" (Rev. 2:21). But when this time, of which we are now the masters, shall be ended, we can no longer have a single moment at our disposal: "Time shall be no longer" (Rev. 10:6). It is then that our Lord's time will have arrived, that time that He has fixed, and then He will ask how we have employed that which He had given. Ah, what a severe account will He not demand!

Let us examine ourselves and see how we employ our time. Is it employed in useful things, or is it frittered away in seeking after vain pursuits?

God gives us this time in order that it may assist us in working out our salvation, and we lose it, or rather, we make use of it in such a manner as will eventually lead to eternal loss. O! what a use to make of a blessing that ought to be fostered with so much care, and so much wisdom.

We shall know the value of time, when we shall have allowed it to pass away, and when our Lord's time will have arrived; and that time is not far off: "Her time is near at hand, and her days shall not be prolonged" (Isa. 14:1).

The wise man is not satisfied with comparing the days of our life to those of a traveler in order to express its short duration; he says, further on, that this short time passes away so quickly that he can but compare it to a shadow.

How likely we are to lose it, and what dangers do we not incur if we do not take especial care to make a good use of that which God has given us.

A traveler pressed for time thinks only of how soon he can complete his labors; he deprives himself of sleep, of his meals, his relaxations, in fact, all that he can shorten or cut off; if we do not make a profitable use of the little time that remains to work out our salvation, what do we not risk?

The loss of your time does not produce an evil less than the eternal loss of your soul.

What, then, is the blindness of worldlings who pass their days in boasting projects of fame and fortune? A traveler whose love of his own dear country urges his return, does he amuse himself on the road with trifles? What are the largest fortunes in the world, or the grandest establishments on earth, in comparison with a happy eternity, to which every Christian should aspire? Nothing but trifles and mere playthings.

My days, alas! are reckoned up, and the number is but very small. I will husband these my days with care, so that I may reach at last the heavenly home.

—Fr. Paul Segneri, S.J. (1624–1694), *Meditations*

∞

God gives me this day to work out my salvation. Ought we not to meditate on this, for are we certain of seeing tomorrow? Today, well employed, may be worth an eternity of happiness and glory. If God had vouchsafed to have given the same grace to those who have finished their career; if a soul could come out of hell, or purgatory, even for one day, with the power of expiating its sins by penance and prayer, what would it not do? In so short, so precious a time, would a single moment be lost? Doubtless, no!

Even those who are in heaven, would they not deem it an inestimable favor if they had another day to merit some new degree of holiness that would unite them more closely to God?

Why should we not make use of this short time in a similar way?

Let us apply to ourselves what the wise man says in Sirach 14:14: "Defraud not thyself of the good day, and let not the part of a good gift overpass thee." Be mindful and do not let slip any opportunity of doing good: we can then listen to, and follow faithfully, the voice and inspirations of God.

Let us do our utmost to carry out the advice of the wise man, and in the most excellent and perfect way: "He hath made all things good in their time" (Eccles. 3:11).

Let us also follow that other advice of Ecclesiastes: Do without delay all that is in your power, because in hell (which is full of souls who have made bad use of time), there will be no time to do good; neither will there be knowledge or wisdom to teach us.

Our life is made up of a number of years that quickly succeed each other; they pass away without a hope of our ever seeing another day or another hour ever return.

This series of years, of months, of days, which God has given us for the purpose of saving our souls, are properly the talent that the Almighty has been pleased to entrust to us. This we ought to make much of, as we shall necessarily have to give a strict account. Since we have been in the world, no year has passed but that it has been the last year for very many, and the year now silently gliding away will terminate the career of many more.

How sad for those who have lost, perhaps, every day of the year? Have we nothing to reproach ourselves with? How have we employed each day? We have worked hard for the world, have we gained much for heaven? For if we have done nothing for eternity, we have lost a year.

Now, at least, let us usefully make use of the little time that remains.

—Fr. Croiset, S.J. (b. ca. 1650), *Exercices de Pieté*

∞

We must not be behind time in doing good, for death will not be behind his time.

The Employment of Time

Happy is the youth, because he has time before him, to do good.
In order to begin well, and to finish better, it is quite necessary to hear Mass every day, unless there be some lawful hindrance in the way.

—St. Philip Neri (1515–1595), *Maxims and Sayings*

∞

There is no greater loss than the loss of time.

—St. Bonaventure (1221–1274)

Faith

Lord, I believe; help my unbelief.

—Mark 9:23

Inquisitive speculation destroys that simplicity that seeks only to bend to authority, and submit the reason and will to the weight of the Divine Word, without wishing to penetrate the depth of the mysteries, and entering into vain and useless arguments.

This simplicity is founded on the respect due to God, and on the deference we ought to pay to His Word.

The mind ought to be as submissive to all that our Savior has said, as the will should be amenable to all that He commands. And as it is our duty to curb our natural inclinations in order to obey the laws of God, so we must control our feelings and repugnances, in order to acquiesce in His truths.

It is not that faith has not reason and prudence, or that it elevates itself above reason, but as St. Bernard remarks, it is not amenable to reason, inasmuch as it is founded on the truth of the doctrine, which it has received. I did not fix my faith on the penetration of my own intellect, but on the authority of God, who can neither deceive nor be deceived. The truth that I do not fathom is enveloped in its origin.

Far from seeking faith out of God by the puny efforts of my reason, I adore it in the bosom of God, where it has existence, invisible though it may be, and hidden from the eyes of men.

Faith

We often hear worldly people say, "Let me but witness one miracle, and I will be converted." They deceive themselves. Their wonder would be excited, but it would leave no impression on their hearts. They would admire the power of the Almighty, but they would not increase in love and charity. They might be convinced, but they would not be converted, and since neither the authority of Holy Writ, nor the interior voice of conscience, nor the preaching of the gospel, nor the inspirations of heaven induces them to believe, the light impression of a miracle would be very soon effaced.

It would require to be renewed in their every action; and the desire of witnessing one is only a pretext, or an excuse for their unbelief, and not a remedy or an assistance they desire for perfecting their faith.

Faith is that column of vapor of which Scripture speaks, which obscures the daylight and enlightens the night. It is that holy mixture of darkness and light, of infallible truths and less evident proofs. It is that enigma mentioned by St. Paul that is seen through a glass darkly.

It is, in fine, the truth that, being revealed, causes the joy and happiness of the blessed, and which, even when veiled, is the hope and comfort of the saints on earth.

It is for this reason that Jesus Christ chided one of His Apostles, "To believe, you have seen and touched me" (John 20:29). You are indebted to your eyes and your hands when you ought to have trusted to my word. You have acquiesced in a visible and palpable truth. It is out of curiosity, not devotion. Rejoice in the grace that I have been willing to confer upon you; but transfer the reward to those who have believed what they have not seen, and who, paying deference to the power of my word, notwithstanding the contradiction of reason and sense, make a public avowal of a truth that is not certainly unknown but is nevertheless incomprehensible.

— Bishop Esprit Fléchier (1632–1710), *Panégyrique sur St. Thomas*

∽

It is far from my intention to quote all the magnificent eulogies that the Fathers of the Church have written on faith, in order to point out the beauties and force of their language. I do not pause to show you that it is, according to the great Apostle, as it were, the spiritual foundation of every virtue, and that it is through faith that man begins to draw nearer to God.

I need not tell you with St. Chrysostom and St. Augustine that it is a purely gratuitous gift of God, preceded by no merit, but from which proceed all merits, and that it is the source and beginning of the righteousness of men.

I will not tell you, with St. Bernardine of Siena, that it is the most excellent homage that man can render to God by subjecting his reason, which is the most ungovernable and the proudest of all his faculties, by a blind deference to all the truths He has revealed, however incomprehensible they may be.

I will not stop to show you that it is to faith that all those good and grand men of whom St. Paul sings the praises, are indebted for so many victories over tyrants and devils, and by which they have overcome all laws of nature and subjected entire cities to the empire of Jesus Christ.

In fine, I do not wish to delay pointing out to you that faith elevates us to a high and sublime knowledge of the grandeur and perfection of the Divine Creator, a faith that is impenetrable to the light of reason and that far surpasses the intelligence of angels. And it has this advantage, in common with the light of glory, that it looks upon God as He is and that it reflects His fullness and magnificence—first in that veiled obscurity that is our comfort here on earth and that will be revealed to us hereafter, in all its plenitude and splendor, as it has been revealed to all the saints in heaven.

—Fr. Pierre de la Font (d. c. 1700), *Entretiens*

∞

Friendship

Blessed is he that findeth a true friend.

—Sirach 25:12

Friendship requires great communication between friends, otherwise it can neither grow nor subsist. Wherefore it often happens that, with this communication of friendship, diverse other communications insensibly glide from one heart to another by a mutual infusion and reciprocal exchange of affections, inclinations, and impressions.

But this happens especially when we have a high esteem for him whom we love; for when we open our heart in such manner to his friendship, we enter into his inclinations and impressions rapidly in their full stream, be they good or bad. Certainly the bees that gather the honey of Heraclea seek nothing but honey; yet, with the honey they insensibly suck the poisonous qualities of the aconite, from which they gather it.

Philothea, on these occasions we must carefully put into practice what the Savior of our souls was accustomed to say: Be ye good bankers or changers of money; that is to say, receive not bad money with the good, nor base gold with the fine; separate that which is precious from that which is vile, for there is scarcely any person who has not some imperfection. For why should we receive promiscuously the spots and imperfections of a friend together with his friendship? We must love him indeed, notwithstanding his imperfections, but we must neither love nor receive his imperfections; for friendship requires a communication of good, not of evil.

True and living friendship cannot subsist in the midst of sins. As the salamander extinguishes the fire in which he lies, so sin destroys the friendship in which it lodges. If it be but a transient sin, friendship will presently put it to flight by correction; but if it be habitual, and take up its lodging, friendship immediately perishes, for it cannot subsist but on the solid foundation of virtue. We must never, then, commit sin for friendship's sake.

A friend becomes an enemy when he would lead us to sin, and he deserves to lose his friend, when he would destroy his soul.

It is an infallible mark of false friendship to see it exercised toward a vicious person, be his sins of whatsoever kind; for if he whom we love be vicious, without doubt our friendship is also vicious, since, seeing it cannot regard true virtue, it must needs be grounded on some frivolous virtue or sensual quality. Society, formed for traffic among merchants, is but a shadow of true friendship, since it is not made for the love of the persons, but for the love of gain.

Finally, the two following divine sentences are two main pillars to secure a Christian life. The one is that of the wise man: "He that feareth God, shall likewise have good friendship" (Sir. 6:17). The other is that of the apostle St. James: "The friendship of this world is the enemy of God" (James 4:4).

—St. Francis de Sales (1567–1622), *Introduction to the Devout Life*

∞

If we consider the friendships of the ordinary run of mortals nowadays, we should find that nearly all human friendships are at a low ebb and are simply kept up by the prospect of gain in the businesses of this life. If you wish to test this, you have only to examine the different causes that bring disunion in families and make you enemies of each other. The reason is that when friendships are founded only on worldly and fleeting advantages, they cannot be true and lasting friendships; they vanish at the least slight, interest, or jealousy, because they are not attached to the soul by bonds that alone cement friendships and render them firm and resolute.

The friendship between persons united in and with Jesus Christ is solid, constant, and invincible; it is not shaken or impaired by suspicion, calumny, dangers, or even by death itself.

He who loves only so long as he is beloved ceases to love when he receives some fancied displeasure from his friend.

—St. John Chrysostom (ca. 349–407), *Exhortation on Matthew 8*

∞

We must not only take care to avoid leading a bad life, but we must also not contract a friendship with those who live sinfully, for that, according to the prophet, is included among the sins.

True friendship exists not in family interests, nor with those persons by whom we are accustomed to be entertained, nor with those who flatter us, and whose company is dangerous; but with those who cherish the holy fear of God and the study of Holy Scripture.

—St. Jerome (ca. 347–420), *Epistle ad Paulinum*

∞

Good Example

Let your light shine before men, that they may see your good
works, and glorify your Father who is in heaven.

—Matthew 5:16

To gain knowledge, one need only watch and see virtue emanating from a saintly man; his very silence, joined to his expressive gestures, plainly show all he would wish to say. So says Emodius.

Every nation, however savage the people may be, however diversified in speech, understands the language of good example, and one need not be astonished at what Tertullian says: "The confidence and invincible patience of the early martyrs has proved to be the first commentary, and the clearest interpretation of the gospel."

It was this mute, but eloquent, philosophy that the primitive Church made use of to enlighten the obscurity of the mysteries of our holy Faith. It was that piety that was imprinted on the faces of the first Christians, that calm demeanor that they displayed when on trial, and especially that unshaken confidence and trust in God in the midst of cruel tortures; it was example like this that touched the hearts of many a pagan.

Even the modest attire of the early Christians (says Tertullian) was a public censure of all the vices of the idolaters. Let us say, rather, that all the early Christians were efficacious preachers.

When the great orators wished to make a deep impression on the judges and their hearers, they often felt at a loss for words, so they betook

352

themselves to action. They knew by experience, that the sight of a body covered with wounds, of a cassock tinged with blood, of a procession of poor little orphans, of a widow bathed in tears were certainly better adapted to excite compassion than all the tropes and figures of the most pathetic of speeches. So true it is that illustrative agents that attract the eye are far more successful than words that tickle the ear. Is it not also true that a general who harangues his soldiers before the battle does not excite their enthusiastic courage half so much as when they see him, sword in hand, lead on the desperate charge and fight in front, covered with dust and blood?

When the sinner contemplates the saint (who has been one like himself, subject to the selfsame weaknesses and frailties), he thinks of his cowardice in the practices of virtue, which he persuaded himself were too difficult, and he reflects, and ends in condemning his folly and malice.

When, for example, your fine people who live in the lap of luxury, or are hangers-on at the court of royalty, deem it derogatory to their high dignity to conform to the precepts of the gospel; when they see a St. Louis, a St. Edward, a St. Casimir, the Eleazars, and others who were in a higher station in life, and more illustrious and valiant; when they read of kings living in the strict observance of the commandments, they are compelled to confess that they have deceived themselves, by fancying that the practice of every virtue is incompatible or inconsistent with their rank in life. When that judge, that merchant, that man of business, looks at David, who, although loaded with the cares of a kingdom, managed to find time to pray to God seven times a day, and to employ hours in meditating upon eternity; when that delicate dame who cannot endure the smell that exhales from the poor sees Sts. Elizabeth of Hungary and Elizabeth of Portugal and many other princesses visiting the hospitals every day, joyfully devoting hours to the care of the poor sick, to dressing their sores, to making their beds, to performing every kind of menial office; in fine, when bad and cowardly Christians contemplate the fervent lives of the saints, they are forced to acknowledge that it is their tepidity, their want of faith, that cramp their feeble efforts, and not the difficulty of sanctity. In truth, says St. Gregory the Great, when God brings before them those irreproachable witnesses, of which Job makes mention, they have no answer, no excuse, but are compelled to acknowledge their guilt.

I know full well that we all have not the capacity to write books on the defense of the faith that is in us, but we can all be living commentators on the perfection of every virtue. We all have not the authority to mount the pulpit and preach against vice, but we can preach, as St. Francis did, by the language of our works, which is far more persuasive than a sermon. We all are not rich enough to give abundant alms, but we can, if we wish, practice charity toward our neighbors in a more excellent way, and that is by good example; we can gently lead them on to God, who is the giver of all good gifts. This we all can do, if we wish.

It is related of St. Bernardine, that he had so grave and modest an air, that his presence alone inspired recollection in his companions. We read also, that many were converted by only looking upon St. Lucian the Martyr.

—Fr. Claude Texier, S.J. (1610–1687)

∞

Good Works

In all things, show thyself an example of good works.

—Titus 2:7

The forgetfulness of our good works is, in itself, our surest safeguard. If you publicly display gold and precious vestments, you invite thieves to find out the means of robbing you; but if you keep them hidden in some secret corner of your dwelling, they will be safe. As it is with riches, so it is the same with virtues and good works. If we keep them in our memory and, as it were, expose them for sale, we arm our enemies against us and invite them to deprive us of the merit. But if they are known only to Him who knows everything, we shall possess and keep them in hopeful security.

Do not, therefore, expose the riches of your good works, for fear of their being taken from you, as was the case with the Pharisee who, carrying on his lips the treasures of his good works, gave Satan the opportunity of robbing him. He spoke only of giving thanks and displayed his good works to God; nevertheless, that did not shelter him, for it was not to return thanks to God, but to seek to be praised by many, to insult others, and to raise himself above them all.

If you return thanks to God, think only of pleasing Him alone; do not seek to be known by men, and do not judge your neighbor.

—St. John Chrysostom (ca. 349–407), *On Matthew 3*

∞

When we neglect nothing and are careful to store up the little gains we can make, we shall insensibly increase our riches; it is nearly the same with spiritual riches.

Since our Divine Lord and Judge will keep an account of a glass of water, there is no good action we ought to despise, however small it may appear, and we must not be grieved if we cannot do great things. Little things naturally are the forerunners of great actions. Neglect the former, and you will not be capable of doing the latter.

It was to prevent this misfortune that Jesus Christ has promised to reward us for little things.

There is nothing easier than visiting a sick person. Nevertheless, God has fixed a great reward for this good work, however easy it may appear.

— St. John Chrysostom (ca. 349–407), *Opuscules*

∞

As the prospect of an abundant harvest soothes the labors and cheers the heart of the husbandman — so in like manner hope and reward ought to support us and relieve our fatigues. The harvest will be ours, for "In due time we shall reap." We cannot cherish a doubt of this, without questioning the fidelity of the Lord our God.

The laborer, notwithstanding his wise precautions, his indefatigable care, his well-founded hopes, may, in a single night, find his fields torn and spoiled by a mighty storm or by some other accident. But the just man has nothing to fear. Let him but persevere in the practice of good works, and nothing in the world can hinder him the fruit: "And in doing good let us not fail; for in due time we shall reap, not failing" (Gal. 6:9).

Some commentators explain those words of the Apostle in another way. It is right, say they, that we should sow without respite; since, in heaven, the harvest will be eternal: "We shall reap, not failing." This is the opinion of St. Augustine.

Good Works

Do not relax in your efforts, says the holy Doctor, and God will not fail to reward you. But if you tire of your work or flag in your efforts, the judgments of the Lord, says a prophet, will overwhelm you, like those bitter weeds that grow in the midst of the wheat. The words of the Apostle signify that we should not cease from preparing for the harvest: "We shall reap, not failing."

The husbandmen do not allow themselves to be overfatigued, although they reap with joy; but the saints who gather in heaven what they have sown partake of the purest pleasures in unalterable joy and pleasures ever new.

Who could have a disrelish in the abode of glory: "What shall come of thee by the pleasure of the Most High" (Sir. 41:6 [RSV= Sir. 41:4]). The fruit of a few years is there, provided the work be persevered in. The choice of seed, the good soil, the beauty of the season do not produce a good harvest if the seeds are not protected from the birds, who swarm to carry them away. That signifies that we must conceal from men the good we do, and not seek for their esteem and praise, for this will deprive you of the merit in the sight of God. If foolish souls, by displaying the good they do, do not lose all the merit, they, at least, lose the greater part. You have sown, but you have reaped but little; the birds of heaven have eaten what you have sown. That is to say, the thoughts of vanity that are in your heart, and which you have complacently encouraged, will have deprived you of the reward that was prepared for you. Conceal then, with humility, your good works, when they are not necessary to be witnessed.

The time will come when you shall receive the reward a hundredfold. "For in due time we shall reap, not failing."

—Fr. Paul Segneri, S.J. (1624–1694), *Meditations*

∞

Holiness and Perfection

Be you therefore perfect,
as also your heavenly Father is perfect.

—Matthew 5:48

No, I must no longer say that holiness is too high a state for such a miserable wretch as I am to aspire to. I feel sure that God calls me to it, and that He wishes to conduct me, since He has prepared the way. I am sure that He wills that I should dare to aspire to it, and that I should do my utmost to reach perfection.

Indeed, what could I wish to be, if I did not wish to be a saint? I must then be a reprobate, for there is no middle course—either a saint or a reprobate. And I must not say that I am too weak and frail to pretend to become a saint; I know but too well that I am a poor frail mortal, but I also know that my Redeemer, who has spared no pains to make me a saint, has taken upon Himself my infirmities, in order to clothe me with His strength, and that I can say with St. Paul, "I can do all in Him who strengthens me" (see Phil. 4:13).

What, then, have I to do to make me really and truly holy, according to the intention of the Son of God, who calls me to sanctity? I have only to put on the Lord Jesus, as the same Apostle says (Rom. 13:14). Is there anything easier, provided that I have the will? If it were a question of amassing great riches to be holy, many obstacles would have to be overcome, many legitimate pretexts would have to be decided, for each one would dispute who should have them; but holiness partly consists in despising riches, and in not allowing them to retain a hold of the heart.

In the same way, if, to be a saint, it was found necessary to be raised to great honors, or noble employments, or to undertake the management of a city or state, holiness would cost so dear that few persons would venture to accept the burden, and it would afford an excuse to many to decline the trial; but what can hinder us, when we are told that the surest and safest road to sanctification is to cherish a hidden life, to love humility and lowliness?

In conclusion, to be virtuous and holy, if it were necessary to enjoy the pleasures of this life, would it not cost much? Should we not have to go to great expense? And often, even then, should we not find much that was bitter, where we expected nought but pleasure and sweetness? But to renounce sensual gratifications, to be content to suffer all the crosses inseparable from every condition of life, to prefer a mortified life of austerity and penance, is this what everyone can do? And thus, as there is no one who cannot but be holy and virtuous if he likes, it follows that all excuses must be frivolous, and cannot be allowed for, at the judgment seat of God.

What! Is it then so difficult to love the three things that the Savior of men has so much loved, and which contain every essential of a truly sanctified life, namely, poverty, contempt, and crosses?

These three things often accompany a sanctified life, and we have so great a dread of them that we look upon them as mortal enemies. Instead of this we should seek for them, and embrace them as the best means of becoming saints, thus becoming as so many sources of merit, and with these, we heap up treasures that will enrich us for all eternity. It is true that our lower nature feels a natural repugnance to, and rebels against, such strong remedies, but the grace of our Savior, who comes to our aid, gives us additional strength. It is this grace that, being the overflowing of His Divine Spirit, infuses into a soul a love of those things that He so much loved; and He clothes it with a holy strength in order that, by a supernatural virtue, he may embrace that which it fled from through a natural repugnance.

And how many saints, who were men like us, and subject to the same infirmities, have been happier, more contented in their poverty, than the rich worldlings with all their treasures? How many of them have felt a sweeter consolation in the midst of scorn and contempt than the most ambitious have felt, even when loaded with honors? And how many have felt a holier joy, even when carrying a heavy cross, than the sensualists in the midst of their pleasures?

—Fr. D'Argentan, Conference 23

∞

How can a truly virtuous man fail in anything? In what situation will he not be powerful; in what state of poverty will he not be rich; in what obscurity will he not be brilliant; in what inaction will he not be industrious; in what infirmity will he not be vigorous; in what weakness will he not be strong; in what solitude will he not be accompanied? For he will have for company the hope of a happy eternity; for clothing, he will have the grace of the Most High; for ornament, the promises of a halo of glory!

Let us recollect that the saints were not of a more excellent nature than ours but were more orderly and regular; that they were not exempt from sins, but that they took pains to correct their faults.

—St. Ambrose (340–397), *De Joseph*

∽

Human Respect

Do I seek to please men? If I yet pleased men,
I should not be a servant of Christ.

—Galatians 1:10

Human respect outrages the dignity of God, for the grandeur of the Creator requires that it should not be put in comparison with man, whom He has drawn from the slime of the earth; and all other greatnesses can be only regarded as nothing.

Now, wishing on the one hand to give yourself up to God, and kept back on the other hand by the fear of man, you say to Him: O Lord, I would devote myself to You, and I would serve You in preference to anyone else, if, situated as I am, I was allowed to serve You without exposing myself to the criticism of the world; I would like to be able to break off all connection with the world, and to consecrate all to You alone, if, in declaring myself openly, I did not attract the notice of a thousand dangerous enemies. I feel a very great affection, it is true; You have filled my soul with a wholesome inclination for virtue, and I dream of being relieved from my grievous faults, of which I am a very slave. Nevertheless, I have not the courage to put into practice my wish, for fear of losing the esteem of the world.

I feel that I am called upon to lead a life of piety; however, I drag my chains after me, although with regret, because the world does not wish to love You, and does not even wish me to love You.

Ah! if it depended solely on myself to choose the path, I would be all in all for You, O Lord; You would be the sole master of my heart, and one would see that, from henceforth, I would do that which I have not done in times past. But You well know what a number of bitter reproaches I would have to endure, were I to make known to the world my determination. You know that the world is most unmerciful to those who leave it, in order to enter into Your service, and, since I must say it, I feel that I have not the moral courage to despise the world, and that I have still the weakness of forgetting You, by remaining in its service.

I know what many would say in answer to this. It is sufficient, they say, to serve Almighty God in secret, to give Him our hearts, without making any outward show of our devotion. Is there any need of making a parade of conversion, which can be done secretly, without the world knowing anything about it? Must we give to the public a sight where vanity and vainglory might possibly play a greater part than that of true piety? Can we not give to God a clean heart, and a faith so fervent that He will accept it?

Can a sinner not do good, serve God, weep for his sins, practice virtue, without its being known to men? Can a just and good man not live by faith, without the world being cognizant of it?

I know that we must conform to the decorous usages and customs of the world, that we must accommodate ourselves to the times and places, that we must take certain measures with regard to our position in society, that charity prompts us to conceal much from the eyes of men, that we must be weak with the weak, strong with the strong, all to all, as says the great Apostle, and there is even a merit in hiding the good we do.

But I say that the allegiance we owe to the Almighty is divided between God and a world that we ought to hate, and this world we flatter by concealing our conversion and serving God in secret. It is my opinion that it is being only half a Christian to blush at being all for Jesus, after unblushingly and willfully following the pernicious maxims of the world.

Human Respect

Since a God made man had become the jest of madmen, since He has been exposed to insults innumerable for love of you, can you wish to conceal your duty to Him, and to suffer something for His sake?

O man! how you ought to blush for being so ungrateful, and not give some tokens of affection to your God, who has loaded you with so many blessings, and especially the crowning gift of conversion. I do not say that your declaring yourself openly for God is unworthy of a generous man; but if you believe in His justice, why dissimulate when you have once embraced His service? A soul that has been reared in pious society would not know how to counterfeit. If you have been taught to love our Lord, if you have promised to serve Him, why do you wish to conceal your love?

You pique yourself on having strength of mind, on having a moral courage in the business of this world, and in religion you are weaker than the ordinary run of mortals.

—Fr. Jean Baptiste Massillon (1663–1742),
Discourse on Human Respect

∽

There is nothing we ought to dread more than giving preference to the fear of man over the fear of God.

—St. Gregory (ca. 540–604), *On Proverbs*

Humility

The prayer of the humble and
the meek hath always pleased Thee.
—Judith 9:16

If, for acts of a true and sincere devotion the world shall esteem you mean, abject, or foolish, humility will make you rejoice at this happy reproach, the cause of which is not in you, but in those who reproach you.

What is it to love your own abjection? In Latin, *abjectio* signifies humility, and humility signifies abjection; so, when our Blessed Lady, in her sacred canticle, says that all generations should call her blessed, because our Lord had regarded the humility of His handmaid, her meaning is that our Lord had graciously looked down on her abjection, her meanness and lowliness, to heap His graces and favors upon her.

Nevertheless, there is a difference between the virtue of humility and abjection; for our abjection is the lowliness, meanness, and baseness that is in us, without our being aware of it, whereas the virtue of humility is a true knowledge and a voluntary acknowledgment of our abjection. Now, the main point of this humility consists in being willing, not only to acknowledge our abjection but to love and delight in it; and this, not through want of courage and generosity, but for the greater exaltation of the Divine Majesty, and holding our neighbor in greater estimation than ourselves.

Praise, honor, and glory, are not given to men for every degree of virtue, but for an excellence of virtue; for by praise we endeavor to persuade others to esteem the excellence of those whom we praise; by honor we testify that we ourselves esteem them; and glory, in my opinion, is nothing but a certain luster of reputation that arises from the concurrence of praise and honor. So honor and praise are like precious stones, from a collection of which glory proceeds like a certain enameling. Now, humility, not enduring that we should have any opinion of our own excellence, or think ourselves worthy to be preferred before others, consequently cannot permit that we should hunt after praise, honor, or glory, which are due only to excellence.

Let us incessantly fix our eyes on Jesus Christ crucified, and march on in His service with confidence and sincerity, but yet with wisdom and discretion. He will be the protector of our reputation; and should He suffer it to be taken from us, it will be either to restore it with advantage, or to make us profit in holy humility, one ounce of which is preferable to ten thousand pounds of honors.

—St. Francis de Sales (1567–1622)

ॐ

Humility is the perfume of God. It is the fragrance that He who cannot be humbled Himself, because He is God, leaves behind. It is the odor, the stain, the token that the Creator leaves upon the creature, when He has pressed upon it for a moment.

It must be a law of the world of grace, because we find it in Mary, in the saints, and in the faintest, most nearly indistinguishable way in ourselves. Perhaps it is something inseparable from God. We trace the Most High, the Incommunicable, by it in the Old Testament. We trace Jesus by it in the New. The glory of humility is in the human nature of our Lord, on which the mysterious pressure of the Divine Nature rested for evermore. It is this inevitable perfume that God leaves behind Him that hinders His altogether hiding His traces from us. It is "the myrrh, and stacte, and cassia from His ivory houses" (Ps. 44:9 [RSV = Ps 45:8]).

Mary has found Him, and she has lain down in the lowliest, most flowery valley of humility, and the fragrance of God has perfumed her garments, her "gilded clothing surrounded with variety" (Ps. 44:10 [RSV = Ps 45:9]).

∞

Humility grows far more rapidly, and blossoms more abundantly, in the mere thought of the immensity of God's love of us, and the unintelligible prodigality of His fatherly affection for us, where there is no thought of self at all, even in the way of merited self-reproach. This vision—for it is nothing but a beautiful celestial vision—overshadows our souls. The fires of our selfish passions go out in it. The glare of the world seems softened through it. There is nothing to distract us in the absorbing simplicity of this one sight that we are beholding. There is nothing to awaken self-love and to aim it against the nobler or better thoughts of self-forgetfulness.

Humility is never more intense than when it is thus simply overwhelmed by love; and never can our souls be more completely overwhelmed by love than when they rest, silent and wonder stricken, beneath the shadow of the Blessed Sacrament.

Nothing teaches us humility so much as the Blessed Sacrament. Our hearts for very love are constrained to imitate Him in our own feeble way, and to worship Him in His sacramental presence by a continual exercise of interior humility.

—Fr. Frederick William Faber (1814–1863),
The Foot of the Cross and *The Blessed Sacrament*

∞

Love of Our Neighbor

He that loveth his neighbor, hath fulfilled the law.

—Romans 13:8

In reference to this commandment, St. Bernardine of Siena remarks that we should love our neighbor with a genuine affection, and not in the same way as we love things necessary or useful, such as bread, a house, and other things that are for our use or for our amusement; these we do not love as ourselves, but for ourselves.

St. Chrysostom says that when the Son of God gave us the best of prayers, He did not intend that we should say "My Father" but "Our Father"; inasmuch, as we have a common Father in heaven we should consider all men as our brethren, and in this way we should love each other with a mutual love, with a love stronger in grace than in nature, as we have all an equal right to a vocation to a supernatural life, the same hope of a heavenly reward.

∞

How sweet is this command! exclaims the saintly Jesuit Père de la Colombière; does it not appear to be worthy of the goodness and wisdom of God? Is it not reasonable that men who are endowed with one and the same nature, who have one and the same Father in heaven, who are obliged to live in society, who are all fellow travelers, and who ought to meet again in heaven—is it not reasonable, says he, that we should love one another here below and should help one another in the same degree as we would wish to be helped ourselves?

The love of our neighbor may be placed in the same category as the love we owe to God. Not all who say, "Lord, Lord" (that is to say, not all who say that they love God) shall enter the kingdom of heaven (Matt. 7:21). Good works and proofs of that love are requisite. He alone will enter the kingdom of heaven who does the will of the Father. The same may be said of the love of our neighbor. We must show it by solid proofs.

As a Christian, you are expressly to love your neighbor; therefore, it is certain that you will best show your affection by tendering all the help that it may be in your power to give him.

The love of our neighbor, says St. Paul, is a debt that is not discharged in the ordinary way; that is to say, a debt once paid is paid once for all. This is what St. Paul means: we are always beholden in the love we are obliged to have for one another.

The more you pay in love and charity, the more you will owe, says St. Augustine.

He who, says St. Fulgentius, does not believe that he has aught to pay to his neighbor, as if he had discharged the debt, ought rather to weep for himself as being without charity.

Do not believe that, when you have forgiven your brother, you have canceled the obligation and that you have already given sufficient proofs of your love. We are ever indebted to our brethren, on occasion of the mutual bond there is between us and them.

We are members of the same body, and if charity be not in our hearts, we renounce this bond; and being no longer united with our neighbor, we have no claim on the love of Jesus, our Model and Master.

St. Chrysostom also says, in his *Homilies on St. Matthew*: One loves because he is loved, another because he is honored, another because he thinks that it will be of service to him; but, alas! how seldom it is that you meet with a person who loves his brother as he ought for the sake of Jesus. Nearly all friends are allied by the bonds of an affection which is of the world, worldly.

Love of Our Neighbor

St. Bernard says that he who does not love God cannot love his neighbor with a sincere affection; God therefore must be our first love, in order that we may be able to love our neighbor, in God and for God.

St. Philip Neri tells us that in dealing with our neighbor, we must assume as much pleasantness of manner as we can, and by this affability, win him to the way of virtue.

—From diverse saints

∞

Love of Our Enemies

But I say to you: Love your enemies, do good to
those who hate you, pray for those who persecute you,
and for those who calumniate you, in order that you may
be the children of your Father who is in heaven.

—Matthew 5:44

Let us reflect seriously on the condition made by our Savior when He taught us to say to our Heavenly Father those words, "Forgive us our trespasses, as we forgive those who trespass against us."

How easy it is to obtain pardon, if we do that which mainly depends on our own exertions; for we have a right to ask for pardon from our Lord if we have forgiven those who may have trespassed against us. We could not realize this if we did not meditate on the wondrous wisdom of the Son of God. His design being to establish charity among men, He makes use of our need of His mercy; and since the state of sin is our greatest misery, He is willing to grant us the remission of sin on condition that we grant our neighbors the greatest favor we can bestow—namely, forgiveness for their trespasses against us.

Let us endeavor to walk in the footsteps of those patriarchs and early martyrs mentioned in Holy Scripture. Let us imitate Joseph, who repaid with presents all the outrages he had received from his brothers; Moses, who prayed for that rebellious people who were continually waging war against him; David, who to Saul returned good for evil; St. Stephen, who, when he was being stoned to death, implored God's pardon for his executioners; St. Paul, who, after having been cruelly persecuted by the Jews, worked incessantly for their conversion.

Should not these grand examples teach us to do good to those who are our enemies?

— Archbishop Bartholomew de Carranza (d. 1576)

∞

"I also say to you: Love your enemies. It is I," says Jesus, "who speak to you."

If a mere man had said so, you would point out the gravity of the offense, and the justice of your resentment. If a person for whom you have the highest respect were to entreat you to forgive another, you might, perhaps, answer that you could obey him in all things else, but in this case you have been very deeply wronged. If a prince or king were to tell you the like, you would suspend your vengeance and give some mark of an outward reconciliation, but in your heart you would cherish a hatred that would burst forth sooner or later.

But it is God who speaks; it is God who commands you to "love your enemies, and do good to those that hate you." To so precise a command, what have you to answer? Consider, says Tertullian, the dignity and infinite majesty of Him who commands.

Do not speak of passion, human feelings, the pleasure of revenge, the atrocity of the insult, the indignity of the affront. It is God who speaks, and He must be obeyed. Do not tell me that this is difficult. Was it difficult for David? Was it so for St. Stephen?

It is difficult, I grant, but it is God who has made it. It is difficult, but it is His will that you should surmount the difficulty.

If, in a violent persecution, He were to ask you to lay down your life, as He has done to some martyrs, would you refuse to give it to Him? If He asked for the last drop of your blood, would you not shed it joyfully?

He commands you to love your enemies and forgive them. Is not this enough?

—Fr. Joly (1715–1775)

∞

It is more glorious to bear silently an affront, in imitation of Christ, than to retort with a sharp and sarcastic reply.

If it should happen that the remembrance of an injury stirs up your soul to anger, call to mind what the Son of God has suffered for us, and how comparatively few have been your sufferings. By this means, you will throw water on the smoldering flames, and you will be the better able to smother your resentment.

—St. Gregory of Nazianzen (329–390), *Sentences*

∞

Meditation and Mental Prayer

Before prayer prepare thy soul; and
be not, as a man that tempteth God.

—Sirach 18:23

The precious gift of prayer, so essential to religion, so glorious to the creature, so favorable to the sinner, so beneficial for all men is nowadays either despised or neglected. It is to induce us to practice this that the Church proposes as our model the early Christians, who had no better occupation, no more agreeable duty.

Indeed, O my God, if we were to think of only its advantage and benefit, what consolations, what sweetness, would we not experience from it? Forced to live for a time in this land of exile, far from Thee, and far from Thy celestial abode, what should we do without the salutary exercise of prayer?

What better consolation can we hope for, except by taking advantage by this means of raising up our thoughts to heaven, of placing ourselves in direct communication with Thee, of consulting Thee in all our scruples, of exposing all our wants, of telling Thee of all our troubles, or of offering up all our pains and sufferings?

What other resource can there be for us except by this holy exercise, by which we shall find an anointing grace that can soften our griefs, a charitable hand to dry our tears, a secret, sacred ray to enlighten our path, a Father who will listen to our petitions, a Physician who will cure all our infirmities, a Judge who will interest Himself in all our concerns, a Master who is ever instructing us?

What other consolation will remain, if we have neglected to seek for this potent remedy?

—Fr. Jean Baptiste Massillon (1663–1742)

૭૪

The first thing we must do in prayer is represent to ourselves, by the help of our memory, the point or mystery that we may wish to be the subject of our prayer. Then our understanding must examine this point and consider all the particulars of it. Finally, our will must produce acts, according as the understanding has digested the matter, that have been proposed to it by our memory. But since this discourse of the understanding is the source whence all our acts in prayer flow; and since we can make no act that does not necessarily spring from this our meditation, it follows that we must be particularly careful to make this well.

The truth is, this proposition is self-evident, for anyone who has the least tincture of philosophy knows that the will is a blind power, unable to attach itself to anything, unless the understanding guides it. Hence it is a maxim received by all philosophers, "that nothing can be willed unless it is first known." The will, having of itself no light, must borrow it from the understanding, which goes before it to give it knowledge and to discover what it ought to love or hate. It is this that made St. Augustine say that "we may love the things we never saw, but never those we have not known"; and St. Gregory says, "No one can love what he is entirely ignorant of."

The reason for this is that the object of the will being a known good, we cannot love anything unless we perceive it is good and deserving of love; just as, on the contrary, we do not hate a thing or fly from it unless we conceive it to be bad and deserving of hatred.

It is clear, therefore, that the operation of the understanding is the foundation of all our acts in prayer; whence it follows that meditation is most necessary, and that prayer cannot be perfect unless meditation goes before or accompanies it, as says Hugo of St. Victor.

—Fr. Alphonse Rodriguez, S.J. (1526–1616), *Christian Perfection*

∽

Meekness

Blessed are the meek:
for they shall possess the land.

—Matthew 5:4

We must accustom ourselves to perform all our actions with quiet serenity. Force of habit can correct or subdue the most obstinate bad temper. But because some are naturally so impetuous and violent that it is difficult to effect an immediate cure, it would be well to reflect on the motives that engender impatience, in order to induce us to effect a gradual cure.

When ebullitions of passion come upon us so suddenly that there is no time for reflection, we must at least try to soothe them, if we cannot immediately master them. It is sometimes proper to make a desperate effort; but we must always try to conquer by degrees, more especially when the first bursts of impatience or anger assail us. It is recommended in Holy Writ: give time for anger to evaporate, and then extinguish it entirely. We must not only do what we can to prevent our getting into a passion, but we must use greater efforts to subdue it when it does come on. Those little outbursts of petulance, which are more amusing than bitter, are innocent in children; they fire up and are appeased in a moment, and all is soon forgotten. Let us not be ashamed to imitate children in this; for does not our Savior say, "If you do not become as little children, you cannot enter into the kingdom of heaven" (see Matt. 18:3)?

Never answer an angry person with a haughty haste; if he be ill-tempered, why fall into the same fault? When two flinty stones are quickly rubbed together, sparks will fly out.

If you cannot cure anger by those means that a calmer judgment would suggest, you must have recourse to stratagem. Patience is a great assistant; for time softens the most violent passion. If we should be exposed to the provocations of a person who continually has recourse to sharp, impertinent answers, and we feel that we have not sufficient command over our own temper, we can at least moderate our tongue by keeping silent. Holy Scripture gives us this advice: "Suffer in silence, and do not have recourse to sharp retorts"; you can then seek reconciliation, and do your best to make it lasting.

We have a noble example in the conduct of Jacob. His first care was to keep his mind free from any temptation to break the precept of meekness. If you have not the strength of mind to do this, at any rate, you can bridle your tongue and allow no bitter reply to escape your lips. When you have taken all such precautions, you will find that more is to be done to secure a mild and even temper.

Would you wish to know how to act when any injury or affront is imposed on you? Above all, do not return evil for evil; pay no attention to the malice of another; there is no occasion to be wicked because another is wicked. Take care to preserve self-respect, and do nothing that might be a reproach for you afterward.

The heathens have often quoted a sensible reply of one of their philosophers. One of his attendants had greatly displeased him by an act of gross injustice. "Go, unhappy man," said he. "How severely would I punish you, were I not angry." King David acted in a similar way; at a time when he was tempted to inflict vengeance, he gained a complete victory over his temper by not uttering a single word to those who had wronged him. Abigail, by her entreaties, calmed that gentle prince who was at the head of his soldiers and who was on his road to avenge the insults of Nabal. It is a sure sign of a noble disposition if you listen to sincere petitions and grant what is demanded of you. David always felt rejoiced when he forgave his enemies, and he praised the cleverness of that woman who so well knew his tenderness of heart that she obtained all she sought for. That royal prophet was not insensible to injury, for he cries out, "I am hurt at what evil-disposed persons have said; had I consulted my evil genius, I should have rejoiced to inflict vengeance."

But this glorious and pacific king, on second thoughts, continues to say, "O! who will give me the wings of the dove, that I may seek peace in flight?" And notwithstanding all their insults and outrages, he preferred to remain in peace.

He says in another place: "Be angry, but sin not." This is a moral precept, which teaches us to allay any little asperity that we cannot altogether stifle.

— St. Ambrose (340–397), *De Officiis*

∞

Meekness preserves within us the image of God, but anger blots it out. If any hard or cutting words should inadvertently escape from your lips, apply the remedy and cure, from the same mouth that caused so sensitive a wound.

St. Augustine (354–430)

∞

Modesty

The fruit of modesty is the fear of the Lord,
riches, and glory, and life.

—See Proverbs 22:4

Modesty is a great relief to our words and actions; it prevents us from committing many faults and from giving utterance to words likely to shock those who listen to us. Often an inconsiderate word betrays us and reveals our secret thoughts. Modesty should even regulate the sound of our voice, so that it may soften any violent outburst, and should never depart from the rules prescribed.

Silence, the guardian of our hidden virtues, is also very necessary for the preservation of modesty and is very beneficial when employed properly—not, however, disdainfully or in a contemptuous, haughty way. Modesty should pervade all that is exterior—our walk, our gestures, and our movements. All outside appearances reveal the condition of our mind; although our passions are hidden, they manifest themselves exteriorly. One easily knows if a man is fickle, haughty, or mischievous, or if he is wise, patient, and reserved; the motion of the body is a species of voice that bespeaks all that is passing in the soul.

We often see some people walk as if they were on the stage of a theater, who march as if they were counting their steps or who move about like dummies. I can well understand that a well-educated person should not walk or run hastily, unless necessity or fear compels him to do so: I fancy that he should be neither too fast nor too slow in his movements, nor that he should be as stiff as a statue. There is a medium in all things.

A man of good breeding should, even in walking, keep up a certain decorum and gravity, without affectation or pompous display. This gravity should be natural, devoid of artifice or constraint. All that is counterfeit or unnatural will always be unpleasing.

Modesty is suitable for all ages, and for all classes of persons; for all times and places; it is especially becoming in youth, and is essentially the dowry of all young people. In whatsoever state or condition of life we may be placed, we should carefully cherish decorum in all we do and make this the business of our life.

An old philosopher remarks that we should even regulate our manners with a certain seasoning, or rather a certain something, I know not how to express, that imparts a gracefulness to all we do. We must not, however, let this agreeableness appear affected, for nothing unnatural can ever be pleasing.

The tone of our voice should be firm, and neither mincing nor effeminate. There are some who disguise their words with an affectation of false gravity, savoring somewhat of malice or sarcasm.

We should further examine into what is appropriate for everyone. What would be suitable for one sex would often be ridiculous for the other. Despite all that we may wish to do, however, we cannot hope to please everybody.

Let not your manners appear affected or effeminate, but above all, avoid all that is rude, gross, or impolite. Let us follow all that nature inspires us with. If we try to be natural, we shall the more easily keep within the bounds of decorum and good breeding.

—St. Ambrose (340–397), *De Officiis* 1:18, 19

∞

It is certain that there is nothing more edifying, more winning, than a wise and modest exterior, because men can see only what is outside, and it is that exterior that moves and preaches more than a torrent of words. Indeed, a humble and mortified exterior has often induced people to be devout and has given them a contempt for worldly things; it has excited sinners to compunction and has raised up their hearts to heavenly things. It is a preaching more effective than the most eloquent of sermons; and the reason why men so esteem modesty and propriety, and are so edified by them, is that they always draw this inference therefrom: that there must be much that is good within. The face, says St. Jerome, is the mirror of the soul, and the eyes, dumb as they are, reveal hidden secrets; there is no mirror that better reflects exterior objects.

In the nineteenth chapter of Ecclesiasticus we read: "A man is known by his look, and a wise man, when thou meetest him, is known by his countenance. The attire of the body, and the laughter of the teeth, and the gait of the man, show what he is" (Ecclus. 19:26–27 [RSV = Sir. 19:29–30]) And the Holy Spirit, speaking through the mouth of the wise man, says: "An unprofitable man walketh with a perverse mouth; he winketh with the eyes, presseth with the foot, speaketh with the finger" (Prov. 6:12–13).

St. Gregory of Nazianzen, speaking of Julian the Apostate, says: "A great many knew not Julian till he made himself known by his infamous actions, and by his abuse of sovereignty; but for my part, when I first knew him, and lived and conversed with him at Athens, I never could perceive the least sign of goodness in him. He carried his head extremely high; his shoulders, as well as his eyes, were always in motion; his behavior was haughty and fierce; his feet never stood still; every moment either anger caused his nostrils to swell, or disdain drew them in. He was continually trying to be witty, or would indulge in low and coarse buffoonery, and his laughter was ungraciously loud. He would freely grant and deny the same thing in the same breath; he would speak without rule or judgment; he would ask silly questions and give impertinent answers.

"By such exterior marks as these, I knew him beforehand, long before I was made acquainted with his impiety, and this news only confirmed my former judgment of him.

My Daily Visit with the Saints

"Those that lived with us then at Athens, were they here present, would testify that, having observed his manners, I exclaimed, O! city of Rome, what a monster art thou feeding! This I then said, and at the same time I heartily wished I might be mistaken; and without doubt it had been much better that I had been so, since we then should not have seen those evils that have almost rendered the world desolate."

Thus, you see that an irregular exterior is a mark of a disordered interior; as an exterior modesty is a mark of a composed interior, which is the reason why men are ordinarily so much moved and edified by it.

—Fr. Alphonse Rodriguez, S.J. (1526–1616),
On Christian Perfection 10

∞

Mortification

If any man will come after me, let him deny him-
self, and take up his cross daily, and follow me.

—Luke 9:23

"They that are Christ's have crucified their flesh, and their vices and concupiscences," said St. Paul (Gal. 5:24). Note that he does not say that those who are Christ's have crucified only their vices, but they that have crucified their flesh along with their vices. In order to effect a cure, we must go to the source, and the flesh is the root of the evils of our soul. But in order to effect a perfect cure, we must chastise the body and bring it under subjection, and this the great Apostle said of himself: "I chastise my body" (1 Cor. 9:27).

How do you act in this particular? What harsh treatment of your body do you practice? Do you fast? What are the austerities you practice?

If, instead of mortifying your flesh and bringing it under subjection, you think only of feeding it and procuring for it every comfort, you are not Christ's. Why? Because, "they that are Christ's have crucified their flesh with the vices and concupiscences."

It is not enough merely to crucify the flesh, but we must also crucify the vices. That is to say, we must add interior mortification to exterior mortification. In fact, the one should not be practiced without the other; for it would be of little use to chastise the body and bring it under subjection, if our hearts and affections slavishly cherished inordinate desires.

St. Paul points out two things that we ought to destroy through the practice of interior mortification: our bad habits and our vices. I say "our bad habits," for however careful we may be to mortify ourselves, we always fall into some actual sin; but as for habitual sins, if we fight them with courage and perseverance, we shall in the end totally destroy them. With regard to our vices, we do not entirely destroy them, but we can at least weaken the power they have over us; and if we cannot exterminate them on the cross, we can, at least, attach them thereto, and this we ought to try to do, if we wish to be Christ's, for "they that are Christ's have crucified their flesh, and the vices and concupiscences."

The Apostle does not tell you, "If you live according to the Spirit," but he says, "If by the Spirit you mortify the deeds of the flesh, you shall live" (Rom. 8:13). One can easily live according to the flesh, and that happens but too often; but no man on earth can always live according to the Spirit; that pure spiritual life is to be found only in heaven, where the flesh, then fully under the control of the Spirit, does not feel the least inclination of rebellion.

Thus, what St. Paul recommends to us is to resist the assaults of the flesh by curbing our desires, by checking our ardor, by a continual opposition to the wicked suggestions of our will; in a word, by bridling our passions by these means and thus overcoming every temptation. Nevertheless, the Apostle does not require that kind of mortification that consists in austerities, scourgings, and so forth, although these are useful for humbling ourselves and bringing us under the dominion of the Spirit.

But the ordinary mortification, so indispensable to every Christian, is that which we have just explained: "If by the Spirit you mortify the deeds of the flesh, you shall live."

—Fr. Paul Segneri, S.J. (1624–1694), *Meditations*

∽

The exercise of interior mortification is a kind of penance, which no one has a right to be dispensed from. It has been the invariable custom of all the saints and known to those who have ever had a wish to be perfect. One has only to be attentive to the Spirit of God. The love of Jesus is so ingenious on this point that He inspires the simplest and most unpolished minds with skillful methods of self-mortification that far surpass the comprehension of the worldly wise and might pass off as so many small miracles.

There is nothing that happens that may not give us an opportunity of thwarting our inclinations; there is no time or place that may not be chosen for practicing interior mortification, without in the least interfering with the rules of common sense.

For example, we can be silent when we have a desire to talk; we can close our eyes when we wish to see. The longing to hear the news, or to know what is going on, what is done, what is said; the wish to see a person, to relate an anecdote, to learn the success of a business that interests us; in a word, all overeagerness is a subject of mortification that would prove to be of more than usual merit and of which God alone would be the witness.

Nothing is more plentiful than the opportunities of interior mortification. Mention of a few will be wonderfully instructive. A word said apropos, a harmless joke, just to enliven the conversation—these refrained from, might be the matter of a beautiful sacrifice. There is scarcely an hour in the day that does not afford us an opportunity of mortification.

Sitting or standing, one can never fail of finding an inconvenient seat or posture without being noticed.

A person may be often interrupted when particularly engaged, and as often can reply with as much mildness and civility as if he had not been very busy. The ill humor of a person at home, the annoyances of a servant, the ingratitude of a man who is indebted to you for past kindnesses—all these may exercise the patience of a good, pious man.

In conclusion, the inconveniences, depending on place, weather, or persons, that are endured unnoticed or unheeded are petty opportunities of mortifying oneself, it is true; but the mortification in these trifling matters is not little; it is very meritorious, and it may be said that the greatest graces are the fruit of these petty mortifications.

—Fr. Croiset, S.J. (b. ca. 1650), *Exercices de Pieté*

∞

A man must learn to treat his body as if it were diseased, that is to say, he must abstain from the food he longs for but that would be hurtful to his body, and must submit to take that which would do it good, notwithstanding the repugnance he may naturally feel.

Thus much for bodily mortification, but spiritual mortification is a kind of martyrdom; it has not the visible torture of the iron chain, but it has something far more troublesome, and that is its duration.

—St. Bernard (1091–1153), Epistle to his Brothers

∞

Obedience

*Let every soul be subject to higher pow-
ers; for there is no power but from God.*

—Romans 13:1

There are two sorts of obedience: the one necessary, the other voluntary.
By that which is necessary, you must obey your ecclesiastical superiors
— the Pope, the bishop, the parish priest, and such as are commissioned
by them; as also your civil superiors and those established for administering justice; and, finally, your domestic superiors — your father and mother,
master and mistress.

Now, this obedience is called necessary because no man can exempt
himself from the duty of obeying his superiors, God having placed them
in authority to command and govern, each in the department that is
assigned to him. You must, then, of necessity obey their commands; but,
to be perfect, follow their counsels also — nay, even their desires and inclinations, so far as charity and discretion will permit. Obey them when
they order that which is agreeable, such as to eat or to take recreation; for
although there seems no great virtue to obey on such occasions, it would
be a great sin to disobey. Obey them in matters indifferent, as to wear
this or that dress, to go one way or another, to sing or to be silent, and
this will be a very commendable obedience. Obey them in things hard,
troublesome, or disagreeable, and this will be a perfect obedience. Obey,
in fine, meekly, without reply; readily, without delay; cheerfully, without

repining; and, above all, lovingly, for the love of Him who, through His love for us, made Himself obedient unto death, even to the death of the Cross (Phil. 2:8), and who, as St. Bernard says, chose to part with His life rather than with His obedience.

We call that obedience to which we oblige ourselves by our own choice, and which is not imposed upon us by another, voluntary. We do not commonly choose our prince, our bishop, our father or mother, nor do even wives, sometimes, choose their husbands, but we choose our confessor and director. In choosing, then, we make a vow to obey, as did the holy St. Teresa, who, besides her obedience solemnly vowed to the superior of her order, bound herself by a simple vow to obey Father Gratian.

We must obey every one of our superiors, according to the charge he has over us. In political matters, we must obey our civil leader; in ecclesiastical matters, our prelates; in our domestic circle, father, master, or husband; and in what regards the private conduct of the soul, our spiritual father or director.

—St. Francis de Sales (1567–1622), *Introduction to the Devout Life*

∞

What would become of the world without obedience? To maintain order and discipline, what is more necessary than this virtue? Experience has proved this. Where obedience is not observed, there can be nothing but trouble; disorder glides in, and peace is banished.

A disunited whole is threatened with destruction, and ruin is unavoidable. But, on the contrary, where obedience is kept, all will be edified. In noticing this perfect unanimity, one would see that these contented minds are perfectly united. If there can be anything lasting on the earth, it is when it is united, and when everything is in perfect order, and this can never be the case where obedience is not strictly observed.

The Apostle St. Peter, in recommending obedience, takes every precaution. Had there been any way of dispensing with obedience, it would no doubt be feasible with those who abuse their authority. Is this a legitimate excuse for disobedience? Can we throw off the yoke and absolutely refuse to obey? If you did, you are condemned by St. Peter, for he says, "Be subject to your masters with all fear, not only to the good and gentle, but to the froward" (1 Pet. 2:18).

How mad is the world! The foundation of their joy is that they are free from all control and are masters of their conduct. How many there are to whom every kind of restraint is insupportable and who ever sigh to be free! They are like so many prodigal sons, who cannot endure their father's government; they are enemies of their own happiness; they wish to be their own masters and soon find that they have been woefully deceived.

Unhappy is that man who, following his own perverse will, wishes to be his own master. When God is angry with men and wills to punish them, one of His severest chastisements is to leave them to themselves and let them go according to their hearts: "So I let them go according to the desires of their heart: they shall walk in their own inventions" (Ps. 80:13 [RSV = Ps. 81:12]).

How has God punished infidel nations when, following blindly the inordinate desires of bestial passion, they excited His wrath by committing the most abominable crimes? "Wherefore, God gave them up to the desires of their heart, He delivered them up to shameful affections" (see Rom. 1:24).

But he who willingly obeys need not fear to be punished in this way. As he is resolved not to follow his own will, he need not expect that God would punish him or leave him to the desires of his heart. What, then, can be more advantageous than to obey, since obedience is a sure protection from that rigorous punishment that is so frightful and so much to be dreaded?

Taking into consideration the good results of obedience, we can say only that it is by far more beneficial to obey than to command. There is nothing, in fact, more to be dreaded than being raised to a high post of authority. Wise men have shrunk from its heavy weight of responsibility. And wherefore? Because they know how dangerous it is to command.

To seek for power, and to strive for a high post, is to wish to be your own enemy. Have we not enough to answer for ourselves without the responsibility of having to answer for others? Do you doubt that all those who command are responsible to Almighty God for those under their authority?

See how St. James in his epistle warns his brothers; does he not say, "Be ye not many masters, my brethren, knowing that you receive the greater judgment?" (James 3:1).

Those who are under the yoke of obedience are safer than others, and consequently happier.

—Fr. Lambert (d. 1836), *Discourses on Ecclesiastical Life*

౸

Obedience is better than sacrifice: it is both right and reasonable that it should be preferred, for in sacrifices, we immolate another's flesh, but in obedience, we sacrifice our own will. Consequently, the number of our sacrifices is in proportion to the number of our acts of obedience, because in bending to the authority of a man for the love of God, we overcome the pride that is so natural to us.

—St. Gregory (ca. 540–604), *On 4 Kings*

∞

Order and Regularity

Let all things be done decently,
and according to order.

— 1 Corinthians 14:40

If we knew how to spend our time in observing the order and regularity that is prescribed for all the actions of our life, how rich we would be in a short time! What a mass of merits we would accumulate! What a crown of glory we would obtain! In a word, what treasures for heaven!

Not one of our actions would be void of virtue; there would be neither word nor thought that would not deserve a reward; not a moment that would not be of value for all eternity. There would not be a sigh from the heart that would not be received by God as an act of love. Ah! how precious would be such a life passed thus holily!

Every moment would be worth a year, and every day would be worth an age. It is a short but certain way of acquiring the merit of the most honorable age, since, as the wise man says, it is not the number of years, but the number of good deeds, that do honor to that respectable old age, and that a man who knows how to regulate his time properly finds that he has done more in a few days than he who has lived a whole life of irregularity and disorder.

Alas! Christians, what a waste of time! What a number of days ought to be blotted out from our lives! What a number of years are counted as nothing!

My Daily Visit with the Saints

One who is today sixty or eighty years of age is still only a child if his merits are reckoned by his years; one who is a child, aged one hundred years (who, full of wrinkles and infirmities, must render an account of his life to that just Judge, who looks only at his actions), will then see, that although he has dwelt a long time on earth, yet he has lived but a short time.

If a profane historian had written the history of Saul, he would have argued that this prince must have reigned forty years over Judea, because the sun had run its course as many times; but Holy Scripture, which does not heed the calculations of astronomers, but measures the years by merits rather than by months, says, that he reigned only two years; because, during that time he had lived a holy life, following strictly the commandments of God.

I do not fear to assert that the best way of knowing the interior of a person is to see and watch her exterior behavior, that is to say, how she regulates her time, her actions, her employments, and all that appears outwardly. It is only fair to presume that a Christian so orderly in her exterior actions has a still greater care for all that is more essential and important, which would be to keep her conscience in order, to regulate her desires, her affections, and all the emotions of her soul.

This presumption is so well founded that as one cannot better judge of a cause than from its effect, so in like manner one cannot have a surer sign that that man is really virtuous who, in all his actions, is orderly and regular and does everything with the intention of pleasing God.

We must not allow any hour of a day to pass without taking pains to do what we ought to do, and that, too, in the very best way. This does not mean that we should abridge the necessary hours for sleep, but, as St. Paul says, whether we sleep or whether we are awake, we should do all things regularly, in order that all may lead to our sanctification, and thus refer all that we do to the honor and glory of the Sovereign Master, whom we should always honor and obey. This is the surest proof that we are serving God faithfully and truly.

And what a consolation it will be, at the hour of death, to be able to feel that we have endeavored to perform all for the love of God, and that, if through frailty, we have not been able to do all things well, we have at least tried to be just and holy.

If a single well-employed day is worthy of a reward, what a weight of glory will be in store for us if our life has been one continued round of order and regularity.

—Fr. Haineuve, *De L'ordre*, discourse 10

∞

It is God who regulates everything; and of all that He has done, there is nothing that can be found to be out of order. We are often ignorant of the reason why He has done one thing in preference to another.

There is a rule and order that is necessary in this life, a regularity that leads us to God, if we keep it faithfully; if we fail in this, we swerve from the path that conducts us to His heavenly kingdom; for all is beautiful where there is order, and the Apostle says, all order is from God.

—St. Augustine (354–430), *De Ordine*

∞

Penance as a Virtue

I chastise my body and bring it into subjection:
lest, perhaps, when I have preached to
others, I myself should become a castaway.

—1 Corinthians 9:27

It is an excellent axiom, on which we do not sufficiently reflect, and that nevertheless ought to be the chief subject of our gratitude to God, that the same things that have perverted us are (if we wish) those that should sanctify us, and that, by a wonderful effect of grace and love, we, without going out of our way, find a remedy for our ills in the very instruments that have contributed to bring them on. It is this idea that St. Paul conceived, when, reasoning on this principle, he explains to the Romans what is the essence of Christian penance, saying: "Neither yield ye your members as instruments of iniquity unto sin; but present yourself to God as those that are alive from the dead, and your members as instruments of justice unto God" (Rom. 6:13). As you have yielded your members to commit sins of iniquity, you must make use of them as instruments of justice in order to lead a holy life; for it is by doing so that your conversion will appear to be sincere, if what was in you as an instrument of sin becomes a means of penance, if what you have defiled when you were a slave to the world you consecrate to the service of Almighty God, and make of your members a victim and holocaust worthy of His justice. This is the way by which you can discern the difference between true and false penance.

Penance as a Virtue

As it is effeminacy and sensuality that have withdrawn you from God, you must, if you wish to make friends with Him, counteract these by a severe penance. And to effect this, your penance must be persevering as well as severe. Why? Because God leaves it to you; your penance must therefore annihilate your self-love, and that can be done only by the zeal of a holy and rigorous punishment. If it were a question of condemning others, and of judging of their shortcomings, what a severe penance would you award them; and when it applies to your own bodies, of which you are so fond, and for which you have nought but delicate tenderness, what severity ought you not to exercise; and if you do not do so, what injustice will you not commit?

Have we not very often fancied that faults that appear to us so small when we ourselves commit them, are magnified in our own eyes when committed by others, and that which we took for an atom becomes a monstrous sin in our neighbor? What is the cause of this? Why, nothing but self-love. O! how should we fight against this? Only by severe penance.

We even love our vices; we make a virtue of them, and what is insupportable in others is sweet and agreeable to ourselves. Penance, however, must destroy all this. However selfish we may be, we must not be corrupt judges; and in order not to be so, we must judge ourselves and punish ourselves severely.

It is a delusion, at all times fostered and encouraged by an effeminate world, to imagine that penance should be a virtue solely interior, and that it should reign only over the spiritual powers of the soul; that the heart should be simply changed, that a careful watch should be kept over our passions, and that all these could be solidly practiced without our flesh feeling the effects, or without inflicting pain on that exterior and worldly man, which forms part of ourselves.

If that were the case, says St. Chrysostom, we must curtail entire chapters of Holy Scripture, in which the Holy Spirit upsets carnal prudence by testimonies, as contrary to our self-love, as truth is opposed to error.

It might also be said that St. Paul did not take that worldly view, or that he thought lightly of Christian penance, when he taught that we should make living hostages of our bodies when he wished that this virtue should extend to the chastising of the flesh, when he commanded the faithful, or rather when he made a law for them, to bear really on their bodies the mortification of Jesus Christ. And finally, to give them an example, he himself chastised his body: "But I chastise my body and bring it under subjection; lest perhaps, when I have preached to others, I myself should become a castaway" (1 Cor. 9:27).

Sin must be punished either in the present world or in the world to come, either by the justice of God or by the penitence of man. Let us not therefore wait till God Himself shall inflict due punishment. Let us take care to prevent the rigor of His justice by the rigor of our penance. Inflamed with zeal, let us side with the Almighty against ourselves and avenge His cause at our own expense.

—Fr. Louis Bourdaloue (1632–1704), *Sermon on St. Magdalen*

∞

Perseverance

He that shall persevere unto the end, he shall be saved.
—Matthew 10:22

There are two grand motives for perseverance. The first is, that we cannot begin too soon to serve God, and as that beginning is never too late, we ought never to relax in our duty to Him, so long as we live. We ought, indeed, to love God, from the first moment of our coming to the use of reason. We ought to love Him as soon as we have known Him, and this is perhaps the reason that the best part of our life slips by without our beginning to do good, and without our engaging to serve Him—and this, too, after the sacrament of Baptism, which is, as you know, a solemn promise to serve and love Him, our Divine Master.

We, by rights, ought never to have relaxed but ought to have kept faithfully to the promise made in the sight of heaven and earth. But by a desertion as shameful as it is criminal, we soon find that we have been more guilty than reasonable, from the very first moment of our existence. Is it not just, then, to make up for lost time, or at least to make reparation for time so uselessly employed, that we should consecrate the rest of our lives, in paying off a debt that is owing to Him, our Creator?

We ought, at least, to enter into the feelings of the great St. Augustine, who exclaims, "Too late have I known Thee, O ancient Truth, too late have I loved Thee, O ancient Beauty!" Ah! had I waited for a year, a month, a week, or a day, would it not have been too late for me to begin?

What can I then now do but devote the remainder of my life to Thy service? You have loved me, dear Lord, from all eternity. You will love me for all eternity, if I am fortunate enough to deserve the eternal happiness that Thou hast destined for me; at least if that short interval that hangs between these two eternities be perseveringly and constantly employed in loving and serving Thee.

The other motive is that we should never be weary of serving God, or quit His holy service too soon. For, tell me, what has moved that soul when, with Christian generosity, it has resolved to leave off sinning and has determined to be virtuous and good? It is either the fear of God's judgments, or the wish to be saved, or perhaps a higher motive has been excited, and conversion has lasted for some time.

But this desirable change ceases, tears are dried up, and the course of penitential prayers are stopped.

The goodness, justice, and mercy of God had brought forth our holy resolutions. Have these been the cause of this change? No! God is now just as loving, just as merciful as He ever was. He has not ceased to be mindful of you; why, then, did you not remain longer in His service?

If, then, the fervent zeal that we should always feel in the service of His Divine Majesty should cease for a day, or even a moment, it would be too late, because there is not a single day or hour that should not be devoted to the adoration and service of Almighty God. We should not, therefore, place any limit to our perseverance; for the very moment we cease to be zealous and good, all our past services are reckoned as nothing, and we lose the merit of them.

— Fr. Antoine de la Porte, From his book on grace

∞

Having considered the motives that ought to induce us to persevere, let us see the sad effects that would inevitably result from the want of perseverance. Consider well that as perseverance in the life of grace is purely a gift of God, so the want of perseverance is simply our own fault.

That life of grace that penance renews in us is of its nature as immortal, and as incorruptible as is our soul. If, therefore, against the design of God, we lose this grace, it is to ourselves, and not to grace, that we can attribute this loss, and in that consists our irregularity.

Instructed, as we have been, of the necessity of final perseverance, why should we not always try to merit it? Should we not daily resolve to obtain this precious treasure?

Should not final perseverance be the constant object of our desires, the aim of all our endeavors, and the motive, so to speak, of all our prayers? Let us store up all our merits; let us multiply our graces; for if we have the misfortune of not persevering to the end, if we have the unhappiness of dying in mortal sin, notwithstanding our former innocence and fervor of penance, if we have the misfortune of losing that grace at that moment preceding the last, all these treasures will be lost for all eternity. God, in this case, does not reckon up our past good deeds. We are justly condemned. O! how blind, how mad must we be not to ask Almighty God for the gift of perseverance and for the means of obtaining this grace!

It is in reality this gift that gives such a value to our good works. Without perseverance, the most perfect innocence, the most heroic virtue, the most austere penance, go for nothing.

Saul had been chosen by God by a singular favor; Solomon had been the admiration of the world for his piety and wisdom; Judas was one of our Savior's Apostles and had even worked miracles.

—Fr. Croiset, S.J. (b. ca. 1650), *Exercices de Pieté*

ॐ

The greatest help to perseverance in the spiritual life is the habit of prayer, especially under the direction of our confessor.

Men should often renew their good resolutions, and not lose heart because they are tempted against them.

—St. Philip Neri (1515–1595)

∞

Piety and Devotion

God is a Spirit, and they that adore Him must
adore Him in spirit and in truth.

—John 4:24

∞

As soon as one takes the firm resolution of serving God, or, what is the same thing, as soon as one begins to practice devotion, he is mild, tractable, humble, upright, obliging, and tries to fulfill every obligation of his state of life. There can be no stability in friendship, no good faith in business, no candor in courtesy, if it be not well grounded in goodness and piety. Piety gives us common sense; candor, earnestness, and uprightness.

True devotion consists in fulfilling the minutest duties of that state of life to which God has called us. There are so many obligations in business, society, and diverse employments of life. Nothing is more praiseworthy than trying to do everything in a satisfactory manner, and what is more satisfactory than the constant practice of devotion? Take a survey of the various states of life.

Who is a good father, a good judge, a kind relation, a sincere friend, a loyal subject? What woman more domesticated, what servant more industrious, what workman more hardworking, what priest more exemplary and watchful than he who is a religious observer of God's commandments?

All these virtues are the fruit of Christian piety and devotion.

Neither God nor the gospel disapproves of the duties of politeness nor the amenities of life. God regulates them. He does not command

Christians to live solitary lives in a desert, but He expects them to conduct themselves as good Christians. Thus, far from making people savage and morose, nothing is more likely to civilize and polish them than piety and devotion. We see examples of this daily.

If a man be debauched and sensual, he is irritable, unbearable, peevish, rough, passionate, and vindictive, in fact only fit to try the patience of others. If a woman be without piety, she is vain, capricious, cruel, and hard on her children and servants, and a heavy cross to her husband. But when such as these put on the armor of piety and devotion, they become reasonable, courteous, gracious to all, diligent in work, respectable in society, and worthy of the esteem and veneration of the world.

How sad it is, O Lord, to hear of devout people, that is to say, those who live according to the precepts of the gospel—how sad to hear that they are peevish, uncivil, troublesome, and that they think that they are good for nothing! What! cannot one be good for something in this world, without giving up devotion?

True piety and devotion does not prevent our mixing in society, neither do they forbid amusements, provided they be innocent.

More than that, does the Gospel forbid us from keeping a careful watch over our own property, or even to work hard, so as to increase it by lawful means? Does the Church condemn the care of providing for your family, of taking an interest in the temporal welfare of your children, of cultivating your own land, or of keeping up your dignity and honor? Does she forbid you to perform the ordinary usages of polite society? Does she even consider harmless recreation a crime, or an attire suitable for your rank or station? Certainly not! The Church condemns only excess, covetousness, or a too great eagerness.

—Fr. Croiset, S.J. (b. ca. 1650), *Réflexions Chrétiennes*

∞

Would you wish to know if you are really devout? Then take heed of what you love, what you fear, wherefore you rejoice, or why you sorrow.

Love God alone, or if you love, love the object, for His sake. Fear only to displease God, or if you have any dread of anything, refer all to Him. Rejoice only in God, or if you rejoice in any other object, look upon it only as an attraction that draws you closer to Him. Let the loss of God be your only sorrow, whether your sorrow is occasioned by past sins or by those of your brethren; or if any other loss worries you, look upon it as a proof that He intends to chasten you, in order to make you more united to Him.

The grace of true devotion is an unction that instructs us in all our duties; he alone who has proved it by experience knows it, and he who is willfully ignorant of this cannot possibly know it, because no one can feel it but he who has received it as a precious gift from heaven.

Devotion is the grace that influences the heart, and that alone. After one has tasted the joys of the Spirit, those of the world and the flesh seem to be distasteful. He who yearns for the blessings of heaven cannot relish earthly pleasures, and he who sighs after eternal things will feel only a contempt for fleeting things.

—St. Bernard (1091–1153), *De Verbis Apostoli*

∞

It is well to choose some one good devotion, and to stick to it, and never to abandon it.

—St. Philip Neri (1515–1595)

Poverty and the Poor in Spirit

Blessed are the poor in spirit;
for theirs is the kingdom of heaven.

—Matthew 5:3

It is the grandest miracle of grace to see a man poor in the midst of riches. We could not understand this miracle if we did not know that Holy Scripture does not condemn riches, or the rich, but only those who love riches and those who wish to possess wealth.

The Apostle teaches us this truth when he says that it is not the rich, but only those who yearn to become rich, who fall into the snares of the devil. St. Hilary well explains this by saying that it is not a sin to possess property, but it is a sin if it be not used in moderation. Thus, when the Gospel curses the rich, and closes the gates of heaven upon them, it does not curse those who possess riches, but those who wish to be rich and those who are eager to amass wealth.

This is the meaning of the Apostle's words, and it is indisputable that the love of those blessings we call riches is bad; it follows, then, that the poverty that the gospel commends is not the absence of riches, but the wish to acquire riches, or the desire to love them when possessed.

The wise man depicts admirably this effect of grace by these words: "One is as it were rich, when he hath nothing; and another is, as it were poor, when he hath great riches" (Prov. 13:7). How can we understand, and could we possibly have any idea of a rich man having nothing, or of a poor man being rich, if we did not know that by the grace of Jesus Christ the poor man lives as if he were rich, and the rich man lives as if he were poor? Behold, then, the miracle of the gospel and its grace: that the rich may be as poor as was our Savior in His riches, since He was the Master of the universe but was clothed in poverty.

A Christian should die poor, either in reality or in spirit, because only poverty can enter into heaven, and if the rich enter therein, it must be through the gate of poverty. Thus, the greatest misfortune is to die rich, that is to say, with a love for and an attachment to riches. This is necessary to repeat often to the rich, in order that they may not deceive themselves or be deceived; and they must be warned that poverty is the sole inheritance to gain heaven, and that the rich can be saved only through poverty.

This truth ought to make the rich and the powerful tremble and fear; not because they can open the gates of heaven by making themselves poor, but on account of the difficulty there is of being poor in spirit in the midst of riches, of cheerfully resigning something from the superfluity of wealth, of loving poverty, when they are rich.

This miracle is not impossible to grace; but it will never be accomplished, except through a contempt for riches, looking upon its acquisition in its true light, valuing it as it should be, that is, its being of little or no good.

—Fr. Sarrazin, Advent sermon

∞

Poverty has been called by some the sister of Christ; by others, His bride. It would seem as if the circumstances of His infancy had been providentially contrived with a view to bringing us as many of the incidents of poverty as were possible, without seeming to be unnatural. From Nazareth to Bethlehem, from Bethlehem over the wilderness to Egypt, from Egypt to Nazareth again, and from Nazareth to Jerusalem for the three days He begged His bread; the biography of His childhood spreads itself like an ample net, to entangle in its folds more and more of the varieties and pressures of His beloved poverty.

If He was born of a royal maiden, it was of one who was poor and reduced in circumstances. He would not be born at home, but took the occasion of the Roman census to be, as it were, a child of exile and a waif upon His own earth.

He would be rejected from the doors of Bethlehem, as the least worthy of all the mixed multitude that had crowded thither. He would be born in a cave, a stable, amidst the domestic animals of man's husbandry.

When age grew on Joseph and his infirmities multiplied, the yoke of poverty became yet more galling to the shoulders of his tender foster Son. The poverty that pressed on Mary pressed tenfold more heavily on Him, from the very fact of its having first pressed on her.

Never was there a childhood of hardier poverty than our Blessed Lord's. It was His inseparable companion, and if He loved its austerities with so singular a love, it was only because they were so singular a cross.

—Fr. Frederick William Faber (1814–1863), *Bethlehem*

∞

Poverty in itself is not a virtue; but the love of poverty is so. Jesus Christ has said, "Blessed are the poor in spirit," not those who possess nothing.

—St. Bernard (1091–1153)

∽

Prayer

Let us go with confidence to the throne
of grace: that we may obtain mercy,
and find grace in seasonable aid.

—Hebrews 4:16

Prayer places our understanding in the brightness and light of God, and exposes our will to the heat of heavenly love. There is nothing that so effectually purges our understanding from its ignorance, or our will from its depraved affections, as prayer. It is the water of benediction, which makes the plants of our good desires grow green and flourish. It washes our souls from their imperfections and quenches the thirst of passion in our hearts.

But, above all, I recommend to you mental and cordial prayer, and particularly that which has the life and passion of our Lord for its object. By making Him the subject of your meditation, your whole soul will be replenished with Him; you shall learn His manner, and frame all your actions to the model of His.

As He is the light of the world, it is in Him, by Him, and for Him that we ought to acquire luster and be enlightened. He is the tree of desire, under whose shadow we ought to refresh ourselves. He is the living fountain of Jacob, in which we may wash away all our stains. In fine, as little children, by hearing their mothers talk, lisp at first and learn at length to speak their language, so we, by keeping close to our Savior by meditation, and observing His words, actions, and affections, shall, by the help of His grace, learn to speak, to act, and to will like Him.

Here we must stop, as we cannot find access to God the Father but through this gate; for as the looking-glass could never terminate our sight if its back were not tinned or leaded, so we could never contemplate the Divinity in this world had we not been united to the sacred humanity of our Savior, whose life and death is the most fit, delightful, sweet, and profitable object we can choose for our ordinary meditation.

It is not without reason that our Savior called Himself the bread that came down from heaven; for as bread ought to be eaten with all sorts of meat, so our Savior ought to be the subject of our meditation, consideration, and imitation in all our prayers and actions.

— St. Francis de Sales (1567–1622), *Introduction to the Devout Life*

∽

God listens, says St. Cyprian, to the voice of the heart, in preference to the voice of the mouth; we must, adds he, watch and give up our mind to prayer; we must drive away all worldly and profane thoughts from our heart, in order that our mind and soul may be engrossed with our petitions.

To whom, continues the saint, should we speak attentively, if not to God? Can He ask for less than that you should think of what you are saying? How dare you expect that He will deign to hear you, if you think only of yourselves? You fancy that God will hear you when you pray, you who are so willfully distracted in prayer. Far from pleasing Him, you offend His Divine Majesty by your negligence, in an action that is the only way of gaining favors from heaven.

We must ask in faith, nothing wavering (James 1:6), and this faith ought to be so firm that we should never hesitate, for he who hesitates or wavers is like unto the waves of the sea, ever moved and carried about by the wind. He who, then, continues St. James, prays without this confidence, must not expect to be heard. And what is more capable of moving the heart of our Lord in our regard than a firm confidence in His mercy? Can He refuse those who have placed all their treasure in Him, those who have trusted in His goodness?

When we pray with confidence, says St. Cyprian, it is God Himself who implants in our hearts that spirit of prayer. The Eternal Father must, then, acknowledge the words of His only-begotten Son when we pronounce them, and He who dwells in the bottom of our hearts will regulate and fashion all our prayers.

We must not, says St. Bernard, mingle in our prayers foolish things with the true, temporal with the eternal, low interests with those of our salvation.

To pray well, says St. Augustine, you must seek God alone; to ask, through Him, for other blessings, is praying badly. Do not seek to make God the protector of your self-love, or of your ambition, but the executor of your good desires. You have recourse to God to curb your passions, and often He sends you crosses, of which He knows you stand in need. When He loves you, continues the holy Doctor, He refuses what your self-love asks for, and in His anger, He gives you that which is dangerous for you to obtain. Do not carry to the sanctuary of the altar indiscreet vows, ill-regulated desires, and slovenly prayers. Ask for nothing but what is worthy of Him to whom you pray. Keep strictly from sighing after vain and hurtful benefits; ask for the dew from heaven, and not for the fat of the land. Open your heart before the Lord, in order that His Holy Spirit may dwell in you, and ask, through sighs and moans, for the true blessings that He wishes that you should ask for.

Let us pray, my brethren, but let us ever pray, keeping a watchful eye over our various duties. Do not let us offer up exalted or abstract prayers, or those that have no reference to the practice of every virtue. Let us pray not to become more enlightened, and more spiritual in words, but to become humbler, more docile, more patient, more modest, more charitable, purer, and more unselfish in every detail of our conduct. Without that, our assiduity in prayer, far from being efficacious and fruitful, will be a delusion and a scandal for our neighbor.

Prayer

Full of delusion! How many examples have we not had? How many have we seen whose prayers tend to swell their pride and lead their thoughts astray! And a scandal to our neighbor, for is there anything more scandalous than to see a person who prays without first correcting himself; who, at the end of his devotions, is not less frivolous, less vain, less restless, less passionate, less selfish than before?

—Archbishop François Fénelon (1651–1715), *Select Sermons*

∞

When you ask for temporal favors, however trifling they may appear, ask with fear. Pray that God may grant or reject them as He thinks fit. The doctor, and not the patient, is best able to judge what is best.

—St. Augustine (354–430), *De Verbum Domini*

∞

A man without prayer is an animal without the use of reason.

—St. Philip Neri (1515–1595)

∞

Predestination

And whom he predestinated, them he also called;
and whom he called, them he also justified; and
whom he justified, them he also glorified.

—Romans 8:30

Predestination, properly speaking, is that particular arrangement and conduct that God makes use of to guide gently and freely to their end those whom He has chosen from all eternity to enjoy everlasting happiness. Or, as St. Thomas expresses it in fewer words, it is an arrangement prepared in the mind of God respecting the leading of the reasonable creature to eternal life. This is tantamount to the definition given by St. Augustine: it is the foreknowledge and the preparation of the blessings and favors of God, which do not fail to lead the elect to everlasting happiness.

It follows, from this definition that predestination is a part of the Providence of God and that the office of predestination, as also that of Providence, is to direct the means to the end, or even to choose and prepare the means proper for the end.

But, as it is certain, according to the articles of faith, that man has been created to obtain supernatural beatitude, he must have the means proportionate as well as supernatural. And as these means are in God, who has the will to give them, it follows that there is in God a predestination. It follows, in the second place, that the predestination in God is an act of His judgment, by which He foresees the force of the infallible means that lead to the end to which He destined the elect.

It is, moreover, an act of His will by which He resolves to give to each such and such of those infallible means. As predestination is an act of the divine understanding, it must necessarily follow that it should be an act of prudence and infinite wisdom, which we should prefer above every human consideration.

Besides, as predestination may be said to be a selection that is an act of the will, we must conclude from thence that it is infinitely just and that it is accompanied by a divine holiness and a very ardent love for the creature.

Finally, it follows that predestination is eternal, since it is an act of the judgment and will of God, which cannot change and consequently is from all eternity; so that what is done at the time happens only because God has determined it before time was; thus, the grace is given in time, but the preparation was made from all eternity.

We must, moreover, conclude from this definition, acknowledged by all the Doctors of the Church, that predestination is certain and infallible; that it certainly proceeds from the strength of divine knowledge, which cannot be deceived; and that it extends to every free event that ought to happen, and not by the strength of the assistance that it gives us. If this infallibility proceeded from the means, assistance, and graces, the creature would not cooperate freely, but necessarily, and consequently, predestination being certain and infallible, would have deprived us of our free will.

Fr. Vincent Houdry, S.J. (1630–1729)

∞

"Many are called, but few are chosen." Even had faith not taught us this awful truth, taking into consideration certain maxims of Holy Scripture in which all Christians agree, reason alone would suffice to convince us that the number of the elect must be small.

My Daily Visit with the Saints

Instructed in the truths of our holy religion, knowing the duties of a Christian, convinced of our natural inclination to evil, seeing the licentiousness of the present age, can one come to the conclusion that there will be very many saved? To be saved, we must necessarily live according to the maxims of the Gospel; and can the number of those who do so live nowadays be called great? To be saved, we must openly declare that we are disciples of our Savior. Alas! how many are there now who would be ashamed to own it? We must renounce all we possess, if not in reality, at least in desire; we must carry our cross daily. What unchangeable purity! What delicacy of conscience! What humility! What honesty! What charity! With such outward signs as these, would you recognize many disciples of Jesus Christ? They are, however, the surest signs we can have of our predestination.

The world is the implacable enemy of Jesus our Savior. It is not possible to serve two masters. Judge for yourself which of the two the greater part obey and follow, and by that, you will be able to know how few, how very few, will be of the number of the elect.

—Fr. Croiset, S.J. (b. ca. 1650)

∞

The fear of God is a sign of predestination.

—St. Augustine (354–430)

∾

Prudence

The knowledge of the holy is prudence.
—Proverbs 9:10

On referring to Holy Scripture you will find many examples of the folly of those who trusted in worldly and political prudence.

Pharaoh had cleverly contrived to destroy the people of Israel, but he had not foreseen the obstacle that upset all his plans. An exposed child he intended to put to death was secretly nourished and brought up in his own palace, and this same child destroyed all the power of the Egyptians and saved Israel.

Abimelech caused seventy of his brethren to be slain in order to ascend the throne; but he himself could not avoid meeting with a violent death, for he was killed by a portion of a millstone thrown by a woman.

Men conspired against our Lord and Savior Jesus Christ; and after long consultations, they said to themselves: "What should we do, for this man does many miracles? If we let Him alone so, all will believe in Him, and the Romans will come and take away our place and nation" (John 11:48). It was by reasoning thus that they resolved to put Jesus to death, in order to save their place and nation; but this counsel, fatal as it was, ended in their entire destruction.

—St. Basil (ca. 329–379), *Sermons*

My Daily Visit with the Saints

∞

As Christians, what better rules can we take for deciding prudently, than the eternal truths? Those precepts and maxims we ought to follow in order that we may not swerve from the duty of considering the end for which we were created, and which should be continually before our eyes.

O! if we had always acted on this principle, if we had followed no other guide, if we had had them ever before our eyes, if we had weighed in this balance all our resolutions and designs (which we can now only trace to ourselves), our conclusions and decisions would have been correct and right. We should not have been subject to so many false proceedings, to so many falls, and we should not have been cast among so many rocks. God would have diffused His light to illuminate our path. He would have united His will to ours. Faith would have given us a true esteem of things. God would have made us find out the true worth of His Word. He would have inspired us with a wisdom all divine, often even requisite in the management and administration of worldly business.

But what do we do? Whom do we consult? We consult, alas, neither our Lord, nor His gospel, nor our Faith. It is a false and carnal prudence, a blind reasoning, that thinks it can see everything, and can see nothing. We judge for ourselves; we wish to believe only in self, and on certain occasions, everything appears to favor our plans, and, full of confident success, we begin, we decide, and we trust to chance.

Whom do we consult? The world—the world and its ideas; unhappy source of many delusions, of many specious delights that lead us into error.

Whom do we consult? Passion; it is an insatiable avarice that devours us and biases us ever in the favor of self-aggrandizement; it is an inordinate ambition that goads us onward and drags us on to fortune; it is a bitter resentment that animates us and ever leans to the side of vengeance; it is a guilty attachment that binds us and makes us slaves to pleasure. These are our counselors; these are our masters.

Prudence

I know, says the Lord, how I can frustrate all your false and worldly plans; these will not only not succeed but will lead to your ruin. I will confound the prudence of the age and will leave them to their own guidance. I will let them walk in their darkness and let them fall into abysses from which they cannot extricate themselves.

We see and experience this daily. We undertake important affairs in which self is concerned; God, on His part, attaches thereto even a temporal punishment, for He upsets and destroys them all.

A thousand times wiser and happier is that Christian who examines everything as a Christian should do, who has recourse to God and stores up resolutions to do all that God may be willing to dictate to him; taking care that all the precepts and maxims of the Gospel may be the rule of his life; applying these to everything; making a just discernment of what is allowed and what is forbidden, of what may be done and what to be avoided; seeking advice from those learned in the law; making use of the commandments of God as a sure way of finding out all that His will may propose, and then by putting it into practice.

The beauty of our Faith and religion is to have rules applicable to every state and condition of life in which we may be found, and there is not a single occasion or juncture that may not require us to act with a Christian prudence.

—Fr. Jaques Giroust (1624–1689), Advent discourse

∞

Purity and Chastity

The value of all gold, is as nothing
compared to a soul truly chaste.

—See Sirach 26:20

Purity is a virtue that puts us on an equality with the angels. The purity of angels is more blessed, ours more generous. They have no temptations of the flesh to fight against, as we have. We cannot preserve our chastity, surrounded as we are by so many enemies, without great exertion, and there are but few who are victorious.

Virginity brings us nearer to God. It seeks for a model in God Himself, says St. Ambrose, for the Eternal Father is virgin and Father. God, also wishing to become Incarnate, willed that He should be born of a virgin. God has also an extraordinary love and tenderness for pure souls; it is to these, in particular, that He confers or reveals His secrets, or on whom He deigns to bestow His favors. Jesus Christ bestowed many graces on Peter, on account of his zeal; but it was the virgin St. John who was permitted to lean on the breast and heart of Jesus; it was he who had the privilege of entering His divine sanctuary, and it was he from whom He hid none of His most important secrets.

Confessors, martyrs, and apostles have great privileges; but it appears that to virgins only He has entrusted the privilege of following the Lamb. They are His spouses, and thus this illustrious quality gives them right of entry everywhere.

Purity and Chastity

Virginity is that precious treasure that so many generous souls have sacrificed their lives to guard. The preservation of this treasure is difficult, but the loss of it is irreparable; one may recover grace when lost by sin, but virginity once lost, can never be restored.

Nevertheless, nothing is easier to lose, and we so readily expose ourselves to lose this treasure — nay, it seems to me that we seek to lose it, and we even make a merit of losing that which ought to be a subject of the most poignant grief.

The demon of impurity, wishing to gain a victory over a person who is modest, and has the fear of God before her eyes, uses nearly the same tactics as a skillful general would use; for he, despairing of capturing a city by storm, employs secret emissaries or spies. Thus, the devil makes use of certain propensities that appear innocent enough, or at least but little suspected of having any secret connection with him. Making sure of the interest these evil propensities excite, the devil will enter secretly into their hearts and undermine and eventually make himself master of the citadel.

These propensities (so nearly allied to passions) are vanity, curiosity, and presumption; seemingly these three have but little connection with impurity. But these are the weapons that the devil makes use of in the world, and they will soon conquer chastity.

The passion that does not appear to be allied to the sin of impurity, but which nevertheless enters deep into the heart, is that curiosity that prompts the reading of bad or dangerous books. Nothing is more dreadful, nothing is more injurious to the purity of young persons than those novels and books of gallantry that, under the pretext of elegance of diction or beauty of language, corrupt the educated mind.

If such reading forms the mind, it spoils the soul; if it gives us a knowledge of the world, it destroys Christianity; and thus, by the loss of devotion, by the loss of the holy fear of God, and purity of conscience, such reading leads insensibly to the loss of chastity.

—St. Astère (d. ca. 400), Homily

∞

Show me the man who is able to explain or understand the value and excellence of purity, a virtue beyond all the common laws of nature. It is on earth a perfect type, and a lively picture of the virginal purity that reigns in heaven.

It is that which has passed through air, clouds, and stars, and which, soaring above the angels, has found the Divine Word in the bosom of His Father, and has drawn Him to earth, to be united to it in an inexpressible manner.

Now, after having been so fortunate as to find a pearl of so great a price, on what plea can we allow it to be lost? Nevertheless, it is not I, but the Son of God Himself who assures us that the pure and chaste will be like the angels in heaven. And at this we need not be astonished if such souls are placed in the rank of angels, souls who have for their spouse the King and Lord of angels.

—St. Ambrose (340–397)

∞

Religion and the Religious State

Walk worthy of God, in all things pleasing,
being fruitful in every good work, and
increasing in the knowledge of God.

—Colossians 1:10

There is no one who ought to be vainglorious for having bid adieu to the world; he ought rather to return thanks to Almighty God. St. Athanasius said as much to his disciples. I would have here the right to use the same phrase. Do not let us feel proud at what we have done for God when we entered into the religious state, but let us praise and bless Him a thousand times for having done so much for us.

In consecrating ourselves to the Lord, we have parted with blessings but they are benefits that, when possessed, are a heavy burden: so says our Lord. For does not Holy Writ mention that it is a sin to be attached to the goods of this world, or to be grieved at their loss?

We resign benefits that cannot be retained without being overwhelmed with their burden; blessings that cannot be loved without our being soiled with avarice; benefits that we cannot lose or fear to lose without being anxious about their probable future loss.

Thus, it is a grace and a blessing that God has inspired us with the will to deny and conquer ourselves. And when I ponder on all the truths that the Faith teaches, what conclusion can I come to, but that I am forced to be astonished at the sight of that wondrous grace that God has bestowed upon me when He called me to the religious life: a state of life that spares me so much trouble, protects me from so many dangers, and compels me to offer unlimited thanks for that singular mercy of my Lord, who has induced me to embrace a vocation that is not only the most perfect and the safest, but also the easiest and the most favorable, to the work of my own sanctification.

For let us not be deceived; it is easier to be deprived of worldly wealth, as we are, than to possess riches and not become attached to them. It is easier to give up the pleasures of the world than to use them as if we used them not — than to be in the midst of honors and distinctions, and not be elated with them.

It is much easier to submit to the will of another than to keep our own liberty and free will within bounds. To make use of the world as if we used it not, is what every Christian is obliged to do; but who are those who do this?

To possess temporal goods as if they possessed them not is a condition attached to all who wish to be saved; but, tell me, where can we find people in the world who are of this opinion?

"What shall I render to the Lord for all the things that He hath rendered to me?" (Ps. 115:12). Ah! Lord, we ought say: You have broken my bonds with the world. And it is for that that I will sacrifice to you the sacrifice of praise; and I will call upon the Name of the Lord, and incessantly invoke Your holy Name. It is for that, that prostrate at the foot of Your altar, I am resolved to begin to make a sacrifice of myself. What can I not do from henceforth, without delay? Have I not the strength to deprive myself of that fatal liberty, which can only lead me to some other object besides Thee?

But You wish me to go further than this; that I should unite myself to You, by indissoluble bonds, after having put myself to the test. Give me the consolation of being able to do, with a hearty goodwill, all that is permitted, and to say with heartfelt gladness, "I will pay my vows to the Lord in the sight of all His people."

For thus I can return love for love, sacrifice for sacrifice. I shall have the advantage of being able to spare nothing for You, who have spared nothing for me; in fine, to be Your victim, as You have been mine.

—Fr. Louis Bourdaloue (1632–1704), *Sermon for a Profession*

∞

But, my dear brethren, while so many holy daughters of the Church are about to resign all earthly ties, while they, by day and night, will try to please their Creator, what shall we do for our salvation? Shall we continue to live in that frightful negligence and ingratitude to God—in our forgetfulness of death and eternity?

Who would believe it? To see on one side their fear and vigilance, and on the other side, our carelessness and idleness.

That young girl, buried, as it were, in a cloister, thinks herself fortunate if she can, after a seclusion of several years, prepare for herself a happy death; while that other worldly girl, is busying herself with the pleasures of this life and perhaps has never thought seriously of death or eternity.

That young man deprives himself of everything, as if he had only a moment to live, while another one thinks only of hoarding and multiplying riches, as if he could live forever. The one passes his life in mortification, the other in pleasure.

What can one say to this? Are there two paths to heaven, one broad, the other narrow? Is it that paradise is given to some for doing nothing and is reached by others only at the sacrifice of their blood?

You will tell me that we are not all religious, all monks or nuns. This is true, and it is that very thing that astonishes me most. For what obligation has this person to bid adieu to the world? What has led her to renounce the pomps and vanities of the world, if not to lead you, and others, to do likewise?

—St. Claude de la Colombière (1641–1682)

∞

O! how safe is a holy religious! The man lives there in innocence and purity; he seldom falls; he often is the recipient of heavenly blessings; he tastes a sweet tranquility; and when he dies, he breathes out his last sigh, full of hope and full of love for his Redeemer. His purgatory is over sooner, and his reward is plentiful. What he leaves behind are but worldly possessions, transitory and of very little value, and those he aspires to are infinite.

I say more than this, and what I say is true: he exchanges darkness for light; from a stormy sea, he anchors in a safe harbor; freed from a wretched slavery, he sighs after a happy freedom; and finally, he passes from death to a life of everlasting bliss.

—St. Bernard (1091–1153), *Epistle 14*

❧

Retreats

I will allure her, and will lead her into the
wilderness: and I will speak to her heart.

—Hosea 2:14

O solitude! Ladder of heaven, mother of contrition, mirror wherein we see our sins reflected, source of sweetness, companion of humility and of the fear of God, light of the soul! O solitude, which teaches us to know our thoughts, to discern the promptings of our heart, which is the foundation of salvation, the curb of intemperance, the school of prayer, the peace of mind, the agreeable yoke, the light burden! O solitude, effectual remedy against temptation, the enemy of imprudence, the joy of the soul, the guardian of the eyes, ears, tongue, and the cooperatrix of every virtue. The friend of poverty, the fertile field of all good fruits, the wall and rampart of all those who wish to fight for the kingdom of heaven.

—St. Ephrem (d. ca. 379)

❧

Withdraw from the crowd and the noise; come and seek God in solitude.

It is God who calls those who wish to speak to Him; it is an appointment He Himself has made. Go into retreat, and He will find you out; there He will speak to your mind and heart, and He will condescendingly be glad to confer with you every time you hopefully trust in Him. He will speak a language that perchance you never heard before, and you will listen for the first time, and you will hear Him henceforth, with consolation and with joy. You will learn truths without number, which you will be surprised you never heard before. You will become indifferent to things that before interested you, and you will take as much care in fulfilling the duties of a Christian, as you formerly did in not thinking of duty at all.

I do not now urge you to quit the world and spend the remainder of your life in solitude; this is devoutly to be wished for and would be the surest way to secure your salvation; but your state of life does not allow of this, and if I were to ask as much, I fear that you would not acquiesce in my request. On the other hand, a retreat of one hour or even a day is not sufficient. You must give God the time to speak to you; you must give yourself the time to listen to what He says, to understand what He will reveal to you, to implore Him to sanctify your will and intellect, so that you may be able to resist temptations, which have not hitherto been resisted. And for this, you are asked to devote a week. I dare to say, and I prophesy, that you will find in this retreat, as did the Israelites in the desert, a column of fire to enlighten your darkness, and a column of cloud to defend you from the false glitter of the world, and to hinder you from being dazzled.

God will be your guide as He was theirs. He will conduct you as He conducted them; He will nourish you, as He did them, with the bread of angels; and as He led them up to the mountain of His sanctification, so He will lead you, if only you have the courage to follow Him, and will make you saints.

Perhaps, however, you will tell me that a retreat, of which I have been speaking, is a recent invention, a new practice, of which you have never heard speak. You have always had an affection for antiquity in all things, but more especially in matters relating to religion and devotion; you have always avoided show and singularity. But I fancy that I hear you say that it would be absurd to alter our usual behavior at our time of life; it is too late to begin to despise the world altogether; we can save our souls without going into retreat, and we must try to do so.

Retreats

What! my brethren, is it a recent invention to do what the Son of God and His Apostles have practiced, of which they have given us so many examples? Read the history of the Church, and you will see that retreats have always been the practice of the saints.

St. Gregory of Nazianzen went into retreat immediately after he was consecrated, and he made so long a retreat, that, on his return, he publicly apologized to his flock. You know the long retreat that St. Jerome made; and that St. Augustine entered into retreat more than once, and the earnest entreaties that he made to Valerius, his bishop, to allow him to make one about every two months. Then, coming to our last centuries, we find that the glorious Archbishop of Milan, St. Charles Borromeo, recommended all the clergy of his diocese to make four retreats before he ordained them priests; and no year passed without his going into retreat, and very often he made two retreats in the year. I need not speak to you of St. Philip Neri, St. Francis de Sales, St. Francis Borgia, and a number of others, who were sanctified by these means.

Is it not written, "You shall be holy, for I am holy" (1 Pet. 1:16), and again, "Be you therefore perfect, as also your heavenly Father is perfect" (Matt. 5:48)?

But do you believe it to be possible to reach perfection without making a retreat? Have you ever seen or heard of persons being made holy by frequenting balls, assemblies, or by mixing with the noise, bustle, and intrigues of the world? Is it in such places as these that God has been accustomed to shower down His special graces? Ah! if we wish to receive His sanctifying grace, we must be in a position to profit by it.

—Fr. Louis Le Valois (1639–1700),
Letters on the necessity of retreats

∞

It is necessary to seek occasionally for a spot where you can be free from the worry and bustle of temporal affairs; a place wherein God is alone with you, and you are alone with God.

"Enter, you and your family into the ark" (see Gen. 7:1). It is as if the Lord had said to the just man: Enter into thyself and meditate; thou wilt there find salvation. A deluge is to be dreaded outside the ark, for there is danger around.

—St. Gregory (ca. 540–604), *On the Book of Kings*

∞

Riches

Riches are good to him that hath no sin in his conscience.
—Sirach 13:30 (RSV = Sirach 13:24)

The love of riches is far more pernicious and more powerful than the devil himself, and many obey this love more blindly than the pagans, who put their faith in idols. For there have been many pagans who did not obey their devilish idols at all times, but people who hanker after riches unreservedly respect everything that tends to feed their covetousness. As if covetousness says to them: "Be revenged on society, forget the feelings of nature, despise God," they obey this to the letter.

To the idols were sacrificed animals, but covetousness seeks to force their worshippers to sacrifice their own souls, and they sacrifice these without remorse. If you despise worldly blessings, you will be more worthy to possess heavenly blessings.

—St. John Chrysostom (ca. 349–407), Homily 64 on St. John

∞

Poverty is not of itself holy, neither are riches criminal, says St. Ambrose. You may have seen poor people, overwhelmed by the weight of their misery, grumble and rebel against the dispensations of Divine Providence, but you may also have seen some rich who are not dazzled with their gold, who possess property as if they possessed it not.

If riches are a sword in the hands of the foolish, "the crown of the wise is their riches" (Prov. 14:24). If riches in the hands of prodigals and misers cause them to heap iniquity on iniquity, they are in the hands of the just and prudent a source of merit. But alas! where shall we find that just and prudent man, or rather where is he who has not bent his knee before the idol of the world and fortune?

Let us seek among all the rich for one who has not made a god of his gold, who has not believed that riches are all his strength, and who, charmed with his treasures, has not said to the precious metal, "You are my confiding hope, and you are the tender object of my love; you are my crowning desire, and the end of my labors."

It must be confessed that a poor man is more likely to be honest and virtuous than a rich man. It is a rare thing to see a rich and virtuous individual. It is very difficult to be good and pious in the midst of riches, and more difficult to be saved in the midst of wealth and plenty: "For they that will become rich fall into temptation, and into the snares of the devil," says the great Apostle (1 Tim. 6:9).

Temptation follows those who wish to acquire riches, because to gain their end they do not hesitate to employ fraud, injustice, theft, perjury, and homicide; in fact, they make use of every vice to satisfy their cravings.

One sees that in every condition of life crime is the willing attendant on those who inordinately desire to be rich: the shop of the merchant is full of snares, to tempt and deceive the purchaser; the judge is tempted to deprive the widow of her field, and the magistrate eagerly gives his warrant, when there is a question of money accruing to him. The poor child, tired of being the son of poor parents, employs every artifice, just or unjust, to accumulate a fortune; and the rich child, tired of being the son of a rich father, becomes a cruel parricide, in order to inherit and possess all his property.

The lover of wealth, says the wise man, despises every commandment: "There is not a more wicked thing than to love money" (Sir. 10:10).

Show me the wisest woman, if once the love of gold and silver enters into her heart. Ah! she will soon be corrupted, and Solomon will be right in saying that he could not find a strong woman, because no woman can resist this temptation.

It is very, very difficult to have much property and much religion at the same time. One cannot add to fortune what one steals from Christianity; one cannot dream of possessing the treasures of heaven, when we hoard a superfluity of wealth on earth. In a word, religion demands an undivided affection, but the possession of temporal blessings stands sadly in the way. For if the rich man give a portion of his wealth to religion, does he not reserve the greater part to feed his love of riches? And when he prostrates himself before the altar of the Lord, it often happens that in his heart, he is adoring his gold.

This is what St. Paul says: that he who gives his heart to riches is not less excluded from the kingdom of God than he who burns his incense to idols. O! monstrous effect of riches, thus to stifle every sentiment of religion!

—Fr. Jean Baptiste Massillon (1663–1742)

∽

You possess many acres of land; some are planted with trees; some fields are well tilled. Besides these, you have vineyards, undulating hills, beautiful prospects, woods, rivulets, and pleasant promenades. Of what use are all these blessings to you! Six feet of earth await you at the end.

—St. Basil (ca. 329–379)

∞

Excellence of Soul

What doth it profit a man, if he gain the
whole world, and suffer the loss of his own soul?
Or what exchange shall a man give?

—Matthew 16:26

According to St. Paul we have two natures, one exterior, the other interior, and these are the body and the soul. Thus, as we have two sorts of lives, we are subject to two kinds of deaths. We have the corporal life, which we share with all created animals, and we have the life of the soul, which renders us like the angels.

This latter is the spiritual life, pure, holy, and detached from all that is earthly. The source of the life of the body is the soul; the source of the life of the soul is God, who, dwelling in the soul by grace, maintains life in a supernatural and divine way, just as the soul supports the body in the natural way. And in the same way that the soul separates from the body when dead, so in like manner the soul dies as soon as God abandons it and is separated from Him.

Again, as the soul is incomparably greater in value than the body, and as God is infinitely above the soul, so when God abandons it, this death of the soul, caused by the withdrawal of God, is more dreadful, more frightful than the death of the body when the soul departs from it. If there is anything that ought to make us detest sin as being the greatest of all evils, it is that it kills the soul by depriving it of the life of grace, and causing the loss of God, who is the sovereign good and who alone can make us eternally happy.

It follows, then, that mortal sin deprives us of all the merits we may have acquired during our life, in the same way as death deprives men of all the goods and riches they leave behind them.

—Fr. Vincent Houdry, S.J. (1630–1729)

∞

Let us reflect on what God has done for us; we shall find sufficient matter to enlighten us on the love He has shown to our souls, "Come and see," says the prophet, "and I will relate the wonders God has done for my soul" (see Ps. 9:2 [RSV = Ps. 9:1]). If the Eternal Word came down from heaven and became Incarnate, it is for the sake of my soul; if He was willing to be born in a stable, surrounded by vile animals, it was the immense love He had for my soul, and this it was that compelled Him to lower all His greatness. In coming among us, His first thought was to save my soul.

Doubtless, all love the object to which they give their first thought; confess it, you who pollute your hearts for the sake of the love of a miserable creature. But the first and uppermost thought that God the Son had was the salvation of our soul; this was, is, and ever will be the wish of His Sacred Heart. With this love in view, let me address you in the words of the Apostle: "Let this mind be in you, which was also in Christ Jesus" (Phil. 2:5). Let all your actions tend to the salvation of your souls, and let your first thoughts dwell on this only important object.

Has it been your conduct throughout life? Has the safety of your soul been the first thought of your heart?

—Fr. F. Nepveu, S.J. (1639–1708)

∞

O adorable Savior, do not let us fall into so deplorable a blindness as to prefer the good things of this world to our soul. Ah, what have You not done to save our soul, that soul that cost You so much and for whose salvation You have shed the whole of Your Precious Blood! What a misfortune, or rather, how mad shall we be, if we lose it for a mere trifle! What is there in the whole world that can be compared with the soul, or what can we offer in exchange for it?

Consequently, let us value it more than anything else; let us forsake everything rather than run the risk of losing our soul, and then we shall inherit an eternal happiness. To this, St. Chrysostom calls our attention, for in his Homily on the Gospel of St. Matthew he says: "He who has lost his house, money, servants, and all his property, may one day find them replaced and recovered; but if he should happen to lose his own soul, he cannot replace it by another."

—Fr. Étienne de Bretteville (1630–1688)

∽

Would you know what is the value of your soul? The only-begotten Son of God, wishing to redeem this soul of yours, has given, not a whole universe, not the earth or sea with all its treasures, but His own most Precious Blood, and from this you can judge of the greatness of the price. When, therefore, you come to lose your soul, after it has cost so much, at what price could you redeem it?

—St. John Chrysostom (ca. 349–407), *On Psalm 48*

∞

Peace of the Soul

*Peace I leave with you, my peace I give unto you:
not as the world giveth, do I give unto you.*

—John 14:27

True peace is a certain mark of predestination. All those who possess this peace being children of God, it is clear that the heavenly inheritance belongs to them: "Whosoever are led by the Spirit of God, they are the sons of God" (Rom. 8:14).

It is this that our Savior means when He says: "Happy are those who have a peaceful mind, for they shall be called the children of God" (see Matt. 5:9). He gives to the elect the glorious title of sons of God, because they act not as slaves, but as true children of God. Slaves are submissive to their master through fear of suffering punishment; children, on the contrary, are submissive to their father through respect and love, and they obey him with joy.

Such is the conduct of the saints, of those glorious just of the first class, to whom we here allude. They, with their whole heart, were so resigned to the will of God that they unreservedly placed themselves at His disposal, and thus they showed that they were worthy to be children of God, since those "led by the Spirit of God, they are sons of God."

But why does our Savior say that those that are led by the Spirit of God will be called children of God? Because these extraordinary saints are not merely sons by adoption, like the ordinary just, but they are acknowledged and reverenced by the world.

It was also said of our Savior Jesus Christ that they shall call Him the "Son of the Most High" (Luke 1:32) because His holiness, humility, patience, wisdom, and meekness ought to prove (except to those who willfully close their eyes to the true light) that He is the only Son of the Almighty. You are perhaps a child of God because you are pious, but do you live in such a way that you could feel within that you are a child of God? The surest sign you could possibly show would be to place all you have and all you want at the disposal of your Heavenly Father. But how can you lay claim to this title — you, whom the slightest opposition disturbs and provokes?

Peace, however, is like unto those rivers whose course flows on in one continuous stream; why are you not mindful of my precepts, says the Lord; your peace would be like a river (see Isa. 48:18).

He who, by dint of perseverance, has at last conquered himself, passes his days in peace. He is at peace with all men, because he is without ambition, without envy, without attachment, to the good things of this world. He is at peace with himself, because his moral courage controls all sensual inclinations. He is at peace with God, because he obeys Him in all things, and as he always seeks to do His most holy will, his conscience never reproaches him.

How beautiful is this peace, says the prophet. How this peace surpasses human understanding! It is full of sweetness and charity.

St. Augustine's definition is that peace is a tranquility which is born of order. The order that is seen in a well-guarded city, but frequently disturbed by civil wars, is not sufficient to prove that peace is therein enjoyed, because its order is without tranquility. The tranquility that may be found in a peaceful city, badly regulated for want of subordination, does not suffice to prove that peace would be lasting, because tranquility would there be without order. To enjoy true peace, tranquility and order must be firmly united.

Let us now see who are those of whom our Savior speaks — those who are peacemakers (Matt. 5:9). This cannot be said of the wicked, who, however tranquil they may sometimes be in their condition of life, are nevertheless continually tortured in mind and conscience. It is therefore true to say that "there is no peace for the wicked." They are not even the good, who have only ordinary virtue, and do not enjoy tranquility; for although they may be on the right way, they nevertheless yield to temptations against the Spirit, and this troubles them incessantly. "They have looked for peace, and behold trouble" (see Jer. 14:19).

Thus the only ones who can lay claim to the title of "peacemakers" are those perfect Christians, who are dead to themselves, in whom the flesh is brought under the subjection of the Spirit; those who are entirely submissive to God's holy will, obeying Him like children, and allowing themselves to be guided in all things by the Holy Spirit.

—Fr. Paul Segneri, S.J. (1624–1694), *Meditations*

∞

We enjoin and entreat you to live in peace with all men, as much as it may depend on you. Exhort your parishioners and flock to be of one mind in the Body of Jesus Christ, by unity of faith and the bond of peace, to settle amicably all disputes that may arise in your parishes, to put an end to dissensions and quarrels as much as lies in your power.

It is a duty for you, my brethren, to love peace, since God is the Author of peace. He has recommended it to us. His wish is that peace shall reign on earth as well as in heaven, and from this peace, all that is eternal depends. "My dearly beloved," says the beloved disciple, "if God has so loved us, let us love one another" (see 1 John 4:11).

—St. Edmund (d. 1242), Letter to his clergy

∞

Peace is serenity of soul, tranquility of mind, simplicity of heart, the bond of love, and the union of charity.

—St. Augustine (354–430), *De Verbum Domini*

∞

Salvation

With fear and trembling, work out your salvation.

— Philippians 2:12

The wisdom of the pagan philosophers and the eloquence of their orators were confounded at the extraordinary sight of the death and triumphs of the early martyrs. The tyrants and judges were seized with astonishment when they witnessed the faith, courage, and even the gaiety of these holy champions of the Faith. What will be our excuse at the tribunal of Jesus Christ if, after having been saved from persecution and torture, we have nevertheless neglected to love God or even attempted to work out our salvation?

What a contrast! On one side, the martyrs, ever attached to God in the midst of the severest trials; and on the other, the greater part of Christians, who, in the bosom of a quiet peace, refuse to give to God a heart that He certainly has a right to demand.

Once more, what could we do on that dreadful day on which our eternity depends? While the martyrs, full of a holy confidence, would show Jesus the scars of their wounds, what should we have to show Him? Can we offer Him a lively faith, a sincere charity, a disinterested detachment from earthly things, successful victories over our passions, souls fond of silence and solitude, hearts pure and chaste, alms given to the poor, prayers, watchings, and tears? Happy the man who is the bearer of these good works, for he will appear with confidence before Jesus Christ and His angels.

Salvation

Holy martyrs, who have merited by your triumphs to be intimately united to God in heaven, deign to intercede on our behalf. We are but miserable sinners; but if you will give us the help of your prayers, the grace of Jesus Christ will enlighten our souls, and our hearts will be inflamed with the fire of divine love.

—St. Ephrem (d. ca. 379), *Homily on the Holy Martyrs*

∞

If a man were to give immense treasures to the poor, that good deed would not be equal in merit to that of a man who contributes to the salvation of one soul. This almsdeed is to be preferred to the distribution of ten thousand pounds; it is worth more than the whole world, however large it may appear in our own eyes, for a man's soul is more precious than the whole universe. God has nothing so much at heart, nothing gives Him so much pleasure, as the salvation of souls.

—St. John Chrysostom (ca. 349–407), *On Genesis*

∞

The work of our salvation is, properly speaking, our own individual work, because all the profit that accrues therefrom is for ourselves. In other affairs, he who works is not he who has the profit. A husbandman sows and reaps, but, more than often, it is not for himself. A father works hard to increase his business or income, but it is to enrich his children, and they often turn out to be ungrateful. A judge is careful in his summing up and becomes, as it were, a victim of the public. What does it come to? Simply a vain honor.

He who sows, says the Lord, is not often he who reaps: "It is one man that soweth, and it is another that reapeth" (John 4:37). But in the work of our salvation, he who works is he who alone has all the profit; no one can share it with him. "If you sow," says St. Paul, "you shall reap a harvest in proportion to the seed you shall have thrown in."

If you pray, if you fast, if you bestow alms, if you mortify your senses, if you crucify your flesh, all the profit will not only be your gain, but it will increase a hundredfold in this life and will last forever in the next.

Salvation is our own work, because if it meet with ill success, the loss will be our own; no one can share it with us.

In profitable but hazardous large businesses, people form themselves into a company, and seek for others to insure them from loss; they prefer a smaller profit provided they lessen their risk, and thus share with others the profit, provided they share the loss. But in the affair of salvation, there can be no company formed, no insurance from loss; we must alone take the chance; all the profit or all the loss will be our own, and in this work, each works on his own account.

That zealous good man who has manifested so much anxiety for your salvation, who has taken so much pains, who has made your business, as it were, his own, will have a share in the profit if he succeed, but he will not share in the loss if he does not. That which will be your loss and your condemnation will be his profit and his merit.

—Fr. F. Nepveu, S.J. (1639–1708), *Réflexions Chrétiennes*

∞

Temptations

Watch ye, and pray that ye enter not into temptation.
—Matthew 26:41

If God does not stop those temptations with which you are assailed, He does it for reasons that are sure to result to your advantage. First of all, He wishes you to know and feel from experience that you have become stronger, more powerful than your enemy. He wishes also that this temptation may keep you, as it were, in a balance, and that the dangers that threaten you prevent you from being exalted on account of the graces you have received.

God wills also that you should be tempted in order that the devil, who is in doubt if you have renounced him, at length knows by your patience that you are still true to your Lord and Savior. More than this, God's intention is that your soul should be fortified through temptation, and it thus remains stronger than ever.

In fine, God permits the enemy to attack you in order that you may realize by that how great and precious is the treasure He has entrusted to you. For Satan would not have attacked you so violently had he not seen you elevated to a condition more glorious than that in which you were before. It was that which irritated him so much when he saw Adam living in so glorious a garden; and it was that which made him so vexed against Job when he saw that God even bestowed on him so many praises.

—St. John Chrysostom (ca. 349–407),
Commentary on the Book of Matthew

∞

You must be courageous amidst temptations and never think yourself overcome so long as they displease you, observing well this difference between feeling and consenting: namely, we may feel temptations even though they displease us; but we can never consent to them, unless they please us, since the being pleased with them ordinarily serves as a step toward our consent.

Let, then, the enemies of our salvation lay as many baits and allurements in our way as they please, let them stay always at the door of our heart in order to get admittance, let them make as many proposals as they can. Still, so long as we remain steadfast in our resolution to take no pleasure in the temptation, it is utterly impossible that we should offend God.

With respect to the delectation that may follow the temptation, it may be observed that, as there are parts in the soul, the inferior and the superior, and that the inferior does not always follow the superior but acts for itself apart, it frequently happens that the inferior part takes delight in the temptation without the consent—nay, against the will of the superior.

This is that warfare that the Apostle describes (Gal. 5:17) when he says that the flesh lusts against the spirit, and that there is a law of the members and a law of the spirit.

St. Francis De Sales (1567–1622), *Introduction to the Devout Life*

∞

To encourage us in temptations, it will be a great help if we consider the weakness of our enemy, and how little he is able to do against us, seeing that he cannot make us fall into any sin against our will. "Behold, my brethren," says St. Bernard, "how weak our enemy is; he cannot overcome but him who has a mind to be overcome." If a man who is going to fight were sure to overcome if he would, how joyful would he be? Would not he think himself sure of a victory that depended only on his own will? With the same confidence we should fight against the evil one. For we know very well that the devil cannot conquer, if we ourselves will it not.

St. Jerome remarks the same upon the words that the evil spirit said to our Savior, when, having carried Him up to the pinnacle of the Temple, he counseled our Lord to throw Himself down headlong. "Cast Thyself down," said the tempter (Matt. 4:6); and this, adds the saint, is the true language of the devil, who desires nothing so much as the fall of all men. He can indeed persuade them to throw themselves down, but he cannot throw them down himself. The voice of the devil says, "Throw yourself down into hell." Answer him, "Do so yourself; you know the way; as for me, I will not," for he cannot have the power to make you, if you have not the will to do it.

It is related in ecclesiastical history that the Abbot Isidore was attacked for forty years by a violent temptation and yet never yielded to it. We see also a great many examples of the holy fathers in the desert who, all their lives, were attacked with violent temptations, which they always sustained with a steady and equal confidence. "These were those giants," according to the prophet, "who were expert in war" (Bar. 3:26). We ought to imitate them in this; and St. Cyprian, desiring to inspire us with the same confidence, makes use of the words of God in the prophet Isaiah: "Fear not, for I have redeemed thee, and called thee by thy name: thou art mine. When thou shalt pass through the waters, I will be with thee, and the rivers shall not cover thee; when thou shalt walk in the fire, thou shalt not be burnt, and the flames shall not burn thee; for I am the Lord thy God, the Holy One of Israel" (43:1–3).

Those words also of the same prophet are well fitted to strengthen us in the same holy confidence: "As one whom the mother caresseth, so will I comfort you" (66:13). Imagine with what marks of love a mother receives her infant, when, being frightened at anything, he casts itself into her arms; how she embraces him, how she presses him to her breast, how she kisses and tenderly caresses him; but the tenderness of God for those who have recourse to Him in temptations and dangers is, without comparison, far greater.

—Fr. Alphonse Rodriguez, S.J. (1526–1616), *On Temptations*

∞

During life's pilgrimage on earth we cannot be without temptations; we profit and advance only through temptations; we would not acquire self-knowledge unless we were tried. No crown without a victory, no victory without a struggle, and no fight without temptations and enemies.

If we were never tempted, we would never be tried. Is it not, therefore, better to be tempted than to be censured without being tempted?

—St. Augustine (354–430), *On Psalm 69*

∽

Vocation to a State of Life

Let every man abide in the same
calling in which he was called.

—1 Corinthians 7:20

There is nothing more important, nothing better, than to enter into a state of life to which God has called us and to choose that vocation that His providence has destined for us. The whole universe is, so to speak, the house of God; all mankind are His family, both as His subjects and His children. It is the master who assigns to each his office. God is a Father and an infinitely wise Master, and He knows what each one is fitted for. But He is as good as He is wise, and thus it is that He will not fail to assign to each of us a proper post, if only we leave everything to His divine management.

This is not what the majority do; it is mere chance, caprice, a spirit of interested ambition, or a blind love that leads them onward; it is such irregular motives that lead them to adopt a particular state of life. Can they fail to go astray if they put their trust in such bad hands? But, alas! they not only go astray, but they fall into the precipice. If nothing is so easy as to fall, so nothing is so difficult as to retrieve oneself.

The consequences of this failure are terrible; since when once we have gone astray it is difficult to limit its extent. From this it follows that if we are not in that state of life to which God has called us, if we are not in that position that Providence has marked out for us, nothing can succeed.

God had given us the qualifications and talents suitable for the state of life to which He had called us; if we had accepted this, we could not have failed, with these dispositions, to have done well. We have taken or rather chosen another path; we are engaged in another employment that God had not destined for us because we were not fit for it. Can we then be astonished if we manage affairs badly, or if nothing succeeds with us?

And again, does not the success of our enterprises and the happiness of our life depend on God and on His blessing? People only wonder that a man who is so clever, a man with so much talent, merit, and understanding, should meet with so little success, that all his efforts seem to be unavailing, and his business seems to diminish daily. It seemed to them that he could scarcely fail of success. Nothing was wanting but the blessing of God, and that alone was the cause of his failure. But how was it that God had not blessed his endeavors? It was that he had entered into that state of life, into that employment, without consulting God, without a vocation.

A bone that is out of place is very painful and causes the whole frame to suffer. So also a man who is not in the proper place that Divine Providence marked out for him is full of grief and vexation; he suffers much and is the cause of suffering to others.

Is not this the reason why you see so few people content with their employment? Is not this, perhaps, the source of all their troubles?

—Fr. F. Nepveu, S.J. (1639–1708), *Réflexions Chrétiennes*

∞

He who alone knows our strength who sounds the depth of our hearts; He who has fixed from the beginning the way that He wishes us to take—He alone should be the first to be consulted in the choice of a state of life we are about to select.

As it is, God, who in His eternal council has prepared the proper and necessary means to effect our good, should be consulted in the first steps we take to arrive at a desirable determination; for all those motives of interest, of rank, of birth, of talent, which have usually the uppermost voice in our choice of a state of life, are but deceitful guides and almost always induce us to make a change.

He who does not follow the will of God in his choice of a state of life is always in danger, and on the other hand, he who follows the path that our Lord has marked out for him is always safe.

God wished that you should walk one way, and you have followed another. He had prepared sufficient grace to help you in the state of life He marked out for you, and He withholds it when you have chosen for yourself.

By His way He wished to lead you to salvation, and you have thwarted His will. He had given you an inclination to be pious and good, a heart devoid of deceit and vainglory; all that showed that He destined you for the altar, and that solitude was your place. You, however, have selected a busy employment in the world. What obstacles do you not meet with in your wish to be saved? What dangers do you not encounter?

—Fr. Jean Baptiste Massillon (1663–1742), *Lenten Sermons*

Part 8

∞

The Four Last Things

∞

Death

Thou art dust, and unto dust thou shalt return.

—Genesis 3:19

The time of our death is absolutely unknown to us. There is nothing that can make us certain of a single moment of our life. On the contrary, how many chances there are of our being deprived of life in an instant!

Death can carry us off in a thousand ways; it may seize us boldly; it may take us by surprise. Perhaps, alas! death may be near, perhaps it may be within you, without your knowing it.

Picture to yourself a fish in a net; it is caught, and it does not perceive it; it plays, it darts about with other fish that are without fear. Nevertheless, its career is ended; and who knows how near your end may be? Perhaps the net is cast, and it may be drawn up without your being aware of it. Jeremiah the prophet says: "I have caused thee to fall into a snare, and thou art taken, O Babylon, and thou wast not aware of it; thou art found and caught, because thou hast provoked the Lord" (Jer. 50:24).

Why do you not then open your eyes, and see the danger in which you are? Hold yourself in readiness, be on your guard, prepare quickly, and make as good a confession as you would wish to make on your deathbed, for you know not when the time will come. The hour of your death — is it still far off? You can wish it, you can hope that it is so, but you do not know it. It is the Son of God even who says that you do not know it, for He tells it to all. Can He deceive us? Is not His testimony — His Word — sufficient?

Do not rely on your youth, on your health, on your good looks, on your strength of mind; possessing all these blessings, you know not if you will be alive tomorrow.

Our Savior says it to everyone—whoever you are, young, old, in sickness, in health—watch and pray, for you know not when the time will come. Look at that man of the world: he fancies that he is happy, and yet he is the most wretched of men. He at least anticipates approaching happiness; he, nevertheless, is pursuing only a phantom. How could he be happy? He knows neither true happiness nor the way to procure it. He is as one asleep and dreams of castles in the air; he mistakes appearances for the reality, and at last he wakes at the moment of his death and finds himself denuded of everything.

How awful is this slumber! for the worldling wakes and finds that there is no time for repentance, no time to seek for the true happiness he has so oft despised, and the pleasures that seduced him have exhausted all his strength.

Do not allow me, O my God, to fall into a sleep so frightful. And if I have fallen into sin, do not wake me at the moment of my death, like that madman to whom You said, "This night thy soul shall be required of thee" (Luke 12:20).

—Fr. Paul Segneri, S.J. (1624–1694), *Meditations*

∞

The act of dying is very simple and very short. Yet all men fear it, and some fear it so much that it casts a shadow over their whole lives. It is the separation of body and soul, the end of that companionship between them, which is a mystery we have never been able to fathom, and which we should have imagined, if we had not been otherwise taught, involved our very existence, our personality.

The act of dying is, moreover, a punishment, and the most ancient of all punishments. It is the Creator's first punishment of the sinning creature, invented by the Creator Himself, the first promulgated invention of

His vindictive justice. It can therefore, under any circumstances, hardly be a light one, whether we consider the Being who thus punishes, or the thing punished, which is sin. Indeed, it is a penalty that nothing could render tolerable to the creature, except the Creator Himself suffering it, and diffusing the balm of His own death over the universal deaths of men. It is true that men have desired to die, and they have sinned by the desire, because it was the fruit of an unsanctified impatience. Others have desired to die, but then they were men who had also in them the grace to desire to suffer. Some have desired to die because they pined for God, and the pains of death were a small price to pay for so huge a good.

Some deaths have been so beautiful that they can hardly be recognized as punishments. Such was the death of St. Joseph, with his head pillowed on the lap of Jesus. Yet the twilight bosom of Abraham was but a dull place compared with the house of Nazareth, which the eyes of Jesus lighted. Such was Mary's death, the penalty of which was rather in its delay. It was a soft extinction, through the noiseless flooding of her heart with divine love.

All who die well are safe with God. As the life is, so shall the end be.

—Fr. Frederick William Faber (1814–1863), *Sermons*

∞

On a Good or Bad Death

*The souls of the just are in the hands of God, and
the torments of death shall not touch them.*

—Wisdom 3:1

How consoling it is to see a just man die. His death is good, because it
ends his miseries; it is better still, because he begins a new life; it is excellent, because it places him in sweet security. From this bed of mourning,
whereon he leaves a precious load of virtues, he goes to take possession
of the true land of the living.

Jesus acknowledges him as His brother and as His friend, for he has
died to the world before closing his eyes from its dazzling light. Such is
the death of the saints, a death very precious in the sight of God.

But, on the other hand, see how shocking is the death of the wicked.
The least evil is the loss of all the good things of this world; the separation of body and soul is more dreadful still; but the worst of all is the
devouring flame, the gnawing worm that never dies.

—St. Bernard (1091–1153)

∞

When that frail frame, that body, of which he was far from being indul-
gent, begins to succumb under human infirmity, to sink under the laws
of nature, what keeps it back? What delays its final extinction? The fruit

is ripe; it begins to loosen from the pending stalks; a gentle shake will make it fall upon the ground.

How consoling to hear the good man say to himself: I am dying, I have soon to bid adieu to the world; that is to say, I am about to resign worldly blessings, which I have hitherto despised, and which, in fact, are of little value to a Christian soul. While I was master of my body, I could not trust it, and I was not allowed to pamper it with delicacies. What use, then, will it be to wish to preserve that which I am told not to love?

I die! That is to say, I shall sigh no more in this land of exile; I shall no longer be exposed to dangerous enemies, to uneasiness, to vexatious troubles, inseparable from a life that is always full of trouble. I die! That is to say, I shall not, O Lord, offend Thee anymore. I shall have no more temptations to struggle against, no sins of thought, word, or deed, no more dangerous battles to fight.

If this detachment is not always so perfect as here described, it is always with a resignation that belies every sentiment opposed to the divine commands; it calls to mind the holy thoughts that have been fixed on his memory from early youth; it makes a virtue of that which God thinks necessary, and making use of death in order to fortify himself against death itself, he gives up blessings, for the very reason that they were given to him, as transitory benefits.

Thus far, this good man looks upon himself as a victim that God sacrifices to His glory. No other altar than the bed on which he lies, where he is humbled under the hand that strikes him. It is there that the victim is prepared and sacrificed, there glory penetrates his bosom, there the fire of divine love consumes him, and there the holocaust is perfected.

Thy will, O Lord, be done; this sacrifice is due to You, and I am well repaid if Thou deignest to accept it. At one time he looks upon himself as a culprit, whom God punishes, and mercy ends by purifying and chastening him. For when we say "a just man," we ought not to understand by that, that he is a saint of the first order, one free from the slightest imperfection, one whose merits exceed what God in justice asks from

His creature. The sick penitent condemns himself and blesses the Judge who punishes him in order to forgive him, and does not spare himself, in order that he might the better be spared.

At another time, in submissive humility, he adores the almighty power of the Creator who made him and who disposes of His work as He pleases. God so wills it; God ordains it; may His holy will be done. At last, at the sight of Jesus on the Cross, he feels encouraged, and at the same time confounded. You have suffered, O Lord, before for me, and how incomparably greater have Your sufferings been. Like You, I die on the cross; happy shall I be, if I may reign with You in heaven.

—Fr. Jaques Giroust (1624–1689)

∞

At the hour of death nothing is more frightful to the wicked than the recollection of their sins. At that hour God will repay them with all the fears and remorse that may have lain dormant during life. His judgments then will be much more just and much holier.

St. Chrysostom sums this up in a few words, for he says there is a weight and a weight, a measure and a measure; a weight during life, a weight at the hour of death. During the life of that libertine, impurity passed off as gallantry; at death it is an unbearable fire within, equal to the flames of hell: weight and weight. A cruel usury is looked upon as a clever stroke of business; at death, it is theft and robbery: measure and measure. An alms coldly refused during life, is allowed; at the hour of death it is cruelty and homicide: weight and weight. A calumny is enjoyable, an allowable revenge during life; at death it is harsh injustice: measure and measure. In fact, there is a difference in looking at a sin clothed in the garb of alluring pleasure and a sin exposed to view in all its ugly nakedness; and it is at the hour of death that the wicked will see their sins in the latter form or shape. Thus it was said formerly by the prophet, "The sorrows of death surrounded me, and the torrents of iniquity troubled me" (Ps. 17:5 [RSV = Ps. 18:5]).

On a Good or Bad Death

In vain will an able confessor try to drive away the vision from his mind, in order to prevent the man from falling into despair. Everything, even the sacraments of Jesus Christ, will remind him of his sins.

—Fr. Vincent Houdry, S.J. (1630–1729)

∞

We must accept our own death, and that of our relations, when God shall send it to us, and not desire it at any other time; for it is sometimes necessary that it should happen at that particular moment, for the good of our own and their souls.

—St. Philip Neri (1515–1595)

∞

The Particular Judgment

It is appointed unto men once to die,
and after this the judgment.
—Hebrews 9:27

The time appointed for the particular judgment is the precise moment of death. For although God, by a particular arrangement of His justice, might have been willing to condemn some sinners before their death, in order to keep men in fear by an exemplary punishment, nevertheless it is His will to judge in an invisible manner, when the soul leaves the body; and at this very moment, all will be tried, settled, and finished. The Judge hears the accusers, pronounces the sentence, and puts it into execution without delay.

It is, then, this dreadful moment I ought to have ever before my eyes, since it will be the beginning of either my happiness, or of my eternal condemnation.

O fatal moment that leads to eternity! The soul that is summoned to appear will at this moment be alone, deprived of its body, separated from all visible creatures, accompanied only by its deeds. For, before its separation from the body, parents, relations, friends, and priests may be found around the person's bed; there is not a single soul who can follow his soul, not one who can protect it in the other world.

The soul of a king is of no more value than that of a peasant; the soul of a rich man may be poorer than that of the meanest beggar; the cleverest may be outrivaled by the most ignorant; dignities and riches are only fleeting advantages, and talents are of no consideration in that other life, where only good works are rewarded.

Meditate, my brethren, on this last moment, and employ well every moment of your life; for on this last one depends a life that will never end.

—Fr. Louis du Pont, S.J. (1554–1624), *Meditations*

∞

Conceive, if it is possible, what must be the horrible dread of a soul that feels that it hangs to its body, as it were, by a thread, and that in two or three minutes, it will have to appear before the awful tribunal of God.

At that time, its conscience will be its worst enemy; it is the conscience that will, even before the last sigh, make manifest every thought and word, and, so to speak, will foreshadow the judgment and sentence. It feels that time will soon be no more, and it begins to see the horizon of an awful eternity; the uncertainty of its fate, the fear of eternal punishment, the reasons it should fear it—all reduce the soul to a state that may be called an anticipated hell.

This poor soul, on the point of appearing before God (that supreme Judge, whom it well knows it has so often insulted), finds itself laden with debts, and there is now no time to pay them, no means of canceling them. It would certainly have been able to find enough in the merits of the Precious Blood to satisfy the divine justice; but is it in a state to say that it is worthy of the promises of Christ?

Troubled and frightened as it is, has it the presence of mind and the tranquility sufficient for that?

But this person expires, and at the very moment the trial has commenced, the judgment is pronounced, the sentence is executed. At that very moment, that person's soul enters into an awful eternity; at that instant, if it be damned, it feels the extent of the torments it will ever have to suffer. No regard will be paid to age, employments, or quality; of all the titles, the only one that will remain, the only one that will be taken into consideration after death, is that of Christian, and on that title we shall all be judged.

The promises made in baptism, the strict obligations that have been contracted, the precepts of the Christian law, and the maxims of the Church will be examined at this judgment. If this soul should be in a state of mortal sin, even if it be a guilty desire, or a sin of thought, it is at that moment condemned to everlasting flames. Howsoever hard may be this judgment, howsoever frightful may be the sentence, the soul itself feels the justice of its sentence.

There, excuses are useless; no need of alleging weakness, surprise, bad example, or violence of temptation. The soul sees, it feels all its error, all those vain pretexts, all those frivolous reasons that served during life as excuses or palliations. These will then serve to increase our regret, and will enkindle within us nought but anger and indignation.

All is lost; time, all means of salvation, the infinite price of the blood and death of the Redeemer; all is lost for me, and all is lost forever, since I lose God Himself.

—Fr. Croiset, S.J. (b. ca. 1650), *Retreats*

∞

The Last Judgment

*The day of the Lord shall come, a cruel day and full of
indignation, and of wrath and fury, to lay the land
desolate, and to destroy the sinners thereof out of it.*

—Isaiah 13:9

The last judgment will not only be favorable and honorable to, but
anxiously longed for by, the just and the elect. For their glory, says St.
Chrysostom, will shine in the light of day, and their happiness and even
the crowning of their desires will be that not only their sincerity of purpose, but their purity of intention will be at last displayed; their glory
will be that they are thoroughly known, since not to have been known
was the original cause of all their disgrace.

This, ye faithful souls, who, notwithstanding the corruptions and
vices of the age, have served your God in spirit and in truth, this is what
must, amidst the hardships of life, have strengthened your resolution and
filled you with consolation.

At that dreadful moment, when the book of conscience will be open,
your hope, enlivened by the sight of the Sovereign Judge and on the
point of being fulfilled, will support you and well repay you for the unjust
persecutions of the world.

While the reprobate, confounded, troubled, and astonished, shall
advance with downcast eyes, you, because that will be the hour of your
justification, will appear with confidence.

My Daily Visit with the Saints

Now envy and calumny cast at you their poisoned darts. Then, envy will be forced to be silent, or, if it should speak, it will be in your favor; calumny will be refuted, and truth will shine forth in all its luster. Nevertheless, you will rejoice in the secret witness of your own heart, which is preferable to all the praises of the world.

Say with St. Paul: It is of little consequence what men think of me, since it is my God who will one day be my judge. "For he that judgeth me is the Lord" (1 Cor. 4:4). Or say with the prophet Jeremiah, "It is Thou, O Lord, who judgest justly, and triest the reins and the hearts, let me see Thy revenge on them: for to Thee have I revealed my cause" (Jer. 11:20).

The Son of God will come to glorify humility in the persons of the humble. It is a justice He will pay to His elect. That humility, that simplicity, that patience in suffering without a thought of revenge, which worldlings will have looked upon as weakness of mind, or meanness of spirit, God will come to crown these and will convince the world that therein consisted true fortitude, true grandeur of soul, true wisdom.

Then, says Wisdom 5:1, "shall the just stand with great constancy against those that have afflicted them, and taken away their labors." It is then that the wise ones of the world, freethinking unbelievers, will be not only surprised, but disconcerted to see those very persons whom they looked down upon as the refuse of the world, placed upon thrones of glory. It is then that many, amazed and almost beside themselves, will cry out, "These are they whom we have often laughed to scorn. Fools that we were! Their life appeared to us to be ridiculous, and their way of life as folly. Nevertheless, now behold them, raised to the rank of children of God, and their inheritance is with the saints."

It is then that the pride of the world will, perforce, bear witness, although by compulsion, to the humility of the elect of God; and the whole effect of our Lord's promise will be perceived clearly, and in a particular manner: "Every one that humbleth himself shall be exalted" (Luke 14:11).

— Fr. Louis Bourdaloue (1632–1704), Advent sermon

The Last Judgment

∞

I am always sure, O my God, of having deserved Your anger; when even I tried to do penance, I was uncertain whether my heart was not deceived, or that I had found favor in Your eye. The day of Your vengeance being near, I have nothing to expect but a judgment without mercy. Have I not reason to fear? But I knew that the fear of Your judgment would be of service to me.

It is that holy fear that has peopled and will people deserts. It would make me fly from the seductions of the world, it would make me wish to go into retreat, and through that, would be to me a haven of safety. Create in my heart, O my God, this wholesome fear that has made the security of the just banish from it that fatal indifference that is the greatest danger of a Christian.

We should indeed be mad, and very blind, not to think of this last judgment, or to think lightly of it. This was not the case with St. Bruno; he was in the constant habit of selecting the last day as his meditation; it was ever present in his mind, and he never lost sight of the severe account we shall have one day to render to the Sovereign Judge. If we try to follow the example of this glorious saint, how changed will be our lives! How soon we shall become new men!

—Fr. Paul Segneri, S.J. (1624–1694)

∞

Purgatory

There shall not enter into heaven anything defiled.

—Revelation 21:27

Let us see what the saints and Fathers of the Church have written on purgatory.

Judas Maccabeus, having made a gathering, sent twelve thousand drachmas of silver to Jerusalem to be offered for the sins of the dead, thinking well and religiously concerning the resurrection (2 Macc. 12:43). Not only does Holy Scripture approve of this, but it praises it by saying that it is a holy and wholesome thought.

Luther and other heretics boldly deny that the two books of the Maccabees are not of the number of sacred books; but, in addition to the fact that these books had for more than three centuries been acknowledged as canonical, we have an express decree of the third Council of Carthage, at which St. Augustine assisted, and who subscribed his name thereto, along with the other Fathers. Before this Council there were many authors who doubted of their authenticity, but since the decree of this council, the whole Christian world have received them as canonical books.

St. Chrysostom teaches us what has been the practice of the Apostles, for in his Forty-Ninth Homily to the people of Antioch we read: "It is true that the Apostles had decreed that when celebrating the divine mysteries a commemoration for the dead should be made, for they well knew that the dead would profit by it." It is thus that the saintly Doctor speaks, and he affirms that it was by order of the Apostles that prayers should be said for the faithful departed.

But if we wish for a witness of the apostolic tradition, can we desire one more satisfactory than that of one of the disciples of Jesus and His Apostles? It is St. Denis, the Areopagite, who distinctly explains, in the *Ecclesiastical Hierarchy*, wherein he tells of many things instituted by God in favor of those who have departed from this life in a Christian-like way. He says that the priest should offer up a devout prayer for the dead; he adds that this prayer is to implore the divine mercy to pardon all the faults of the deceased that he may have committed through human frailty.

We cannot question this truth after the decision of the third Council of Carthage, attested by St. Augustine, and since confirmed by the Sixth Synod. This council not only declares that the two books of the Maccabees are canonical but also forbids the celebrant of the divine mysteries from offering up the Holy Sacrifice unless he is fasting. This is why, says he, if, after dinner, you are obliged to pray to God for the repose of the souls of the faithful departed, you should make use of simple prayers. Moreover, the Council of Nice speaks in somewhat a similar strain. When a bishop dies, notices must be sent to all the churches and monasteries in his diocese, in order that prayers and Masses may be offered for his soul.

Who can teach us the holy customs of the early Church better than so many prelates and Doctors, no less illustrious for their piety than for their learning, who have been ocular witnesses of what they have written about?

This is what St. Augustine says: "We read in the books of Maccabees that sacrifices were offered up for the deceased, but one can find nothing like unto this in the ancient Scriptures. The authority of the Church, which approves of so holy a practice, ought, however, to be of great weight."

Again, among the several prayers that are recited at the altar, there are some offered to God for the faithful departed. We must therefore conclude, from the words of this great saint, that when we might be mistaken as to what he says of Purgatory, as Calvin wished (which is very erroneous), we must confess that what he has said about the custom of praying for the dead (a custom acknowledged by the whole Church) must be incontestably true. How could so learned a Doctor not know of a custom that was in use throughout the whole Church, a custom he was a daily witness of?

We have other testimonies quite as genuine, such as those of St. Athanasius, St. Basil, St. Gregory of Nazianzen, St. Cyril, St. Chrysostom, Tertullian, St. Cyprian, St. Ambrose, and St. Jerome. All these are quoted by St. Bellarmine, in his *Treatise on Purgatory*.

If the general feeling of all nations and tribes who acknowledge that there is a Supreme Being is an invincible argument against the atheists, who do not acknowledge one, it is an argument no less convincing against those heretics who reject the doctrine of Purgatory, for this belief is common to pagans, Turks, Jews, and to the majority of civilized persons who pray for the dead.

The light of reason will tell us that there are three classes of persons in the world. The first are those who are so virtuous and holy that they merit an eternal reward. The second are the wicked, and those who die in the state of mortal sin, and these are justly condemned to everlasting fire. The third class retain the middle state; they have, in truth, performed many good deeds worthy of reward, but at the same time they have committed venial sins, which deserve a temporal punishment at least. Thus, these said sins may not have been punished or atoned for in this world; consequently we must come to the conclusion that they will be expiated in the other.

∞

Hell

Go, ye cursed, into everlasting fire, which has
been prepared for the devil and his angels.

—Matthew 25:41

There is, alas, a difference between the sufferings of this world and the torments of hell. The sufferings of this world are limited and do not affect the whole man. The mind suffers only in proportion to its union with the body, and one member alone endures pain in proportion to its sympathy with the brain. But the tormenting fires of hell enter into every power of the soul, and every member of the body.

The pains we suffer on earth are, so to speak, but momentary, and death puts an end to them, but in hell they have no end. Death has no power there, and immortal bodies partake of the immortality of the soul.

Again, in this world we always find some little consolation, or some temporary relief from pain, but in that place of torture every pain will be extreme, and without intermission. Our friends, from whom we might have expected some consolation, will then be our enemies; for if they are saved, they will have no sympathy with our sufferings; and if they are lost, as we are lost, they will only increase and aggravate our pains.

The fires of hell will perform two frightful functions with regard to the damned: one will serve as a chain to bind them to the place; the other will be a horrible mirror reflecting their sins, and their frightful consequences, the sight of which will increase their torments.

My Daily Visit with the Saints

Although they say that hell is a region of darkness, that the action of light will be merged in the power of burning, it can, however, be said that there will be a certain dark and opaque light that will reflect all that is detestable and hateful, and that this fire that surrounds them will be like a blazing theater that will show them a thousand horrid phantoms. But the most terrible image that this mirror will reflect will be that of the justice of Almighty God, eternally incensed; and it is the opinion of some theologians that the greatest punishment of this fire consists in being the sign of the anger of God, which will continually show them, by an inevitable necessity, a God always angry with them and always ready to damn them.

—Fr. Jacques Biroat (d. 1666), Third Friday of Lent

∞

It is fearful to think upon the union of God's power, wisdom, and justice, in producing this world of punishment, this wonderful, mysterious, and terrific part of creation, which is, in its desolate mysteries, as much beyond our conception as the joys of heaven are in their resplendency. Nevertheless, we will leave the great evil, the loss of God, out of view, and all the horrible details of the cruelties of physical torture. Bating all these things, what sort of a life will the life in hell be, after the resurrection?

It will be a life in which every act is the most hateful and abominable wickedness. We shall understand sin better then and be able more truly to fathom the abysses of its malice. Yet in every thought we think, every word we speak, every action we perform, we shall be committing sin, and committing it with a guilty shame and terror, which will be insupportable.

To this we must add the mental agonies of hell. Envy, despair, spite, rage, gloom, sadness, vexation, wounded sensitiveness, weariness, loathing, oppression, grief, dejection, wildness, bitterness—all these are there, in all their kinds, and in unspeakable intensity. Think of a violent access of sorrow now; think of the rawness of lacerated feeling; think of a day's leaden load of oppression. Now, without pause, without alleviation, without even vicissitude of suffering, here is a blank, huge, superincumbent eternity of these things, with an undistracting multiplicity of wretchednesses, far beyond the worst degrees they could ever reach on earth.

The life in hell is a life from which there is a total absence of sympathy and love. This is an easy thing to say, but it is not so easy to penetrate into its significance.

The life in hell is also a life of terror, and a life, too, without pauses, diminutions, or vicissitudes. No angel ever wings his way thither on an errand of consolation. All the united eloquence of hell could not bring one drop of water from earth's thousand fountains to cool the torture for one lightning's flash of time. All is unintermitting.

Yet this is the bright side of hell! How bitter the words sound; yet it is not bitterness that prompts them, but the intense fear that pierces through me like splinters of ice at this moment. This is hell, with the hell left out, the crowning woe, the loss of God.

—Fr. Frederick William Faber (1814–1863), *Spiritual Conferences*

∞

Heaven

God shall wipe away all tears from their eyes:
and death shall be no more, nor mourning, nor
crying, for the former things are passed away.

—Revelation 21:4

I believe, O my God, that if I serve You faithfully in this life, I shall be eternally happy after my death, and that You will bid me enter into the palace of Your glory, where there will be all that I can wish for, and where there will be nothing to fear; where there will be good without evil, pleasure without pain, glory without confusion, peace without war, joy without sadness, repose without trouble, and life everlasting. I hope that in heaven I shall see You, that I shall love You, that I shall possess You, that I shall rejoice with You; that I shall see You, the first cause, that I shall love essential beauty, that I shall possess sovereign goodness, that I shall enjoy a happy eternity. I believe that in You, O God, I shall see all that is beautiful, that I shall love all that is good, that I shall possess all that is rich, that I shall taste all that is sweet and shall hear all that is melodious.

—Fr. Jean Crasset (1618–1692), *La Foi*

∞

Paradise! What is it? It is the most wonderful invention of the wisdom of God, the masterpiece of His mighty power, the boundary of His liberality and magnificence, the worthy cost of the Precious Blood of God; a boon so grand that God, all-powerful as He is, could give us nothing better than Himself, says St. Bernard. For it is He Himself who is given to the blessed in heaven, and can He give anything better than Himself?

To obtain this happiness, He asks us for only a little restraint on our passions, a sigh or tear from a contrite and humble heart, a drop of water given for His sake. Is this too much? If we refuse so small a tribute, do we not deserve to be deprived of the reward forevermore?

Paradise is an immense boon, since it is the final touch of the magnificence of God. God manifests His riches, His liberality, in all other gifts, but it is only in heaven, says the prophet, where He appears to be magnificent. The earth, the sea, the sky, the stars, and all the wondrous and visible works of the Lord, manifest His power and majesty; but in Paradise alone His wondrous magnificence is to be seen. Every blessing that God bestows upon His creatures here below are but as globules dropping from that torrent of joy that will inundate the souls of His elect. Sometimes God, in His mercy, allows His servants to feel a foretaste of delight, and He does it to make them understand that if so much sweetness be granted to them while here on earth, what an ocean of joy is prepared for them in Paradise.

— Fr. F. Nepveu, S.J. (1639–1708), *Réflexions Chrétiennes*

Sophia Institute

Sophia Institute is a nonprofit institution that seeks to nurture the spiritual, moral, and cultural life of souls and to spread the Gospel of Christ in conformity with the authentic teachings of the Roman Catholic Church.

Sophia Institute Press fulfills this mission by offering translations, reprints, and new publications that afford readers a rich source of the enduring wisdom of mankind.

Sophia Institute also operates two popular online Catholic resources: CrisisMagazine.com and CatholicExchange.com.

Crisis Magazine provides insightful cultural analysis that arms readers with the arguments necessary for navigating the ideological and theological minefields of the day. *Catholic Exchange* provides world news from a Catholic perspective as well as daily devotionals and articles that will help you to grow in holiness and live a life consistent with the teachings of the Church.

In 2013, Sophia Institute launched Sophia Institute for Teachers to renew and rebuild Catholic culture through service to Catholic education. With the goal of nurturing the spiritual, moral, and cultural life of souls, and an abiding respect for the role and work of teachers, we strive to provide materials and programs that are at once enlightening to the mind and ennobling to the heart; faithful and complete, as well as useful and practical.

Sophia Institute gratefully recognizes the Solidarity Association for preserving and encouraging the growth of our apostolate over the course of many years. Without their generous and timely support, this book would not be in your hands.

www.SophiaInstitute.com
www.CatholicExchange.com
www.CrisisMagazine.com
www.SophiaInstituteforTeachers.org

Sophia Institute Press® is a registered trademark of Sophia Institute. Sophia Institute is a tax-exempt institution as defined by the Internal Revenue Code, Section 501(c)(3). Tax I.D. 22-2548708.